AN INTRODUCTION TO TOWN PLANNING TECHNIQUES

MARGARET ROBERTS

 HUTCHINSON EDUCATIONAL

Hutchinson Educational Ltd
3 Fitzroy Square, London W1

London Melbourne Sydney Auckland
Wellington Johannesburg Cape Town
and agencies throughout the world

First published 1974
© Margaret Roberts 1974

Set in Monotype Garamond
Printed in Great Britain by
R. J. Acford Ltd, Chichester, Sussex
and bound by Wm. Brendon & Son Ltd,
Tiptree, Essex.

I S B N   0 09 116890 2 (cased)
          0 09 116891 0 (paperback)

Contents

Preface   vii

PART 1—Introduction

1   Introduction   3
2   The Land Use Planning Process   13
3   What is Planning?   43

PART 2—Stages of the Land Use Planning Process

4   Information   63
5   Preliminary Analysis   81
6   Models   93
7   Plan Design   109
8   Evaluation   125
9   Implementation   161
10 Communication   179

PART 3—Land Using Activities

11 Population   191
12 Employment   220
13 Housing   265
14 Shopping   297
15 Leisure   327
16 Transport   372
17 Perception   395

v

To my son Daniel

Preface

I have written this book in the hope that it may be useful. It is, more than anything else, a 'digest'—a compilation of explanations and examples of planning techniques, each of which can be found elsewhere, but which many practising planners and students may appreciate finding gathered together.

I am not offering any new theoretical insights into land use planning, although my own orientations may show somewhat in the choice of material. The content is intended to reflect what actually goes on in planning today, with the addition of a few pointers to new directions. When I first worked in planning, it was not usual for anyone to be taught any planning techniques; 'how to do things' was a skill acquired on the job. Now, most students of planning receive explicit instruction in techniques, and journals regularly contain accounts of their development and use. There remains, though, a lack of comprehensive texts, and it is that need—which has been expressed to me often, both by students and by planners working in offices—that I have tried to meet.

I cannot possibly acknowledge individually here all those who have provided the stimulus which has sustained me in the long endeavour of producing this book; they include my teachers, my colleagues and my students. Whatever value this book may have derives, of course, not from me, but from all those who have developed the methods and carried out the studies which are here described. Two particular debts must be recorded—to Adam Hilton and to Ella Kramek, for their help.

I would end this Preface with the plea which is obvious, but which I feel deeply, that whilst we cannot function effectively as land use planners without techniques, let us never forget that the purpose of planning is to achieve improvement in the lives of people, and that techniques are only a means to achieving that end.

MARGARET ROBERTS

PART ONE
Introduction

1 Introduction

This is a book about techniques of planning, written especially for land use planners. It will be useful as an introductory manual for people starting work on a shopping study or a population forecast, and working for examinations. But it is just as important to know when and why to use a technique, as how to use it.

I hope that by the time the reader has completed the three chapters that together form Part 1 of this book, he will have received an adequate introduction to three things:

1 the activity of 'planning',
2 the more specific activity, 'land use planning', and
3 the part played in land use planning by 'techniques', which are, of course, my central subject.

Therefore, in this first, introductory, chapter I begin to deal with what planning is, and what land use planning is. Chapter 2 will discuss different recent interpretations of the land use planning process, and provide an illustrative land use planning sequence, with examples of techniques that might be used in it. Chapter 3 will conclude the introduction by developing some of the ideas which are essential to an understanding of what the activity 'planning' really comprises.

The key points, to start from here, are that planning is a part of the organisation of society and that some control over the use of land is, and will continue to be, an important component of that organisation. It does not follow, however, that there need necessarily be separate planners of land use and it seems at least possible that the profession might give up its present special identity.

Meantime, there is great and harmful confusion about what land use planning can achieve, which in part derives from an inadequate attention to the function of 'planning' and relatively too much concentration on the study of land use patterns and influences upon them.

'Planning' consists of making choices among the options that appear open for the future, and then securing their implementation, which depends on the allocation of the necessary resources. Elements of decision theory can, therefore, be helpful, particularly in treating both the value and the uncertainty of different possible futures. As planning is a decision making and resource allocating activity it is 'political', in that options have to be selected that will not benefit equally, or equitably, all members of society. Since the only thing about the future that is unambiguous is that we cannot foretell it, there is much to be said for playing down the recent emphasis on goal setting in land use planning, and paying greater attention to matters amenable to successful treatment in the short-term, with more of a 'contingency planning' attitude, emphasising flexibility, to the more distant future.

The fact that we have 'land use planning' defined as a separately practised component of planning is partly an accident of history. A peculiarly British combination of practical reforming legislation, such as the early Public Health Acts, and visionary thinking —by men like Owen, Geddes and Howard—has produced a profession that seems extraordinary to a Frenchman or a Russian. Whether or not a separate profession dealing with land use goes on existing, however, their functions will continue to be important, and to need skilled attention. Thus whatever option the profession eventually decides to try to exercise about its future, techniques will continue to be needed in the planning of land use. Of course, many such techniques are also used for a wide range of other planning activities. Perhaps the profession in discussing its future may make some progress in clarifying the ambiguities in what land use planning today is, and what it claims to be about. The many confusions and delusions affecting land use

4

planners are inhibiting improvement of methods and hence of results.

The bulk of this book is a discussion of techniques—in Part 2 as related to different conceptual stages of the land use planning process; in Part 3 in the context of various activities which generate demand for land. I shall no doubt be criticised for adopting a form of organisation that emphasises boundaries. My defence is that although the interactions are crucial, in the practical manner of the best division of my material all the alternatives explored were more confusing. Further, although it is now orthodox to stress the 'system-like nature' of land use planning's subject matter, in the day-to-day work of a planning office, or the programming of a study, work is defined largely in the compartments I here use. What I hope will emerge clearly, though, is that land use planning is not like a jigsaw puzzle, where there is only one possible whole and satisfying resolution, but much more akin to producing something from a set of building bricks, where the final form depends in some part on the bricks themselves, but also on the preferences of the builder.

Planning's relationship to the political process

At anything above basic subsistence level, no man has precisely the same needs and wants as his neighbour. So, too, for groupings of people—families, teenagers, the inhabitants of different areas. When a number of men are living together in one society, it is apparent that there is not total compatibility between their wants —either at any one moment or over a period of time. Sadly, what would help to satisfy some would at the same time impinge on the welfare of others. So some method is used to resolve the conflict, whether it be brute strength, traditions or statutes. Such mechanisms for conflict resolution we give a generic term—politics—the means for deciding what wants and whose wants the available resources should be used to satisfy. The complementary process of identifying and choosing among various possible uses of productive resources, and then ensuring that the preferred uses are achieved, is planning.

It thus goes without saying that planning is a part of the political process—that is, the enunciation, establishing, weighing and reconciling of different views held within a society about how it should be organised, how its resources should be deployed, and how far the individual may be restrained, constrained or coerced in the interests of others.

Historically, the particular place in this political process of the town planner—better called land use planner—has been through a degree of control over the use of land—one of society's key resources. It has become steadily more obvious to land use planners that they could not carry out their work without an increasing degree of attention to the forces that generate demands for the use of land, and the forces that influence the availability of those resources needed to complement land in any use of it. Thus a growing concern for the entire socio-political and economic context, as well as a shift of attention from uses of land to activities. Actions taken ostensibly about the use of land and other productive resources must act to the specific advantage of various individuals, and, quite frequently, to the specific disadvantage of others. This is true both of actions which influence how much is available for distribution in total (the size of the cake), and actions which focus on how and to whom it is distributed (how it is sliced up). Usually, too, the interests of present population versus those living in the future are being balanced.

How does 'land use planning' relate to the wider process of planning?

There are so many different agencies in society that are actually planning—each with different powers, different explicit and implicit objectives and using different methods—that it is difficult to see the whole picture. Statutory obligations to plan are often only a small part of the whole.

How does land use planning fit in? And why differentiate a land use planner from any of the other planners, when it has been suggested already that there is one embracing definition of what 'planning' is?

I mention later what I regard as an important issue—the wide divergence between what land use planning commonly claims to be about and for, and the powers it really has and actual achievements it can point to. Techniques are sometimes stated to be

6

merely adding to the confusion, and it is true that complex techniques can help to cast an obscuring smoke screen. But I would argue that the fundamental point is that proper supervision of the uses of land will continue to be a necessary activity. Further, that a significant body of knowledge and awareness builds up among people dealing regularly with the same type of situation. Thus the sum of preoccupation, experience and information acquired in his daily work—as well, of course, as his professional education—will differentiate the land use planner from any other planner, although there will be degrees of overlap in their interests, intellectual approaches and methods.

Such demarcation of types of planner exists only as long as considered useful, and it seems certain that the boundaries will change. Indeed it is not out of the question that the land use planner as such may disappear (see the Royal Town Planning Institute's statement of future options[1]). Even in that eventuality, many of the working methods and techniques used by land use planners now—and discussed in this book—will remain relevant. Already, there are so many skills and backgrounds represented among land use planners that if you scratch one you may find an architect, engineer, surveyor, geographer, economist, sociologist, political scientist, mathematician or operational research man.

What is unfortunate is how many land use planners are able to gloss over the true nature of their work. Since some of the instruments of land use planning are technical, people are able to convince themselves that they are engaged in a technical process. This they may define variously as concerning co-ordination, or facilitating what would happen anyway, or protecting 'public goods'. Unfortunately, efforts to increase understanding of the urban system through development of theory, modelling techniques or whatever, may serve in practice to divert attention from the qualitative and social aspects of land use planning in operation and from any clear understanding of the process that is 'planning'.

A major debate, particularly among younger planners, now focuses on community action—remedying obvious defects in the physical and non-physical functioning of areas—and the more complex concept of community development, which involves an increase in self-awareness, self-confidence and self-direction on the part of people, even if this sometimes militates against the most rapid improvement in conditions in the short-term. At extremes this becomes the familiar dialogue about progress through evolution or revolution. Land use planning may be construed as a way of papering over society's cracks. Shelter began only as an agency to produce amelioration of bad physical conditions, but found it necessary to move to a direct recognition of the root socio-economic causes.

This perhaps leads on to the question of goals in land use planning. Over the last five to ten years there has been much more emphasis than hitherto on goals. Indeed, Chadwick recently wrote that the 'crucial matter of goal-formulation is not only the most important but also the most neglected part of the planning process'.[2] A great deal has been written about the nature and function of goals in planning. Partly in reaction, perhaps, arguments then developed about whether goal-setting and problem-solving are actually the same thing inversely expressed, the opposite of each other, a difference in emphasis or what? And what implications follow for land use planning?

In terms of its actual functioning, it seems fairly clear on reflection that, from day to day, the land use planner is a problem-solver within the parameters of set policies and traditions. What is crucial, is how the implicit hierarchies of the most important policies and the most important problems actually emerge, and how often the parameters for daily action get changed as a result of feedback from observation of results. The balance being struck is essentially between immediate problems affecting a known group of people, and more distant goals that might achieve benefits that appear more diffuse. It is of interest that economists marry the ideas that land use planners express in terms of goals and problems into net benefit (net of cost) and the discounting of values over time.

A related point here is participation. To a human being in dire poverty, it may well be that the overwhelming priority is for an improvement in physical conditions, whatever may be the implications for their pride, sense of independence and self-identity. But it is certain that, as material circumstances become less abject, they assume less predominance. Thus the paternalistic, restrictionist, establishment characteristics of public action,

8

which includes land use planning, will become increasingly unacceptable. The needs for a sense of control over one's own destiny, some personal differentiation from the millions around, ability to decide one's own priorities are strongly felt by many. Furthermore, they are considered reasonable requirements. This line of argument was well developed (if rather poorly resolved) in a recent paper by Arctander—'The process is the purpose'.[3]

The functions of land use planning—some confusions

Perhaps it would help to clarify the present position of land use planning if we asked ourselves, 'What is good land use planning? How do you recognise it?'

Suppose we went to a town and discovered that people had a short journey to work, a home and a shopping centre. That happens infrequently enough, but how much of it would have been achieved by land use planning? Land use planning cannot produce a short journey to work because it cannot produce work, or a sufficient income for people to pay for a home, or, in itself, suitable sizes and types of houses. It may play a hand in providing a shopping centre, but cannot ensure it contains shops, or, if it does, that they succeed, nor can it see that people have a car to get to them and so on.

Even on restricted terms, therefore, land use planning does not have powers to do many of the things it is aiming at. If the terms are broadened it could be asked how great a part of a person's happiness or fulfilment is a short journey to work, a home to Parker Morris standards and a shopping centre? Land use planning plays only the most minute part in providing people with a happy family life, enough money, a sense of identity and security, good television programmes and so on.

Why is it then that, whenever a planning study now appears it contains a section with worthy sounding goals, like 'maximise individual happiness and opportunity and choice', with no acknowledgement that land use planning alone can achieve none of these things, and, in truth, plays a fairly minor part even in facilitating them. Would it not be more honest if the goals said—'to reduce the average journey to work from 30 minutes to 28', and 'to point out to a departmental store where there is a vacant

6

site', and 'to prevent the local builder from putting green tiles on house roofs'? Ironically, my argument is coming full circle to return to the position before the early American advocacy planners criticised land use planning for its mundane objectives, commenting that traditional planning tried to deal with the problem of alienated man with a suggestion to shorten his journey to work. It now seems, however, that only confusion arises from trying to make land use planning a remedy of ills in society which people rightly deplore, but which land use planning has no power to affect. Our concern for alienated man must be expressed in more humane and effective *overall* social and economic policies; all that can result from an unrealistic ambition for land use planning is cynicism and disillusionment with what it can achieve.

I am thus, in sum, making two points:
that those people working in land use planning should continue to strive for the efficiencies and improvements that land use planning is able to achieve, *but* with more realism about its limitations and with less extravagant promises of what it can do for mankind.

At the same time, it should be tirelessly emphasised that the crucial benefits to mankind cannot be achieved unless other policies and procedures are strengthened and created. Furthermore, that all the resource allocation mechanisms of society—social service policies, economic planning, fiscal measures and so on, as well as land use planning—ought to be viewed as integral parts of one mechanism, with critical repercussions on each other, and interdependencies.

Much of the confusion alluded to above stems from the failure of land use planners to define adequately three separate elements, and to clarify their influences on each other. The three elements are 'land use patterns', the 'activity of planning', and the 'land use planner'. Let me explain these a little further.

1 *Land use patterns*

There exists today a pattern of uses of land which is the expression of exceedingly complex influences of demand and supply that have interacted over a long period of settlement by man. The study and understanding of these forces is both fascinating in itself and a vital prerequisite to any attempts to control the forces at work, and hence the patterns of land uses in the future. However, whilst this understanding provides a vital and major component of the land use planner's sphere of interest, it is not the totality of his concern. Urban and rural land use, and related activities, are studied also by geographers, economists, sociologists and others, who may seek simply to understand and explain, whereas the land use planner is characterised by seeking to influence, change and control land use.

2 *The activity of planning*

Planning has already been defined as an activity concerned with making choices about future options, taking into account probabilities and the value of what may be achieved, and then securing the implementation of the chosen option. It is an activity applicable to many different functions within contemporary society, both in the public and the private sector, and indeed is also a part of individuals' lives. There is much to be learned about how to plan, which has been relatively neglected by land use planners.

3 *The land use planner*

The land use planner must be interested both in the forces shaping land use patterns and in how to plan. Like any other worker, he must too pay some attention to defining his particular function, purpose and role in society and in the organisations within which and with which he must perform. This leads on to a concern for education, intra-professional communication, relationships with others and so on.

Different schools of thought about land use planning see the relationship of these three elements quite differently. For example, the systems approach moves logically from 1 to 2 to 3—analysis of the land use system defines the possibilities for planning and hence the role of the planner. This contrasts with the view of the relationship implicit in advocacy planning, which focuses on 3—the role of the planner—because of profound concern about 1—the forces allowed to shape the patterns of land uses in contemporary society—and an impatience with the cumbersomeness and insufficient relevance of 2—the planning process as practised. In Chapter 3, the suggestion that, in general, land use planners have recently paid too much attention to land use patterns to the detriment of an adequate understanding and development of the process of planning, will be developed further.

The place of techniques

The central subject matter of this book is the land use planner's techniques. The development of such techniques takes up numberless man hours, receives large sums of research money, calls upon computers to handle many millions of bits of data and draws on an increasing range of disciplines. But unfortunately this development effort is accompanied by considerable incomprehension and mystification, not only of the public, but of the majority of land use planners too. For most of them need only an extremely restricted range of techniques for their own particular work and are far too busy to be able to keep abreast of the ever widening land use planning spectrum. Further, of course, techniques do not actually deliver any goods, decision making techniques do not make decisions, housing techniques do not build houses, and employment techniques do not provide employment. But they do play a vital part in establishing and assessing issues and options. They are essential for land use planning, and many of them could also assist with wider and more effective planning if machinery of an appropriate range and power is ever set up.

References

1 Royal Town Planning Institute, *Town Planners and Their Future,* (1971).
2 Chadwick, G., *A Systems View of Planning,* Pergamon (1971).
3 Arctander, P. 'The process is the purpose', in the *Journal of the Royal Town Planning Institute,* page 313, **58** (1972).

2 The Land Use Planning Process

Introduction

The central subject matter of this book is the various techniques land use planners employ to carry out their work. Obviously, techniques are a means helping to achieve ends; thus techniques must be carefully appraised before a particular use is undertaken. Preoccupation with techniques for their own sake marks an unbalanced planner. Similarly inadequate though, is the planner who focuses on the desired end-product without knowing the best means (most suitable technique) of achieving it.

The different techniques that a planner uses are his tools, and, like any similar equipment, they should be efficient, labour saving, reliable and fit for their particular purpose. Through selection of the wrong tools a job will be impossible to carry out; through selection of poor tools it may be done badly, or with unnecessary effort; occasionally a tool functions in such a powerful way that it predetermines the characteristics of the finished article it produces.

For a long time, land use planners debated three things—whether the process of plan-making was (could be or should be) totally rational; whether planning was (could be or should be) value-free; whether there was a 'best' plan for every situation, that is, should planners seek to optimise?

These matters are less frequently debated now as separate and specific issues. Instead one can find adherents to a variety of overall conceptions of the plan-making process. So, for example, the rational camp consists primarily of followers of the 'systems approach'. In contrast, the idealists are likely to be found in the 'action planning' camp, and for them 'the problem . . . is no longer how to make decisions more 'rational', but how to improve the quality of the action'.[1]

For those who believe in commitment there is 'advocacy planning', with no possibility of being value-free: 'Appropriate planning actions cannot be prescribed from a position of value neutrality, for prescriptions are based on desired objectives.'[2] As for optimisation, the planner often has his cut-off point defined for him, whether he likes it or not, since 'the decision-maker stops short of pursuing the optimum at some satisfactory point . . . Activists are frequently intolerant and even mocking of what they consider to be planners' temporising tendencies and what they think is a dysfunctional preoccupation with studies.'[3]

The goals versus problems debate is discussed elsewhere.

As a preliminary to any review of planning techniques and the use made of them, it is essential to examine the various conceptions of the plan-making process touched on above, since they form the 'envelope' within which techniques find their context. I shall first look at four current conceptions of land use planning, with particular regard to the degree of emphasis placed on techniques.

Comprehensive planning

Using a chronological approach, we begin with a short section on 'comprehensive' or 'traditional' planning, which is rapidly losing its adherents.

'Traditional' planning, referred to in the USA as 'comprehensive' planning, prevailed in this country until the publication of the PAG Report[4] and in the USA until 1967, for various reasons a significant year for American planning.[5] I prefer the American name, since it is less ambiguous and more expressive in its emphasis. Comprehensive planning has been defined as the devising of a plan to cover developments which use land, in order to maximise the overall benefit, and then ensuring adherence to the scheme. The techniques employed are mainly those of survey and fairly simple analysis, and technique as such is not greatly

14

emphasised. Altshuler defined the functions of comprehensive planning thus:

'One, to create a master plan which can guide the deliberations of specialist planners; two, to evaluate the proposals of specialist planners in the light of the master plan; and three, to co-ordinate the planning of specialist agencies so as to ensure that their proposals reinforce each other to further the public interest.'[6]

As Friedmann puts it, 'the city planner views himself as the stern guardian of the public interest'.[7] Hansen saw the two key characteristics of comprehensive planning as being its entirely physical scope and its detachment from the decision-making process. Thus he said that traditional planning in the USA before 1967 'tended to be physical in scope, detached from decision-making and technically and administratively primitive'.[8]

The more recent conceptions of the land use plan-making process have developed in reaction against comprehensive/traditional planning. They are—structure planning; the systems approach and advocacy planning.

Structure planning

Structure, or strategy, planning is more *activity* than land-use oriented and is more explicitly concerned with implementation and decision-making factors. It is often referred to in the USA as the 'new' or 'action' planning. As Friedmann says, 'It is still the old language, but the perspective is new: planning and action are brought together and fused.' Structure planners are, therefore, said to require 'normative thinking, analytical thinking, futurist thinking and strategic thinking'.[9] Technique is regarded as important—mostly up-dated methods of survey and analysis, plus techniques for goal definition and evaluation. Closely allied is the idea of adaptive planning, which emphasises the planner's function of *steering* the forces for development and change in society in desired directions. For this, techniques are important in understanding the forces at work and in defining the room for manoeuvre. The steering view of land use planning superficially allows a neat sidestep of many of the philosophical and ethical difficulties which ought to be confronted by any land use planner.

We have all at some time been told of the most influential

early definition of the land use plan-making process—Geddes' 'survey, analysis, plan'. Some recent versions are not in essence so very different, although it is normal to find at least two additional stages made explicit—'definition of objectives' and 'evaluation of proposals'. For example, Hansen's Metropolitan Plan-making Process had eight stages—see Figure 2.1.[10]

It is now normal for structure planners to differentiate between the two levels of concern to the land use planner, the *structural* level and the *development* level. (What Chadwick called the policy level and the technical level.[11]) The distinction implied is between 'the guidance of change through time in accordance with evolving policies' and 'the design of finite schemes of localised change for execution in the near future'.[12] Cripps and Hall attach significance to the structure plan's 'emphasis on activity and interaction' which 'distinguishes the content of the structure plan from the design of adapted spaces and leads to the two-level approach to plan and policy formulation now accepted in both the USA and this country'.[13] A recent example of structure planning is the 1969 Nottinghamshire/Derbyshire Sub-regional Study.[14] The plan-making approach is described in an appendix, 'The Technical Process'; three broad stages are defined (see Figure 2.2).

The first stage

'The survey and preliminary analysis and the formulation of objectives for the strategy'. This entailed research into the physical potential of open country for existing uses and for urban development, into improvement needs and possibilities in existing built-up areas, and into anticipated growth and change in population and economic and social characteristics of the sub-region over the next 30 years.

The second stage

Strategy formulation and testing. Alternative strategies were based on 'indications of need, opportunity, potential and trend derived from the survey and analysis'. The alternatives were tested in terms of their feasibility, flexibility and acceptability.

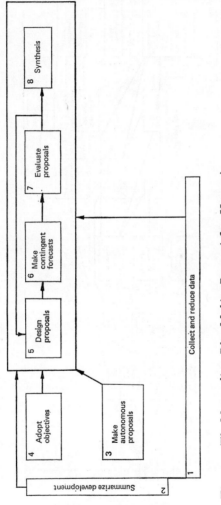

Fig. 2.1   The Metropolitan Plan Making Process (after Hansen)

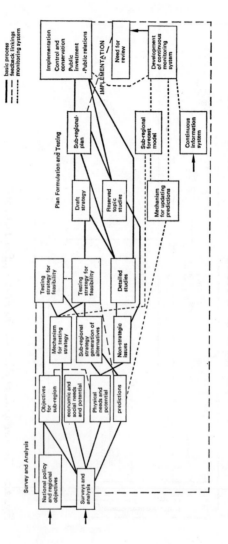

Sub-Regional Plan-Making Process

Fig. 2.2 The Notts/Derby Study Plan Making Process

The third stage

Advice on implementation, including a monitoring system and a programme for development.

It is worth emphasising that there are two components of this elaborate process that are most critical for the final outcome—the initial selection of lines of investigation and the methods of testing alternatives. Thus the planning unit began the process by taking 'six main theoretical concepts' to guide its lines of investigation:

1 development in areas with the greatest welfare problems
2 development in areas where the opportunities (economic, residential, communications, the ability of rural areas to accept large growth) were greatest
3 development in areas where physical and organisational restrictions were at a minimum
4 development employing ideal urban spatial forms
5 development in areas with the greatest potential for future growth
6 development following trends.

From these concepts, the unit identified different spatial patterns, which gave a total of 47 *representative strategies* for testing. The testing process, however, seems to have had an unduly heavy dependence on gravity-based models of various kinds. (See page 105).

Systems approach planning

The systems approach to planning places the greatest emphasis of all the different views of planning on technical expertise—in analysing the urban system, in forecasting future change and in simulating alternative futures. It is characterised by its view of the subject matter of planners as systems and sub-systems of man's activities, with their physical manifestations and their inter-relationships.

In a recent paper exemplifying the systems approach, Cripps and Hall expressed their purpose thus: 'We are concerned to identify the system of interest to the planner through a review of recent theories of urban growth and development and to agree about the process of planning the urban system.'[15] It can be

19

argued that in the planning profession, at least, there is no general agreement on either the nature or the context of the planning process, although recent theory and practice are beginning, in a few places, to bring some coherence to the process of urban and regional, town and country planning.'[16]

This coherence, they believe, is founded on the systems approach, and they quote from McLoughlin: 'The system that lies at the heart of the planner's concern is composed of types of *human activities* connected by flows of people, materials, energy and information. The physical framework for the system consists of buildings and their curtilages, open spaces, agricultural land and other *adapted spaces,* while the flows are accommodated by roads, railways, pipelines, wires and cables serving as communication channels.'[17] This definition based on Chapin's ideas, is expressed in Figure 2.3.

Objects	Activities	Physical Infrastructures	Land	Policy
Population		Buildings	Land in different uses	Decisions
	Residing Education Shopping	Houses Schools Shops		
Goods	Production of goods and services	Factories Offices		Goals
Vehicles	Making trips	Transport facilities Roads Railways Airports Ports etc.		

Fig. 2.3   Basic Entities For Planning System (after Chapin)

Cripps and Hall also drew attention to Chapin's distillation of a theory of urban growth and development from a considerable range of contributions (mainly American) 'and although there are marked differences between each particular theory, mainly due to the differing backgrounds of each contributor, a general theory of urban spatial structure and change based appropriately on general systems theory is beginning to emerge'.[18]

If a coherent systems-based theory is now beginning to emerge, what of the techniques it requires? 'There still remains, in the planning profession at least, a gulf between concept and the knowledge of the technology required to turn theory into practice. If the profession becomes convinced that we are dealing with matters that are system-like, a new technology for urban planning will undoubtedly be necessary.[19]

Bayliss underlines this point: 'We are in a regressive situation, where our knowledge and expertise are being left behind by the problems they are being applied to.'[20]

Undoubtedly, the systems view of planning and the plan-making process is now quite widely held, both among theorists and practitioners. In practical terms it has recently been used as a basis for the Leicester/Leicestershire Study.[21] The network diagram (Figure 2.4) shows their *simulation process*. The methods used for this study under McLoughlin's direction may be compared with his theoretical analysis of the planning process cycle.

1 The decision to adopt planning

2 Goal formation and identification of objectives for physical planning

3 The study, with the aid of models of the urban system, of possible courses of action (These studies show how the urban system might change through time under the impact of a variety of influences arising from private actions and public actions and interventions)

4 Evaluation of these courses of action in order to select an operational course by reference to assumed social values and the estimation of costs and benefits

5 Action to implement the plan, including both direct works and the continuous control of public and private proposals for change (The essence of control is to study the impact on the urban system of proposed changes in order to see whether or not they would deflect it from the course charted for it in the plan—using Stage 3 models).[22]

McLoughlin continued his exploration of the systems approach to planning in a three-stage project concerned with 'control in urban and regional systems'. The first fruit—a review of the literature on 'cybernetic and general-system approaches to urban and regional research' included an introduction which explained the project's purpose:

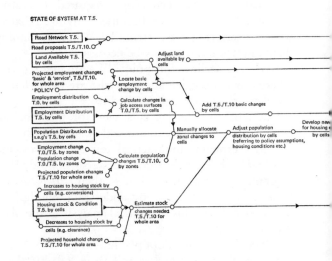

STATE OF SYSTEM AT T.5.

Fig. 2.4   Leicester/Leicestershire Study Simulation Process

'The *raison d'être* of the whole project is an intuitive belief that human settlement patterns may be regarded as particular kinds of systems, namely complex, dynamically interrelated sets of elements with characteristics of growth and change which may exhibit certain qualities of intrinsic organisation such as are found in other kinds of complex systems. A deeper understanding of these organisational mechanisms in general and in similar specific systems may lead to enhanced understanding of urban-regional organisation, help to illuminate the whereabouts of intrinsic order and the sources of disorder, and perhaps suggest the most appropriate strategies for deliberate or extrinsically applied controls, including statutory planning as understood in Britain.'[23]

In order to achieve these aims—'The research project itself has been designed to pass through three major stages: first, exploration of the literature and the setting up of a conceptual framework; second, fieldwork in British local planning authorities, and third, a closing stage which will try to draw conclusions for

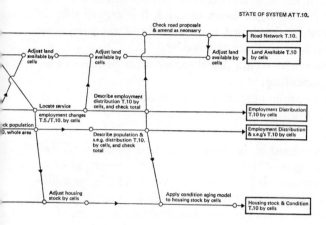

the improvement of practice (and especially the deliberate control procedures). This latter stage is likely to be intellectually exacting and will need to relate theoretical notions, both highly generalised and very specific, to the hard realities of practice as learned from the empirical stage of our work.'[24]

Having mentioned above the influence of Chapin, I should like to refer to one of his most often quoted articles—'Activity systems and urban structure: a working schema'.

'Since the immediate concern here is with human settlements, whether in the form of towns, metropolitan complexes, or megalopolitan belts of urbanisation, to be useful the framework should provide a basis for understanding and discovering an essential order to the way concentrations of human beings come

23

about. It is argued here that the key to understanding this order and its evolution is to be found in the study of activity patterns of urban residents and how human satisfactions and dissatisfactions affect choices in activities. Further, it is argued that activity patterns, particularly those that relate to the way in which people use city space and community facilities, affect their choice of residence . . . In short, if the needs of human interaction hold the key to the spatial organisation of cities, it is argued that thf framework must be developed from a study of the origins oe these needs and how they are satisfied.'[25]

Chapin continues by saying that there are three elements of the concept he is presenting:

1 a value system component, that operates on—
2 the choice mechanism, which produces—
3 an activity component

The basic relationship is applied to both short-term and long-term behaviour—'The satisfaction levels generated from outcomes at one time scale (e.g. weekly) provide a basis for evaluating outputs at another scale (e.g. life scale). He suggests, therefore, that 'A form of activity analysis based on time accounts of the way people spend their time and move about in the city offers a means of describing and eventually simulating living patterns.'[26]

Chapin thus holds his focus steadily and specifically on human needs and their satisfaction, which unfortunately cannot be said for many systems theory adherents. What Chapin has been to the American systems oriented planners, Chadwick has been to their British counterparts. In his recent inaugural lecture, which was entitled 'The alternative futures of alternative futures', he explained both the systems approach, and the part techniques play in systems based planning.

First Chadwick describes three kinds of system—engineering, ecological and social; 'Systems of the first kind are such that their behaviour is fairly predictable for they are essentially (not exclusively) deterministic, their guiding criteria being set externally either in the process of their design or as part of their operation.' In contrast, 'Systems of the other two kinds are essentially probabilistic and their behaviour is often counter intuitive and thus difficult to predict, because of their feedback

24

loop complexity. Open systems such as these import negative entropy from their environment, which offsets the positive entropy which develops inside the systems, thus making growth of the system possible, as well as homeostasis, the maintenance of critical variables.' Systems do not always grow or persist in harmony, however, 'When negentropy cannot be imported from the system's environment, or its quantity becomes insufficient, the system will move towards maximum entropy, and thus death. Thus interference with the balance of entropy and information which the system may dispose of—for example by pollution or over-competition—will lead to the disappearance of that system or systems.'[27] (For a much more detailed exposition, see his recent book[28].)

Chadwick then moves on to the unique characteristics of *social* systems—'But there are differences between ecosystems and social systems, I believe, in that the response to change within ecosystems occurs as a result of change external to a given animal or plant community, whereas in a social system individual actors set *their own* criteria for action. In other words, human beings respond to external change by decision from within—and they can also *cause* external change by their own decision: they are both actor and acted upon.'

This raises the crucial point of control—to what extent, and how can it be applied—'It follows therefore that the 'control' of ecosystems and social systems is necessarily different from that of engineering systems, for the controls of the former are inside the system and are capable of being reset or modified from within and thus only partly susceptible to external influences. The idea of 'steering' a social system, in the way that an engineering system can be controlled, is thus not possible.'

What, then, in this systems view, can planning be? Planning 'is I think [says Chadwick], the attempt to achieve a consensus by which there is some interference in the matrix of market and political decisions to give a wider spectrum of choice. This interference has normative aims which are arrived at by reviewing the probable outcomes of different courses of action and events and by presenting these outcomes as a basis for decision, both public and private. Thus planning, although seen as a rational activity, in fact must recognise the bounds of rationality, and the limitations of control which I have described: it cannot pretend to be an entirely objective way of making decisionst However, it can be normative: it can attempt to show wha. behaviour will produce what outcomes, and what courses of action should be followed if certain futures are desired—or at least, it may suggest what course should not be followed if certain futures are to be avoided.'[29]

The techniques needed to follow through a systems approach to planning are also discussed by Chadwick. The 'broad brush' methods, such as scenario writing (see page 34), will give way to more specific techniques as one approaches the more usual professional tasks of the town and regional planner; and at the technical level of producing alternatives which are functionally based and related to specific spatial locations we are, of course, in more charted territory. Some of the methods and techniques involved are now well understood, some are well tried, and some are known, but appear to require further application; they may be listed briefly.

Firstly, Design Method may be employed to devise the solution directly from the problem by, as it were, turning it inside out—context becoming form through the agency of a defined tolerance of 'fit'.

Secondly, there is allocation spatially using gravity or potential concepts, for example, in the now well-tried Lowry model.

Thirdly, there is simulation via multiple regression analysis of existing development to discover rules for allocation and Monte-Carlo type simulation over time using these rules, as in Chapin's Greensboro model.

Fourthly, there is linear or dynamic programming as in Schlager's model at Wausheka, Wisconsin.

Fifthly, there is dynamic simulation as practised by Jay Forrester at MIT.[30]

The systems approach holds sway at present in British land use planning, but comes under heavy criticism—sometimes for what it inherently is and emphasises, sometimes more for the fact that it appears rather easily half or mis–understood, and thus dangerous in its actual influence and application.

Advocacy planning

In the USA there has, perhaps, been more overt opposition to the systems approach than in this country; it did, of course, gain currency earlier there, and there are increasing signs of a similar movement here. This opposition frequently takes the form of advocay planning.

Advocacy planning contends that the planner should be a pleader of particular needs and approaches to their solution and that he requires technique to build up a weighty and convincing case.

The justification for such an approach is often based directly on spotlighting the inadequacies of other approaches to land use planning. Thus in an early plea for advocacy and plural planning, Davidoff stated: 'City planning is a means for determining policy. Appropriate policy in a democracy is determined through political debate. The right course of action is always a matter of choice, never of fact. Planners should engage in the political process as advocates of the interests of government and other groups. Intelligent choice about public policy would be aided if different political, social and economic interests produced city plans. Plural plans rather than a single agency plan should be presented to the public.'[31]

Davidoff draws attention to what he sees as the deficiencies of a systemic view of the planning process by quoting from an article by Britton Harris (written in 1960) as follows: 'We have suggested that, at least in part, the city planner is better advised to start from research into the functional aspects of cities than from his own estimation of the values he is attempting to maximise. This suggestion springs from a conviction that at this juncture the implications of many planning decisions are poorly understood, and that no certain means are at hand by which values can be measured, ranked and translated into the design of a metropolitan system.'[32] Davidoff counters, 'While acknowledging the need for humility and openness in the adoption of social goals, this statement amounts to an attempt to eliminate, or sharply reduce, the unique contribution planning can make; understanding the functional aspects of the city and recommending appropriate future action to improve the urban condition.'

The planner should 'be an advocate for what he deems proper'; he should 'represent and plead the plans of many interest groups.'[33]

The level at which planners have so far been content to define their objectives comes under fire from advocacy planners. 'The contemporary thoughts of planners about the nature of man and society are often mundane, unexciting, gimmicky . . . Planners seldom go deeper than acknowledging the goodness of green space and the soundness of proximity of linked activities . . . We cope with the problem of the alienated man with a recommendation for reducing the time of the journey to work.'[34]

Another plea for more emphasis on goal definition as an activity central to planning came recently from Young: Planning may be defined as the process of determining goals and designing means by which the goals may be achieved' . . . 'The delineation of goals assumes equal importance with the design that is meant to achieve them'; at present planners often have goals 'more a part of their creed than a result of rational enquiry'.[35]

Which one is right?

Anyone who attempts to follow the currents of thought in the planning profession must often feel in sympathy with successive students who inquired why they always found the same questions on their examination papers and received the reply, 'The questions stay the same, but we change the answers.'

Having discussed above the four different conceptions of planning which have governed and still are governing what planning is thought to be and what planners ought to do, is it possible to say that one conception is 'the right one'?

It should be emphasised that land use planning must, of course, be evolutionary and responsive: first, to its own history of development (as is any field of study or profession), building on previous debate, but also reacting against whatever views have recently been current—in planning there is often a dangerously strong intellectual backlash to ideas which have previously been excessively embraced. The overall result is thus a premature jettisoning of much of potential value. Secondly, planning is evolutionary and responsive in relation to the developments taking place in society as a whole—whether the appearance of

28

new needs and opportunities for planning or changes in the general socio-political climate that defines the planner's own role. 'Planning must also understand something of the socio-political-cultural system in which planning is popularly understood, where it takes on its meaning and is eventually effectuated.'[36]

Eversley, in his paper 'New horizons for planners' gave a sensitive and thorough analysis of the scope of planning, which is reflected in his definition of the office of the planner—note, *not* the land use planner—'He is still concerned with the physical environment, but he is equally deeply involved with the efficient functioning of the economy, the growth of communities and the correct use of scarce resources for which there is competition from many directions. This means the planner becomes a listener, a researcher as well as a decision maker. The office of the planner is to gauge trends in the economy and in society, to pinpoint shortcomings and sources of friction, and to make proposals for solving the immediate problems of the community in which he works. The grand design is at the back of his mind, but in practice he is a gradualist, a social engineer capable at best of improving the immediate function and environment of his area, one section at a time, according to a scheme of priorities which he himself must help to shape. In this process the planner cannot work in isolation. Not only is he in partnership with planners for other areas, and his fellow professionals, like architects and traffic engineers, but unless there is continuous consultation with the public and private interests affected by changes in the physical environment, his planning is not merely in some abstract sense undemocratic, but is bound to fail because the technical objective becomes divorced from the social goal.'[37]

Amos also reviewed the planning scene in order to draw his conclusions about planning, in his paper 'The development of the planning process'. Those conclusions were:

'First, there is growing acceptance of the fact that many activities in society are too fragmented and insufficiently forward looking to be effective. Consequently the planning process is being seen as a useful means of co-ordinating effort and of solving problems. Second, the planning process is no longer seen as a means of achieving a fixed objective. It is now seen as a cyclical process reviewing the current situation and adjusting action to achieve the most desirable end, of those ends which are achievable. Third, in its new cyclical form, the planning process is inextricably involved in the management process. Fourth, the newly evolved planning process is applicable to a very wide range of problems in different fields of public administration and in different levels of government. Fifth, the planning process is an intellectual discipline which may be developed and applied in many fields of knowledge and which has no specific affinity to physical planning. Sixth, the Institute's (the RTPI that is) current posture concentrates attention upon the application of the planning process to physical planning at various scales, to the exclusion of direct applications of the process to social and economic phenomena and to the neglect of management planning of coincident physical, social and economic factors.'[38] (When the Institute's incoming President says that to its Annual Conference, one can feel for a rare moment that, although land use planners undoubtedly still have a long way to go in their self-awareness, they have also come a long way!) Pahl had a slightly different message for land use planners in his paper 'Planning and the quality of urban life'. He concluded that 'Planners must continue to make judgements and that no magic techniques, computers or experts are going to make things any easier for them. Indeed, making judgements is getting more and more difficult as we get to know more about the factors involved. But judgement must still remain the basic element in planning and part of the pathology of the present situation is the planners' fear of making judgements . . . ' He elucidates: 'The planner is concerned with the spatial distribution of scarce urban resources and facilities. Some people lose and others gain: very often the same people lose all the time and are at the bottom of the heap for housing, income, job opportunities, educational opportunities, health facilities, legal facilities, knowledge of welfare provision and so on. Some planners may share my values and argue that the same people should not be at the bottom of all the heaps all the time. . . This is a judgement and those making such a judgement should be prepared to defend it. . . . If planning . . . can live with the ambiguity that this move from technocratic certainty entails, it

30

may play a vital part in improving the quality of urban life.'[39]
The next chapter develops further my analysis of what constitutes a 'planning process', and thus points up some of the deficiencies of present approaches. But before embarking on that more detailed discussion, the next section presents a sketch of a typical land use planning process, as currently accepted, with the techniques relevant to each part of it, so that the reader has a clearer overall picture of what land use planning attempts to do.

The planning process and techniques

Having discussed in a highly oversimplified way various different concepts of what land use planning is about and that, to varying extents still prevail today, in an equally oversimplified way, I shall now try to present a conceptualised land use planning process to make clearer what a typical land use planner is actually doing. I shall also try to illustrate the place of different techniques used by land use planners within such a 'typical' sequence of planning activities. Any particular planner may find himself concerned with only a part of the sequence—with action area implementation, or population forecasting, say—and may not actually need to be concerned from day to day with how his own work fits into the broader planning context. However, it is crucial in studying land use planning techniques to appreciate what a multi-faceted and open-ended activity land use planning is, and to consider how all the various parts of the process relate to each other. I have tried to show in Figure 2.5 a comprehensive sequence of planning operations, together with the techniques which might usefully be employed at each stage. I must stress that my concern has *not* been to perfect a model of the planning process—the purpose here is more to illustrate just how the various techniques which are described in more detail in the other parts of the book might relate to the overall process of land use planning. Three different elements must be differentiated —namely, facts, value inputs and decisions. I think much confusion can arise from a failure to distinguish whether a particular piece of work is intended to furnish facts, value inputs or decisions, or some combination of the three.

The next part of this book (Part 2) looks more closely at different stages of this land use planning process—information assembly, for example, or evaluation—and the following part (Part 3) is organised on an 'activity' topic basis, that is, Shopping, Leisure and so forth. In a normal working context, of course, whether it be in a local authority office, private consultancy or community action group, most working tasks comprise a *type* of technique—such as a method of forecasting, or evaluating alternatives—being applied to a particular *topic*, or activity—for example, forecasting housing needs, evaluating alternative transport proposals—so it is most helpful to the reader to adopt related approaches in this book. In reality in any land use planning organisation most of the conceptualised discrete stages of the process are occurring simultaneously and it is currently accepted that the land use planning process must be a fluid and continuous one.

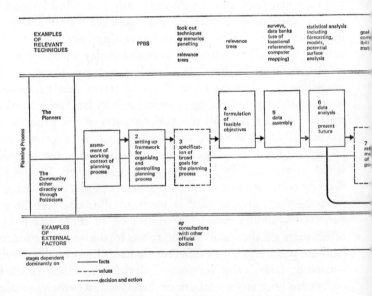

Fig. 2.5 A Comprehensive Sequence of Planning Activities—Together With Suggestions on Techniques

The planning sequence

Let us then look at the sequence in Figure 2.5; and try to specify the techniques relevant to each stage of it.

Stage 1—Broad assessment of context

Conceptually, a land use planning process may be said to begin with the institution of some form of organisation that will subsequently decide that one of its proper functions is land use planning. The basic attitudes of such an organisation, for example whether it favours in principle public sector activities, market guided *laissez-faire*, or community self-help, and the total range of its responsibilities will be extremely relevant to the scope allowed to its planners and other employees, and to the types of decision it is likely to take. It has been pointed out that whether or not techniques are used successfully depends as much on the characteristics of the organisation as on those of the technique.[40]

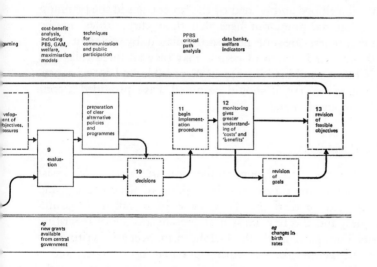

Stage 2—Decision on framework for organising and controlling

Once the organisation is in being, the second stage is the setting up of a framework for the organisation and control of all subsequent activities. The current acceptance of a Planning Programming Budgeting System by many authorities with planning responsibilities provides one example (see page 162).

Stage 3—Specification of broad goals

With Stage 3, we embark on the process of land use planning as more narrowly understood. In the light of fundamental principles held by those responsible for making the decisions (who we shall term 'the decision makers'), those responsible for suggesting possible actions (who we shall call 'the planners'), and taking account of the attitudes of all others involved and affected (who shall be called 'the community')—broad policy goals are specified, in the knowledge that they will subsequently be much developed and refined by the later stages in the planning process. Let me point out here that these three 'roles' in the planning process are not necessarily played by different individuals—the same group of people may play all three roles and various other combinations are both possible and in existence. All the stages so far, it should be noted, have provided a considerable input of values.

'Look-out' techniques

The first group of techniques to mention are those which assist thoughts about the future and the making of wide-ranging and unconstrained predictions. They have been called 'look-out' techniques, and the best known at present are scenario writing and panelling, particularly the Delphi form. Scenario writing is a disciplined method for structuring possible future states, and is *not* merely an extrapolation of existing conditions. Kahn, at the Hudson Institute, is associated with the development of the scenario. Another look-out method is panelling, where a group of people, each with particular knowledge of some relevant

34

aspect, consider what might happen in the future. Influenced by each other's carefully reasoned views, they eventually reach a consensus. There are many variants of panelling, but the Delphi method is perhaps the best known (see page 91).

I would suggest that these, and similar techniques, can appropriately be used in the planning process to assist with formulating broad policy goals.

Stage 4—Formulation of feasible objectives

The broad policy goals, although obviously influenced to some extent by the known realities of the particular situation, were formulated as ideals, to be refined by subsequent examination, and eventually translated into programmes of action, control and influence. The refinement begins with the postulation of specific objectives that would ensure progress towards the policy goals, but which can be made into achievable, testable and clearly understood proposals.

A type of technique which can assist with the structuring of feasible objectives from broad policy goals is the relevance tree. There are also other forms of tree which are applicable (see page 89).

Stage 5—Data assembly

The next step is to assemble the data needed to amplify and assess the objectives. Techniques for assembling data, including surveys and the use of published material, are always given much attention in the planning literature, and are dealt with thoroughly in a later chapter (see page 63).

The crucial part played by information gathering in the planning process is not to be denied, although the common assumption that better information will automatically mean better planning is more open to question.

Stage 6—Data analysis

Collection of data is simply the preliminary task to its analysis to provide understanding of the existing situation and of likely futures. It is highly desirable that it is known before the data is assembled what analytical techniques are to be used, even if some modification proves necessary.

Techniques for analysing data relevant to planning are extremely diverse, and have been borrowed from many other disciplines. They include those to forecast the future, as well as those which help to clarify the present. Sometimes the analyst knows exactly how the results of his work will be used, and this determines the patterns he looks for in the data; for example, an analyst of demographic data may know his work is required to predict needs for primary schools. Other analyses may be more open-ended, seeking any patterns meaningful to planning that can be discovered in the information available.

It is perhaps helpful to distinguish three groups of techniques here, first, those that classify data into like groupings; secondly, those that uncover relationships, whether correlative or casual; and thirdly, those that attempt to replicate relationships and study the results, for example many of the models used by planners. Chapter 5 discusses this stage of the land use planning process.

Stage 7—The refinement of goals

At this point, much more is known than at the beginning of the land use planning process about the actual situations with which the planners are confronted, both in the present and the future. It is, therefore, appropriate to revise the objectives, and possibly even the goals, which were formulated in relative ignorance, in the light of the known circumstances. This can be followed by the development of alternative programmes of action.

At this stage it is necessary to see how much complementarity or conflict exists between different objectives (each desired in itself) and hence in any land use proposals. Such techniques as a goals compatibility matrix (see Figure 2.6) can help to reveal which goals are reinforcing, and which require a choice of priority. Such methods as 'potential surface' analysis, which take account of the characteristics and policy demands on any area of land, showing potential land use conflicts, may appropriately be used here (see page 82).

Stage 8—Development of 'objectives' measures

As a necessary preliminary to the evaluation process, in which alternative possibilities are carefully compared according to *predetermined* criteria of usefulness, *objectives* measures must be established. In practice, this means measurable targets which can be assessed to give the benefit side of a balance sheet against costs. The more apparently sophisticated the evaluation techniques used, the more crucial this stage of the process is. Even

Fig. 2.6   Goal Compatibility/Conflict matrix

if a fairly simple technique is used, in which each step of the calculations can be seen and understood, it is extremely important that these objectives measures should be thought out before the evaluation is undertaken. It will be explained below that they are also needed at a later stage, when the effectiveness of action

37

is being assessed. Any evaluation techniques require some measures of benefit, as they do of cost; value inputs must be supplied to the rational framework such techniques provide. In view of the central part they ought to play in the planning process, measures of benefit or welfare have been remarkably little developed, although they are currently beginning to receive more attention, both here and in the USA. There has, however, been some work done on approaches which can help to reveal people's preferences and comparative weighting of alternative possibilities. Such techniques include gaming, in which the real world, with its possibilities and constraints, is simulated and the choices made by people observed. Such simulations function at various levels of complexity—a simple one which is amusing to use, the priority evaluator, has been described as 'the planner's fruit machine'. Much depends on our efforts to develop better welfare indicators, since these are needed both for evaluation of alternative possibilities and for monitoring the effects of action taken, to ensure a realistic appraisal of their effectiveness.

The measurement both of the likely value of proposals and of their effects in action is clearly basic to any effective land use planning and one of the most glaringly deficient parts of the process at the moment.

Stage 9—Evaluation

This very important stage in the planning process puts together facts and values in a comparison of the alternative possibilities— how well they achieve the objectives specified and at what cost. The evaluation findings must be presented to the decision makers (and possibly as a separate exercise to the community if they are not the decision makers) in the form of clear alternative policies and programmes, with all the assessment of them that the land use planner can provide to help in making a choice.

Evaluation must, therefore, include all relevant aspects of any proposals. Operational tests—for example, a simulation of the traffic loadings on a projected road network to see how well it copes—are clearly needed. However, the form of a land use planning evaluation is usually a comparison of benefits and costs of alternatives under consideration, expressed as far as possible in comparable terms. Operational efficiency may be taken into account as a variable, as also such characteristics as flexibility, acceptability and so on. The best known versions of cost-benefit analysis applied in the planning process are the planning balance sheet and the goals achievement matrix. Possibly, in the near future, welfare maximisation models, based on the same principles, may be operable (see page 153). Without over-complicating at this point the discussion of evaluation techniques, which is presented in Chapter 8 in full, I would like to stress that they can be used in more than one way—for example, as a *sensitivity test* of the plan that performs best, given certain value preferences.

Techniques for communicating

It is clearly imperative that the land use planner should be able to communicate effectively and sympathetically to a wide range of people so that they understand his findings and can express preferences or make decisions as necessary. He must also, of course, be a good listener. Chapter 10 explores this aspect of techniques needed for land use planning.

Stage 10—Decisions

The decision makers make their choice of the alternative courses of action which the land use planners present to them as representing the most reasonable means of achieving the goals originally specified.

Stage 11—Implementation procedures

Once the decisions are made, procedures for implementing the chosen policies and programmes begin. Implementation is a term embracing such a multitude of varied activities that there is no one technique, or even group of them, to ensure that implementation is effective. The range of functions involved includes answering queries from anxious householders as to whether a road scheme will affect their back gardens, encouraging ecumenical co-operation in using a building, statutory control of development and many others. Thus it requires public relations, persuasion and restraint. If an organisation is using an 'umbrella'

39

technique like PPBS, then it will be of relevance to its implementation activities. For some aspects of implementation, organisation techniques such as critical path analysis may be found useful. Chapter 9 deals with this stage of the process.

Stage 12—Monitoring

Monitoring of events provides the information needed to gauge the real success or failure of implementation. That assessment constitutes one of three factors which will necessitate revision of objectives, and possibly even of broad goals. The other two are elements in the pattern of events that were not foreseen (such as a rise in birth rate) and a change in the principles or values held by the decision makers, the community or even the land use planners.

It has already been mentioned that welfare indicators are important at this stage, in assessing the success or failure of action. Monitoring is a systematic observation of what is occurring, and a large quantity of data will need to be held and up-dated. Thus effective techniques for data storage and retrieval are very important, for example by using data banks (see page 70).

Stage 13—Revision of objectives, possibly of goals

It is certain that there will be a need for revision of objectives, and maybe even of goals, due to one of the three possible causes suggested above. We are thus, in effect, back at Stage 7.

As mentioned earlier, in practice many of these so called stages will be going on at the same time.

References

1 Friedmann, J., 'Notes on societal action', in *Journal of the American Institute of Planners,* page 311, **35,** 50, September 1969.
2 Davidoff, P., 'Advocacy and pluralism in planning', in *Journal of the American Institute of Planners,* page 331, **31,** 4 (1965).
3 Dyckman, J. W. 'Guest Editor's Introduction to the practical uses of planning theory', in *Journal of the American Institute of Planners,* page 300, **35,** 5, September 1969.
4 Planning Advisory Group, *The Future of Development Plans,* HMSO, London (1965).

5 See Hansen, W. B., 'Metropolitan planning and the new comprehensiveness', in *Journal of the American Institute of Planners,* page 296, **34,** 5, September 1968.
6 Altshuler, A., 'The goals of comprehensive planning', in *Journal of the American Institute of Planners,* page 186, **31,** 3, August 1965.
7 Friedmann, J., 'A response to Altshuler: comprehensive planning as a process', in *Journal of the American Institute of Planners,* page 195, **31,** 3, August 1965.
8 Hansen, *op. cit.* (5) above, page 295.
9 Friedmann, *op. cit.* (1) above, page 312.
10 Hansen, *op. cit.* (5) above, page 300.
11 Chandwick, G. F., 'The alternative futures of alternative futures', in *Planning Outlook,* New Series, **10,** spring 1971.
12 See McLoughlin, J. B., 'The P.A.G. Report: background and prospect', in *Journal of the Town Planning Institute,* page 257, **52,** 7, July/August 1965; and 'Notes on the nature of physical change', in *Journal of the Town Planning Institute,* page 397, **51,** 10, December 1965.
13 Cripps, E. L. & Hall, P. 'An introduction to the study of information', in *Information and Urban Planning,* CES IP 8, page 32, **1,** Centre for Environmental Studies (1969).
14 Notts-Derby Sub-regional Planning Unit, *The Nottinghamshire and Derbyshire Sub-regional Study,* Nottingham County Council (1969).
15 Cripps and Hall, *op. cit.* (13) above, page 25.
16 Cripps and Hall, *op. cit.* (13) above, page 27.
17 See (12) above.
18 Cripps and Hall, *op. cit.* (13) above, page 30.
19 Cripps and Hall, *op. cit.* (13) above, page 37.
20 Bayliss, D., 'Environmental research', in *Official Architecture and Planning,* page 1329, **31,** 10, October 1968.
21 Leicester City Council and Leicestershire County Council, *Leicester and Leicestershire Sub-regional Planning Study* (1969).
22 McLoughlin, J. B., *Urban and Regional Planning: A Systems Approach,* Faber and Faber, London (1969).
23 McLoughlin, J. B. & Webster, J. N., 'Cybernetic and general system approaches to urban and regional research: a review of the literature', in *Environment and Planning,* page 369, **3** (1970).
24 McLoughlin & Webster, *op. cit.* (23) above.
25 Chapin, F. S., 'Activity systems and urban structure: a working schema', in *Journal of the American Institute of Planners,* **3,** 1, January 1968.

26 Chapin, *op. cit.* (25) above.
27 Chadwick, *op. cit.* (11) above.
28 Chadwick, G. F., *A Systems View of Planning,* Pergamon, Oxford (1971).
29 Chadwick, *op. cit.* (11) above.
30 Chadwick, *op. cit.* (11) above.
31 Davidoff, *op. cit.* (2) above, page 331.
34 Davidoff, *op. cit.* (2) above, page 337.
35 Young, R. C., 'Goals and goal setting', in *Journal of the American Institute of Planners,* page 77, **32,** 2, March 1966.
36 Dyckman, *op. cit.* (3) above, page 300.
37 Eversley, D. E. C., 'New horizons for planners', paper to the Town and Country Planning Summer School, Southampton (1971).
38 Amos., F. J. C., 'The development of the planning process', paper to the Annual Conference of the Royal Town Planning Institute, Edinburgh (1971)
39 Pahl, R. E., 'Planning and the quality of urban life', paper to the Town and Country Planning Summer School, Southampton (1971).
40 Wade, B. F., 'Some factors affecting the use of new techniques in planning agencies', in 'Environment and Planning', page 109, **3** (1971).

3 What is Planning?

The discussion in this chapter aims to deal in more detail with the question, 'what is planning?', which was raised in the introductory chapter, and in the course of the exposition of the traditional and current schools of thought about land use planning in the last chapter. The discussion here begins with a reference to the way we think, which is further developed in the sketch of decision theory that follows. The 'strategic choice approach', which depends to a large extent upon decision theory concepts, but which makes clearer the practical relevance to land use planning, is explained in the subsequent section. The chapter continues with a discussion of 'an introspective but scientific approach', which usefully draws together many threads to provide a cogent answer to the question, 'what is planning?'. The final section considers our general attitudes to the future.

The way we think

When we go up stairs, we do not have to work out each time the way to use our muscles; similarly, our minds have set routines of thinking. A land use planner receives professional conditioning, but, before that begins, he will already have been substantially shaped in his patterns of thinking by his general education and acculturation. Our overall view of life, of the world and our place within it, of the meaning of events as they occur, is only

43

in part a personal reaction. In growing up, we undergo a continuous learning process; every new experience is filtered and classified to fit in with our existing stock of knowledge. The reaction to any new piece of information depends greatly on when it occurs in our own particular sequence of learning. To each person, therefore, an event has some unique significance, but there is also a great deal of common ground between people. This common ground is established by the continuous presentation to us of information, and interpretations of it, by the society in which we live. Our parents, our teachers, our friends, our lovers, our political leaders and our advertising agencies seek to inform us. They have widely varying awareness of what they are doing, and even more diverse motivations. Thus our personal interpretation of the world is shaped to a large extent by the suggestions of others. They assist in the endless process of ordering information and forming it into patterns that is vital if we are not to be totally overwhelmed and disoriented by the array of new experiences continually encountered.

Each individual's knowledge and perception of the world is thus a unique product of his own past, but he will have a substantial overlap with others in his society, resulting both from formal education, and daily exposure to the generally held notions and mores. When meeting new circumstances, then, a person is already possessed of a mental equipment which offers him a range of simplifications and classifications which may be scanned for relevance. To carry out the matching up necessary between new events and existing knowledge we seek key items of information to help identify any appropriate information sets that already exist in our memories. What these existing information sets are will depend to a considerable extent on what our formal and informal education has supplied. Although it is usually intended as a criticism to suggest to anyone that they have a closed mind, how far, in fact, does any of us ever have an open mind?

The above discussion is intended to introduce the matter of a land use planner's patterns of thinking. These will enormously influence, or, perhaps more accurately, constrain, his approach to his work as a whole and to any particular task. Our intellectual tradition is essentially a rational one—incorporating a belief that the world can largely be understood, that facts and events can be ordered into perceptible patterns, that cause and effect can be established, and, by extension, that there are scientific methods appropriate to problem solving. It is true that there is disagreement about the validity of particular methods, but there is much less disagreement that some such method is appropriate.

The formal education process to which most of us have been subjected sought to encourage, above all, clear thinking—analytical approaches to structure propositions rationally—what is termed 'linear' thinking. This is supposedly the way in which the key institutions of our society go about their tasks. It is also widely assumed that the more education a person has the more likely he is to extend the rational approach to every facet of his life.

Recently, more attention has been given to the possible disadvantages of this approach to thinking. It has been suggested, notably by de Bono, that 'lateral' thinking may often be more productive (so advocates of 'the creative leap' have long been arguing).[1] Although the occasional inadequacy of linear thinking—though perhaps not given this name—has always been acknowledged by land use planners, it undoubtedly dominates both definitions of the land use planning process as a whole and the development of specific techniques.

It is as well, therefore, to reiterate some of the implications of the above discussion. First, we do not ever approach our work with an open mind—we cannot expunge all previous experience and knowledge. Secondly, our automatic mode of thought is to seek order and pattern, and thus to superimpose some structure on events or information. Thirdly, we do this in large measure by trying to identify 'key' factors. Fourthly, it follows that we have a preconceived framework for assessing the significance of things. In sum, it is certain that, as land use planners, we will always bring with us some preconceptions to our work, and the dominant influences upon most of us as individuals—which must carry through to our professional approach—have tried to cultivate habits of linear thinking (see Figure 3.1). All these matters need to be given explicit consideration particularly in view of the rapid development for land use planning of methods which aim to be, above all, systematic. These are, on the whole, even more 'linear' than the planner's traditional approaches to his work, since they must be more explicit. Thus, algorithms for problem solving, the use of symbolic models, computer aided plan generation and evaluation do not, within themselves allow for creative leaps, for lateral thinking, unless this has been built into them. They depend upon a structured conception of a problem. They also depend usually upon the identification of patterns and upon the isolation of significant key variables. They

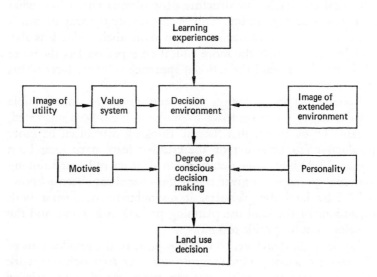

Fig. 3.1 Simplified View of an Individual's General Decision Making Framework (after Found)

SOURCE *A Theoretical Approach to Rural Land Use Patterns*, W. C. Found, Edward Arnold, London (1971)

are thus an embodiment of a person's existing approach to the world—at present likely to be linear—and have the same advantages and the same dangers. The only additional dangers they present are that the use of specific languages that are not commonly understood, and the employment of machines to undertake some of the calculation necessary, have a distancing effect. This is enhanced by the complexity of many land use planning matters and the range of information necessary. Suspicion of such methods

46

is, in many cases, largely fear of the unknown and, therefore, incomprehensible. But there is also a fear present among some of those who do know well what is going on that such methods may increasingly be used in situations where they are not wholly appropriate or adequate (see Figure 3.2).

The discussion of decision theory that follows will develop the proposition that there are three elements to making a decision— the establishment of factual information about available options, the definition of values and the treatment to be given to residual uncertainties. The majority of rational problem solving methods now in use in land use planning tend to be strongest on the first of the three, and play down the significance of the latter two elements.

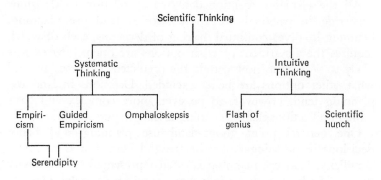

Fig. 3.2   Creative Thinking and Forecasting (after Jantsch)

SOURCE   *Technological Forecasting in Perspective*, E. Jantsch, OECD, Paris (1967)

Decision theory

Few people enjoy making decisions, and those that do so with any great confidence that they are making the right decisions are even more rare. Making a decision is, in fact, choosing between alternatives—to go out or stay at home, to apply for a job in New York or remain in the familiar and comfortable life pattern in London. Any such choice has to be based on an assessment of the likely outcomes of selecting each possibility. Some consequences are easy to predict, others completely unfathomable.

47

Some effects will be pleasant and beneficial, others unpleasant and unwanted. Finally, choices are usually to a large extent mutually exclusive—by choosing to go out, one is automatically rejecting all the pleasures and disadvantages of staying at home. Thus every action we take in life represents a choice between alternative possibilities; the choice may be made after careful judgement, although usually we do not think about all the alternatives foregone. Any such choice is made with a certain amount of knowledge of the possible consequences but also with a considerable measure of uncertainty. In general, we aim to maximise our knowledge of possible outcomes and minimise the uncertainty, then we can compare the alternatives that seem to be open and make our choice or *decision*.

All the elements mentioned above in relation to decisions occurring in personal life apply also to land use planning. Planning involves continual making of decisions, each of which requires the assessment of what options are open, how each is likely to work out, how certain the predicted outcomes are and what other options are being excluded. Decisions in land use planning tend, however, to be even more complex and have more ramifications than the choices arising in personal life.

One general point about land use planning—and hence decisions in planning—must be stressed here. For the sake of simplicity, land use planning is often represented as an activity that can be broken down into many component parts—types of problem or area—which will require a certain kind of treatment within a given time period. This must be recognised for the simplification it is. Planning is a continuous activity, which truly is endless. Any particular phase of action can only serve as a basis for the planner to reassess further action needed. Thus any decisions taken in planning should never be seen as final. They can only be appropriate to one moment in time, and the know-ledge available, the assessment of uncertainties and the concept of goals and priorities that make up the definition of the situation and hence the choices of action to be taken. All these elements must subsequently be reviewed to assess their continuing relevance, and whether there have developed any better ways to meet the revised objectives. Thus, although the word 'decision' has a rather emphatic and final ring to it, because of the nature of planning, decisions in land use planning should bever be regarded as final.

Decision theory is concerned with analysing how appropriate choices can be made in situations where alternatives exist. White points out that, 'There appear to exist, in practice, two different types of problematic situations. In one, the alternatives are given and the decision maker is required to make a suitable choice. In the other, part of the problem involves the search for alternatives.'[2] Ackoff refers to the types as 'evaluative' and 'developmental' respectively. Both types of decision problem are commonly met in land use planning.

Logical decision depends on a *well-defined* state of ambiguity, and thus a well-defined set of alternatives. It involves a decomposition of a situation into its various components, spotlighting any ambiguities for analysis. Thus selection can be made as rational as possible. It is applicable to 'human', as opposed to 'natural', sciences, because:

1 They have a cognitive element—choice behaviour depends on what the individual perceives at the moment of choosing.

2 The systems involved are 'open', in terms of the generation of new conditions.

3 There is generally no possibility of isolating and repeating experiments for the system under consideration.

The theory of decision emphasises the need for a consistent form of comparability between alternatives before choice can be made, otherwise there are no premises for analytical reasoning. So *measuring* becomes crucial to the decision taken, and in measuring the possible outcomes of a situation, two important and complementary concepts are involved—'value' and 'uncertainty'. In a decision situation, as much ambiguity as possible is removed by the analysis and measurement of the value and predictability of different outcomes, and any residual ambiguities then have to be acknowledged and treated as such. In selecting a preferred option from amongst all those options available we are considering and weighing up two separate aspects of each option—how certain it is to come about, how much it would contribute to our welfare if it did. There is no purpose in selecting a blissful option that will never happen or, at the other extreme, one that is highly probable but undesirable.

49

Let me illustrate these ideas, and the key components that influence choice in a decision making situation—uncertainty and value—with a simple example. I am about to go out for the day, and I have to choose whether or not to carry an umbrella. In doing so I must anticipate the likelihood of rain falling. This I do, as best as I can, from the look of the morning sky, assessing the probability of rain falling as twice as likely as not. There is still one major factor, however, that will help decide whether or not I take my umbrella, and that is the 'value' I attach to all the different possibilities. These are four in number, as shown:

	Rain	*No rain*
Take umbrella	Possibility 1	Possibility 2
No umbrella	Possibility 3	Possibility 4

The value I attach to each possibility depends on my personal relative comfort in getting wet or staying dry, carrying an umbrella or being unencumbered. The decision is finally made by considering such values together with the assessment of the probability of each outcome occurring.

There are various guide-lines to making such a choice—simple ones include taking whatever action most safeguards against the worst possibility occurring, or whichever offers the best chance of the highest valued outcome materialising. These guiding rules are fully developed, with all their logical ramifications, and with methods for analysing all manner of situations in the branch of study known as 'game theory'—a 'game' being a situation containing conflict of interest.

Decision theory provides a highly appropriate conceptual framework for land use planning and helps to clarify both requirements for the process as a whole and for its constituent parts. It emphasises the choosing nature of making decisions, the necessity to clarify options, to value the possible outcomes and to blend such values with the probability of the option's occurring. The fact that it is impossible to guarantee the future becomes clear, and also that even the 'right' decision depends largely on which kind of strategy is preferred. Uncertainty thus becomes a recognised major component of decision situations, which can best be handled by assessment of probabilities, but cannot be eliminated, and the right decision is recognised as totally dependent on the values attached to various outcomes. The conceptualised planning process in the last chapter incorporates these notions, and the 'strategic choice' approach which is now outlined builds upon the concepts of decision theory.

The 'strategic choice' approach

Friend has explained how, coming as outsiders to observe land use planning at work, he and Jessop developed their understanding of its most significant characteristics. Their specific interest was to apply to governmental decision making in social policy the approaches of Operational Research. 'By the early 1960's, the practice of operational research, which had its roots in the war-time secondment of scientists to work on the operational as opposed to the purely technical problems of national defence, had become well established in Britain and elsewhere as a service to industrial management' but 'its increasing acceptance in industry had led to a rather . . . restricted understanding of its scope in some quarters, with particular emphasis on certain well-defined classes of problem arising in such areas as the control of production and of stocks'.[4]

To promote the application of OR to problems of social policy, the Institute for Operational Research was set up in 1963, as a unit of the Tavistock Institute of Human Relations. Jessop conceived the idea of 'formulating a long-term project to explore the contribution OR might be able to make to planning and policy making in local government, which he saw as a microcosm of government in general in its problem of reconciling the demands of diverse public services.'[5] The research team began four years of involvement with Coventry City Council's planning problems, and the processes through which they reached their decisions. They observed various committees in action, work in the departmental offices of the Council, and the private group meetings of the two opposing political groups. During their period of observation, they were able to follow through 'several successive stages in the development of certain strategic issues, such as the review of the City's development plan, the future of secondary education and the search for a coherent transport policy'.[6]

Interestingly, their early reaction was an abandonment of preconceptions about the contribution that OR might make. As clearer views emerged as to the planning process that was going on, knowledge gained from parallel studies of architectural design teams and engineering design began to seem relevant, and particularly the technique—AIDA—Analysis of Interconnected Decision Areas. The technique offers a systematic way of analysing complex decision problems with many related elements, but the process of decision making as observed in the land use planning process appeared to be especially continuous and diffuse. 'The way in which AIDA might be applied to this kind of continuing planning process only began to become apparent once we began to link the basic concept to some ideas about the analysis of uncertainty which were then emerging from our experience in Coventry, and some concepts relating to the value of flexibility in planning which had been emerging elsewhere.'[7] The overall ideas about methodology which derived from the research project were presented in 'Local Government and Strategic Choice', illustrated by a series of fictional case examples. The potential of AIDA for land use planning problems was further explored in the six studies selected for the LOGIMP experiment, and the AIDA technique is discussed in Chapter 7 (see page 110).

The 'strategic choice' approach to planning will now be outlined.

The strategic choice approach to planning

'Plan makers are beset by the problems of uncertainty. These arise not only because they are concerned with the future which is difficult to control or to forecast, but because there is much in the present which they do not know or understand, which affects the success and the viability of their plans for the future.'[8] Much of this uncertainty is concealed, partly by use of probabilities and margins of error in facts and figures, and partly because one of the roles of planning is seen as the reduction of uncertainty. But the uncertainties under which planners operate often result in plans not being implemented, or turning out to be poor plans. Attempts to deal with uncertainty fall into two categories, either reduction of it through gaining better understanding or control

52

over the sources of it, or building flexibliity into the system so that adaptation is possible. In practice, both of these approaches have been taken in land use planning in recent years—with considerable research into urban models designed to increase understanding of the urban system, and with new approaches to planning, as recognised in the 1968 Act, aimed at increasing the flexibility and adaptability of the land use planning process.

As already suggested, another response to the recognition of such a large measure of uncertainty in relation to land use planning is to emphasise short term action, preferably keeping as much flexibility as possible for further ahead. This is essentially the philosophy underlying the 'strategic choice' approach. 'Our approach to dealing with the situation is to move away from concentration on the production of a plan and to focus more on current problems and the action that can be taken here and now. We regard planning as not so much concerned with the description of the future—a future over which there is only limited control—but with providing a firmer case for action which there is power to take now. Planning is concerned not so much with producing a plan as with gaining a better understanding of the problems with which we are faced now and in the future, in order that we can make better decisions now.'[9]

In practice, this approach involves exploring a 'range of possible directions that could be taken in the future', and 'exploring the nature of the uncertainties that inhibit our ability to choose a single plan with confidence'. It involves 'deciding what action to take to reduce uncertainty' and also 'what decisions should be made which will lead one in a desired direction, whilst still maintaining a range of options for the future'. And those options must also allow for the opportunity of making further good decisions as time resolves some uncertainties. It will be recognised by the reader that this is an expression of the tenets of decision theory explored earlier in this chapter.

An introspective, but scientific, approach to plan-design and evaluation.

I should like to continue this chapter by referring to a recent paper, with the above title, given by Michael Batty, which expresses most lucidly many key ideas, and synthesises them into a powerful argument.[10]

He begins by suggesting that the present self-questioning of the profession traditionally called 'town planning' is, in large measure, a reflection of wider problems facing society—'of the increasing rate of change in the growth of ideas and in the difficulties of reconciling past with the present'. The reaction of trying to embrace more and more ideas is doomed to failure; Medawar has argued that 'The factual burden of a science varies inversely with its degree of maturity.' Since planning historically has emphasised action rather than research and practice rather than theory it is easy to suggest that the present professional crisis is 'an intellectual class struggle rather than a true search for better ways of improving the lot of society'.

Batty's central argument—one to which I have already referred in this book—is that we pay scant attention to 'planning as a problem-solving method' or to ways of 'how to plan and how to plan best'. Thus the crisis of planning derives from a vacuum at the centre of the profession and of the subject as taught. Much attention is paid to how cities work economically or socially, and some effort is devoted to analysing and understanding the institutions that plan, but there appears to be little awareness of any value in learning about planning methods.

A concomitant of this argument is that the traditional formulation of the planning process, which has been modified rather than replaced over the years, has vital deficiencies. Geddes' original survey-analysis-plan has been expanded by the incorporation of some ideas from decision theory, to become:

but despite talk of 'feedback' and 'cycles' it remains essentially an *unintegrated* process.[12] The links between different stages of the process are not explicit and the whole approach is not in accord with the thought processes most likely to solve problems. (See above discussion on lateral thinking.)

Batty compares the process used for land use planning with other forms of problem-solving for planning and concludes that the land use planning method is uniquely cumbersome and wasteful. 'In psychology, problem-solving is seen as a learning process which is something more than just blind trial and error; the animal-learning is based upon using the results of a particular experiment to try to improve on the next experiment—there is positive and often conscious selection. In science, the process of hypotheses–experiment–observation is replicated and reordered many times in the quest to solve problems. In mathematics, problem-solving is systematic, leading from first approximation to the solution, or from decomposition of the problem into sub-problems whose partial solutions are synthesised into a final solution.'[13]

What each of these methods has in common, he suggests, and what land use planning lacks, is a process of learning from each solution improvements that can be made in the next solution. Batty gives two examples of the deficiency in land use planning— the first is the comparative study of metropolitan planning projects carried out by Boyce, Day and McDonald, in which they found that there is often time to generate only one or two alternatives; the second is the Coventry-Solihull-Warwickshire Study's discovery that alternative plans can be so similar that individual evaluation becomes pointless.[14]

Before suggesting some methods which are genuinely problem-solving approaches to planning, Batty makes a final point that perhaps the most formidable problem for land use planners is defining the 'solution space' within which the optimum solution must fall. He refers to approaches taken in architecture, traffic engineering and design to this problem which are extremely relevant.[15] Of recent land use planning studies, perhaps the Notts-Derby Sub-regional Study has approximated best the cyclical learning approach to problem solving.[16] (for discussion of that Study, see pages 16 and 116).

Batty then briefly explains three approaches to problem-solving that he considers pertinent—linear programming, combinatorial programming and graphical synthesis; these are discussed in the chapter on plan design (see page 119).

Although Batty is only able to make tentative suggestions about how we might in practice plan more adequately, his argument is indeed very convincing.

Attitudes to the future

This last section of my introductory discussion deals specifically with our attitudes to the future. It is a tautology to say that planning is concerned with the future, but there are many different attitudes that may be adopted. The two hypothetical extremes are that nothing can be established with certainty, therefore it is of no use at all trying to think about or prepare for the future, or that it is imperative to know exactly what is in store, and ensure that everything is controlled to achieve a predicted state.

In practice it appears that some middle position is almost always adopted—a compromise that accepts a measure of prediction, a measure of target setting, with an acceptance of a considerable measure of uncertainty. The need to know the future relates to two elements—the effects on welfare that a variation in events may bring about (whether or not there is going to be a harvest failure in an area dependent on one crop), and the ability to moderate actions effectively to accommodate variations in events (making arrangements in good time for supplementary foodstuffs to be brought in from elsewhere). Clearly, if variations in events in the future will make little difference to welfare, or if there is virtually no scope for alternative courses of action, the need to know about the future can be no more than curiosity.

Thus it seems plausible that our increasing preoccupation with probing, forecasting and attempting to shape the future is bound up with a belief that we stand to gain or lose depending on which of various possible patterns of events actually come about, plus a belief that we have some ability to choose among our immediate actions to influence which events come about. It is thus a dual conviction that there are better and worse futures and that something can be done to secure the better futures that motivate the carrying out and publicising of elaborate future forecasting exercises, such as those of the Hudson Institute or the Club of Rome.

The ideas of 'alternative futures'—once regarded as classifiable under 'science fiction'—now have total intellectual acceptability and pedigree. Thus land use plans are no longer rather aberrant attempts to look ahead—they are merely one of a whole range of forecasting operations regarded as obligatory by central and local governments, and institutions of all kinds, whether big businesses, charitable trusts or universities.

There are many interesting aspects to our current attitude to the future, and the appropriate way to regard it and treat it. It must obviously be bound up with a society's ideas concerning free will and determinism. It may be that the so-called 'bomb generation' reacted vehemently against having a passive attitude to the future. There must, too, be some connection with changing majority notions about the likelihood of any after-life, which surely impinges on the relative importance attached to shaping of the existing life. Changes in mortality rates and life expectancy patterns may make a more distant future seem a reality than was the case when average life expectancy was 32 years; thus each individual, and hence the whole community, has shifted in the valuation of the future as compared with the present (what is expressed in our 'rate of social discount'). Perhaps most significant of all, people no longer expect stability; we expect change, and though we may not welcome it, we wish to be prepared for it.

Thus, as stated above, forecasting is now, more than ever before, a major preoccupation of a wide range of agencies and groups all over the world. Associated with the increasing interest has been a considerable development in concepts and techniques relevant to the future and to forecasting. Some of these have already had significant influence on land use planning —others are still waiting in the wings. I shall try to sketch briefly some of the recent changes in the attitudes embodied in land use planning toward the future and to forecasting, which have had considerable implications for techniques.

Land use planning's attitude to the future

Land use planning since the 1940's has embodied a dual conception of its function—reacting in the present to specific proposals regarding the use of land, and seeing those present reactions within the context of preferred options in the future. What varies is how the relationship between these two is conceived, and how it is suggested that the planning process should be carried out in consequence. (And since the whole reason for planning is to ensure tangible achievements, there is a complex interaction between what people think ought to be the rationale and function of land use planning, and what appears able to be its rationale and function, in terms of existing real powers and responsibilities.)

The changes in legislation covering land use planning at the end of the 1960's resulted from suggestions, including those of the Planning Advisory Group on the Future of Development Plans, as to changes needed in the system set up under the 1947 Act. That system was based upon a conception of the way to treat land use planning and the future that had become unacceptable, revolving as it did around the master plan—a blueprint for a specified date in the future that all interim action should be aiming to achieve. The need to set explicit goals was not stressed, since a consensus about what constituted an opportunity and what constituted a problem was assumed to exist; when a land use planner, or his local government committee chairman or an official at the Ministry of Town and Country Planning saw a problem or an opportunity they would know it. That process thus reflected both a general acceptance of the integrity of the British professional and politician, and a society assumed to be substantially united in its wishes.

The still continuing revisions of the 1960's and 1970's to this now apparently grossly simplistic model of land use planning have been complex and wide-ranging. Among revisions that land use planning has now endeavoured to incorporate, the following are particularly relevant to this discussion of attitudes to the future. Planning should emphasise policies, which focus on activities, rather than two dimensional plans, which stressed carefully defined and classified land uses. Planning is a *continuous* activity, therefore it is invidious both to single out a particular moment in the future as in a master plan or development plan, and indeed to emphasise the further future as opposed to the nearer future. (See discussion elsewhere in this book about problem solving versus goal achieving.) It is unrealistic to suppose that there will not always be a considerable measure of uncertainty in planning, therefore any rigidity should be avoided if possible—planning must be *flexible*. Linked with this, should be definite provision for modification of policies, including monitoring procedures to see if things are working out as anticipated, and *feedback* of such information to the policies. As Eddison said, 'We have moved slowly from the era of the blueprint or the master plan into a phase of continuous review—a period when flexibility and adaptability are emphasised. What is happening is that we are coming round to recognising that uncertainty is the future, that no matter how glossy we make our plans, we cannot be sure what will happen. More and more the perhaps unpalatable truth is dawning that one of the greatest certainties is that our plans will be wrong. It is good that this is now being recognised and that our preoccupation should be to devise new approaches and techniques for coping with uncertainty.'[17]

References

1 De Bono, E., *The Mechanism of Mind,* Jonathan Cape, London (1969).
2 White, D. J., *Decision Theory,* Centre for Business Research,
3 University of Manchester, Allen & Unwin (1969);
see also Edwards, W. & Tversky, A. *Decision Making,* Penguin (1967).
4 Rapoport, A., *Fights, games and debates,* University of Michigan Press (1960).
Friend, J. K., 'The origins of the experiment', in *The LOGIMP Experiment,* CES IP 25, Centre for Environmental Studies, page 10 (1970).
5 Friend, *op. cit.* (4) above, page 11.
6 Friend, *op. cit.* (4) above, page 11.
7 Friend, *op. cit.* (4) above, page 12.
8 Wedgwood-Oppenheim, F. *The LOGIMP Experiment, op. cit.* (4) above, page 15.

9 Wedgwood-Oppenheim, *op. cit.* (4) above, page 15.
10 Batty, M., *An introspective, but scientific, approach to plan-design and evaluation,* a paper given at Oxford, during a course on Evaluation, Oxford Polytechnic, 1972; see also Levin, P. H., 'The design process in planning', in *Town Planning Review,* **37,** 1, April 1966; Schlesinger, J. R., *Organisational structures and planning,* Rand Corporation (1966).
11 Medawar, P., *The Art of the Soluble,* Methuen, London (1967).
12 Geddes, P., *Cities in Evolution,* Williams & Norgate, London (1915); see, for example, McLoughlin, J. B., *Urban and Regional Planning,* Faber, London (1969).
13 Batty, *op. cit.* (10) above.
14 Boyce, D., Day, N. & McDonald C., *Metropolitan Plan-Making,* Regional Science Research Institute, Monograph No. 4, Philadelphia (1969); Wannop, U. (*et al.*), *Coventry-Solihull-Warwickshire: A Strategy for the Sub-region,* Coventry City Council (1971).
15 Alexander, C., *Notes on the Synthesis of Form,* Harvard University Press, Cambridge, Massachusetts (1964); Manheim, N., *Hierarchical Structure: A Model of Design and Planning Processes,* Report No. 7, M.I.T. Press, Cambridge, Massachusetts (1966); March, L. & Steadman P., *The Geometry of Environment,* RIBA Publications Ltd., London (1971).
16 Thorburn, A., (*et al.*), *Nottinghamshire and Derbyshire Sub-regional Study,* Nottingham County Council (1969).
17 Eddison, P. A., 'Preface', in *The LOGIMP Experiment, op. cit.* (4) above, page 7.

PART TWO

Stages of the Land Use Planning Process

4 Information

Two kinds of need for information can be differentiated—the first is where a specific subject is being considered with an immediate purpose and the function of assembling the necessary information may be termed research; the second is a more general requirement for amplifying and updating knowledge in a wider field, which we can call intelligence. There has been some controversy in land use planning as to whether or not the activities of research and intelligence should properly be carried out in a separately organised unit, or by the same staff who will subsequently be developing and implementing policy as a result of the analysis of information.[1]

The categories of research and intelligence correspond to a large extent with a distinction I shall make between two types of information, namely, statistical and other, principally literary. Any information in land use planning may relate to a subject, a place, a time, or two of these or all three. Much complication arises from needing information that is complementary in all three of these dimensions, and approaches to making data compatible are mentioned below. First, however, a definition of 'information'—'data' are representations of facts or ideas in a formalised manner, 'information' is what those data mean to someone, when passed through the 'fact filter' of a brain.[2]

Most discussions of information for land use planning tend to concentrate on statistical data and its sources. The chapters in Part 3 of this book, which deal in turn with different activities of concern to land use planners, each contain a discussion of relevant statistical sources. What I deal with in this chapter are more general considerations relating to 'research' information, including a brief sketch of the main sources of statistical data and recent developments in data handling and presentation. Also, I include in this chapter a brief section on 'non-statistical' information needed in research. The information needs for 'intelligence' are dealt with in the chapter on Communication (see page 185).

Land use planning's data requirements

Data is needed in land use planning to provide information about basic distributions and about relationships. For example, in investigating employment, a land use planner will want data about the location of places of employment, and also about how they relate to the location of the homes of employees. A third use for data which is given explicit emphasis now is for 'indicators', both of need and as measures of the effects of action.[3] Any data is either gathered specifically by the immediate user, in which case it is 'primary' data, or obtained at one remove, when it is termed 'secondary'. Where data is being directly collected, it may be from a case study, which probes the detailed facts and relationships of one event in one area or, more usually, in a selective process looking at elements of interest.

The term 'survey' is given to the systematic collection of data, but there are many variants of the survey. One distinction is between surveys aiming at a complete coverage of units and surveys where a sample is considered sufficient. The details of sampling methods are complex. If a survey aims to be statistically valid, careful procedures must be followed to avoid bias. It may be decided to stratify the sample—that is, select from several known different categories of the units to be sampled (for example, age groups in the population), or to weight it—pay more attention to part of the sample than would be obtained on a strictly random basis (if school-age children were of some particular relevance, say). Whatever the sample may be designed to achieve, it must be randomly obtained. Provided that is so, and that it is large enough, and there is an adequate response, it is possible to state what the statistical reliability of the survey has been. For coverage of these matters, the reader is referred to Moser's book, *Survey Methods in Social Investigation*.[4] A survey may, however, be frankly non-scientific—intended only as a guide.

Various methods of survey are used by land use planners, and also, of course, by market research firms or other institutions which often carry out such investigations for planning studies. First, let us mention surveys of people. Often they are contacted at home, and either posted or left a questionnaire, or interviewed, or frequently some combination of the two. An interview may be totally structured—controlled in advance, usually by a questionnaire—or more open-ended. The latter technique in general requires that the interviewer is very well informed as to the overall purposes of the survey, and is more used where it is the attitudes of those interviewed that are of interest rather than factual information concerning them and their habits. People may also be contacted away from their home, at a picnic site in a recreational survey, in their car for a traffic survey, outside a shop for shopping surveys and so on. They may also be reached indirectly by, for example, leaving a card on their car, or by questions in a theatre programme.

However they are contacted, they are usually asked for two categories of information about themselves—the details that relate to the subject of the survey—their travel habits, for example, and also personal information so that relationships between travel habits and personal characteristics can be established. Such personal information is called the 'profile data'. Design and implementation of survey is a highly skilled process, as is, of course, the analysis of results. It is usual for a 'pilot' (a trial survey) to be carried out before the full-scale investment of the time and money required in the proper survey. It cannot be stressed too much how important it is for the later stages of analysis and policy formulation to be thought through before information collection is completed.

Apart from surveys of people, land use planning requires many surveys of objects. These may be carried out by direct observation, as with land use, from a secondary source—age of buildings from an ordnance survey map, or electronically—as in some traffic counts. Aerial photographs and maps are an important source for various types of survey. Finally here I should refer to the chapter on leisure, in which there is a section, based on Burton, on sources of information for recreation, which should be looked at for a discussion of different methods of survey that have been used for planning for leisure.

There have been fears that unnecessary duplication of effort was going into surveys for land use planning—particularly those oriented to topics, rather than those of an area—and the PEP report 'Making fuller use of survey data' was one of the first to deal with this problem.[5] The growth of interest in data banks and information systems, discussed below, stems in part from this, and has now been given official sanction in the GISP Report (General Information Systems for Planning)[6] (see Figure 4.1).

Some of the main sources of statistical information

Central government

Central government collects and publishes statistical information, both as a service and incidentally to other functions. A great deal is produced by the Office of Population Census and Surveys, but other major Departments and agencies operating under the auspices of central government also produce both regular reports of surveys and special publications. (It is as well to mention here that there are guides to government statistics relating to different subjects, published by the Stationery Office.)

The *Census of Population* is perhaps the outstanding government source of statistics used by land use planners. For the Census, information on many aspects of population and housing is collected—at present with full coverage every ten years and a sample survey at the mid-period. The smallest area to which statistics relate is the Enumeration District—one enumerator's area for the survey—and data for these are aggregated in a variety of ways. A fuller discussion of the Census, of what it offers, and its drawbacks, will be found in the chapter on population (see page 195). Changes in the *Census of Population* derive from users' requirements, the experience gained in taking each Census, and from new possibilities opened up by technical advances. At present, attention focuses on making results more rapidly available, and there is interest in machine scanning of

66

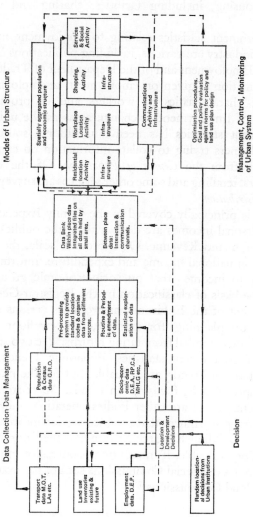

Fig. 4.1   A Suggested Planning Information System (after Cripps & Hall)

SOURCE   'An introduction to the study of information for urban and regional planning',
Information and Urban Planning, CES IP 8, 1 (1969)

forms and automatic processing. The last Census introduced geocoding and the grid square unit as adjuncts to the traditional referencing and areas. The same Census is also a main source of statistics on housing, including facilities, sharing and over-crowding.

Central government statistics relating to employment and to manufacturing industry are various, including publications of the Department of Employment and of the Department of Trade and Industry. Information is given on employment, unemployment, hours worked, characteristics of workers and of producing units. The use of Employment Exchange areas as the unit for many employment statistics has been a traditional source of difficulty for planners trying to collate information on employment with data from the *Census of Population*. Of the other economic sectors, retailing and some other services are surveyed in the *Census of Distribution*.

Expenditure is principally covered in the Family Expenditure Survey, and personal incomes are dealt with in the publications of the Board of Inland Revenue. On a broader scale, the Blue Book has data on national income and expenditure. Information closely relating to income—that on socio-economic group—is produced on the basis of classification by the Registrar-General.

The Department of the Environment produces various series of information for planning, for example, the new floor space statistics, which are compiled from rating returns. The two special compilations of government statistics, Economic Trends, and the more recent Social Trends, are valuable, but for the purpose their names imply, that is, focusing on trends. Apart from the main Departments, there are other bodies operating under the auspices of central government that produce statistical information, for example, the Building Research Station and the Countryside Commission. Very valuable, if intermittent, sources of information, are the reports of special Commissions set up, for example, the Hunt and Maud Commissions.[7]

Regional sources

As they relate to the newest and weakest tier in the land use planning hierarchy, regional sources of information are not well developed. Regional bodies set up with responsibility for economic or land use planning often need to carry out research to produce information, and they also, of course, compile what is already available. A guide to regional information has been produced by Hammond.[8] Reference may also be made to a report on sources of regional statistics prepared for the Standing Conference on London and South East Regional Planning.[9]

Local government

Land use planning departments have certain statutory obligations to collect statistical information, for example for the production of structure plans and various local plans. They need information for other purposes too, as when they are assessing a planning application or appearing at an Inquiry. A standard range of subjects will be considered by any land use planning department, but their special interests will depend on the characteristics of the area, and hence its problems and needs.

The other departments in any local authority also obtain information as a part of their functions, or as research material. Thus work undertaken for education, social services, housing, traffic policies and so on all generate data useful to the land use planner. A special unit may exist in a local authority outside the departmental structure to carry out research and intelligence work. That is one approach—which has strong advocates and opponents —to making a common pool of useful data available to all interested departments. The data bank and information system discussion below deals with this problem again. *Ad hoc* bodies operating at a similar geographical scale to local government may provide useful statistical information—for example, the Notts-Derby Sub-regional Study set up a sub-regional data bank, which had purposes wider than the immediate needs of the study. Consultants' work may make a valuable contribution, too, for example the data collected by the Buchanan team for the South Hampshire Study, or the recent series of reports on historic towns.

The Development Corporations and the Commission for the New Towns compile much statistical information about their affairs (a lot of which is summarised each January in the journal *Town and Country Planning*).

Other sources

Still concentrating on statistical information, there are other sources, which land use planners find useful, apart from central and local government. Sillitoe's *Britain in Figures: A Handbook of Social Statistics* is excellent, although it is, of course, dealing with the national situation only.[10] Welfare agencies produce information—for example, Shelter on many aspects of housing, the Notting Hill Trust on its area. Research bodies, in universities or elsewhere offer the work of staff and students, and frequently have special series of Working Papers.[11] Institutions including the Centre for Environmental Studies, PEP, the Economist Intelligence Unit, and the Institute for Social and Economic Research often produce information that land use planners need; so do private market research organisations, but access to it may be difficult or expensive. I mention in the next section various other sources of information, which are on the whole non-statistical, but there is not a hard boundary; thus the Registers of Research—of the RTPI, the *Architect's Journal* or the Countryside Commission, say, may yield statistical sources, and occasionally this is also true of articles in journals.

Finally, in relation to statistical information, let me enumerate the common difficulties, which are that data is found to be for the wrong areas, the wrong years, the wrong groupings, has no time series consistency, is costly of time and labour to extract, is confidential or is not statistically reliable. It is in part in an attempt to deal with such problems that data banks are being developed.

Data banks

The requirements of the land use planning process for information are so unbounded and so varied that traditional methods of recording and storing data are increasingly inadequate. This is a problem which has been given added emphasis by the development of mathematical simulation techniques, which usually demand a large data base. A solution which is increasingly being adopted is the creation of a 'data bank'.

A data bank has been defined as: a system of storing relevant and useful information in such a way as to be readily accessible, easily manipulated, and capable of constant review. It is quite possible to have a manually operated data bank, but far more usual for a computer to be used.

Lee has suggested that there are three points where conventional manual filing systems fail:

'1 The total stock of raw data is necessarily made up of incompatible and scattered parts. An enormous proportion of effort goes into seeking out possible sources of data, and putting them into a usable form. There is always the suspicion that somewhere there might be more recent, more up-to-date information, but to search all the files is inconceivable.

2 There is a limit to the time that technically qualified staff can devote to manual data processing, but it is becoming more and more vital do do work of this nature.

3 The time consumption of manual methods, both of basic storage and simple manipulation, severely restricts the amount of information that can be brought to bear on each planning exercise or decision.'[12]

Although Lee refers to the use of staff time, it is perhaps pertinent to emphasise specifically how much most staff dislike and resent the routine work of data manipulation, disparagingly referred to as 'number crunching' in most offices. The potential advantages of a computer operated data bank therefore include— the provision of an up-to-date source of information on which to base policy and detailed decisions, the immediate availability of information in an appropriate form, and the elimination of duplication, both of data and effort.

However, it is important that the data bank should fit effectively into the overall information system used by an organisation. They must both be carefully related to the organisation's functions. Since those of a land use planning department are varied, an information system must be able to provide output in a variety of forms. Similarly there are many differing sources of relevant information, so the system must be able to store and process numerical, literary and graphical forms of data. Thus the system must be flexible both in relation to output and input. The main criticism levelled against computer-based systems is that of inflexibility. Also that operational difficulties arise with data banks from the wide sweep of decision making in planning—embracing both daily management decisions and strategic planning, and areas which range in scale from individual properties to, say, an entire metropolitan region.

A data bank may have one of two structures—either a single centralised file of information, or several separate files, linked by a system of reference. In the centralised single file structure, data from all sources is held at the same level, the lowest common level suitable for all purposes—in a planning department, the single property.

There are several attractions to the alternative structure—separate but integrated files. The structure is more flexible—data can be held at different levels and the files added to as needed. In many instances specific aggregation of data will not be necessary, since it is already held at the desired level. The differing levels of availability of data will present no problem. In some situations it may well be preferable to have up-to-date information at a higher level of aggregation than the ideal, rather than older information at the best level. The deciding factor for any planning department's data bank, in practice, is that so much of the information of interest is not available for individual properties, nor is it likely to be in the near future. Thus a structure of separate but integrated files has to be used.

It may be helpful to mention as an example here CLUSTER, a land use system devised for the seven central London local authorities. It involves the creation of a main file of the survey data collected by each of the authorities to answer the requirements of the 1971 Greater London land use survey (collated by the Greater London Council). Data from resurveys, correction of errors and ancillary planning data will be submitted monthly to update the main file. The file can be interrogated to extract details of properties falling within certain locational areas or satisfying certain conditions. The information may be sorted, totalled and sub-totalled at the request of the user, and the data printed at varying levels of detail. The master file consists of the following records:

File Heading Record
Street Heading Record
Main Property Record
—Special Areas Record
—Housing Record
—Public Buildings Record
—Use Record
—Employment Record

The file is maintained in street/house index order. Some of the problems faced by land use planners in securing data compatibility are illustrated by the following list of descriptions which are filed with each property—street, property number, plan number, street block number, parcel number, grid reference easting and northing, traffic zone and sub-zone 1962 and 1971, district plan enumeration area 1966, enumeration district 1966 and 1971, Initial Development Plan zone, New Plan zone. Information filed relates to the building's age, condition and number of storeys, whether it is listed, the owner, various measures of area, building ratio and parking space, whether it includes a restaurant, hotel, shops, houses etc., whether it is in a special area, such as conservation, action, improvement, environmental, Board of Trade shopping area; then land use classifications, and information on employment, including number of workers, their sex and type of occupation. Obviously, the details of this system are specific to the central London context, but the general range of the land use and employment data is what is everywhere required for land use planning.

Data classification

At the heart of ensuring the efficiency of a data bank is the system used for the classification of data. Since the locational identification of data is of central importance in planning, this will now be considered. For a discussion of the other two important aspects of classification—the separate treatment of qualitative and quantitative data, and the distinguishing of 'pure themes' of information relating to the use of land—the reader should look at Lee's article on 'Data Banks for Planning'.[13]

73

The Ministry of Housing suggested that a locational coding system for land use must be able to identify unique locations, must also be able to identify relative locations and should be suitable for electronic data processing. The Ministry, and the Royal Town Planning Institute's Research Group, recommended the use of a co-ordinate reference system based on the National Grid.[14] The advantages of basing a system on a grid (whatever its size) are, first, that the basic unit is uniform in area and shape; thus any differences between units are purely a function of the variable under study; and secondly, that the framework is constant over time. Two difficulties have to be accepted—that the units do not relate to anything recognisable on the ground, and that much existing data is not available for grid squares. However, conversions are possible, and there is increasing acceptance of the need to provide information by grid squares (by the Office of Population Census and Surveys for the Census of Population, for example).

As already mentioned, the method of locational referencing which seems, on balance, the best, is co-ordinate referencing. Data can thereby be grouped into convenient areas, such as transportation zones, or general improvement areas, and the location of services matched to the clients. Such referencing is essential for automatic manipulation of data spatially, which is bound to become more and more the norm.

Point referencing means the application of co-ordinate references to individual point locations on the ground—in planning, the location of land or property units, by choice of a point within them. All dates relating to that location may then be coded, using the same point co-ordinate reference. For vertical sub-divisions of a building, an appropriate common property coding system would be needed. Co-ordinate referencing can thus provide the common code needed to relate the separate information files of a data bank. Such a code is known as a key code. It is suggested that the National Grid Referencing System can be used—a twelve-figure reference would locate a point to a one-metre resolution, an eight-figure reference to 100 metres. The first half of the digits are 'eastings' and the second half 'northings'. Co-ordinates can be established by eye, or using a digitiser, which is a reading table with movable cursor, attached to an electronics console. The degree of accuracy obtainable is governed by the accuracy of base maps—a scale of 1:1250 is recommended as these become uniformly available. Conventions for referencing are being established.[15]

Locational referencing facilitates computer mapping and spatial data processing, which are both important advances in analysis of information for planning.

For illustration of the possibilities of computer mapping, I shall briefly describe the system developed by central government, known as Linmap. Using a standard line-printer attached to a computer, Linmap provides a rapid means of producing maps from large quantities of data, provided the centres of the areas for which data is available are co-ordinate referenced. Virtually any data can be prepared for use with the system, provided a co-ordinate reference is given to the centre of each area to which data refer. As first examples, 1966 Population Census data by wards and parishes, and 1969 Agricultural Census information were prepared for Linmapping.[16]

The data are stored on magnetic tape, and can, if it is wished, be extensively processed before a map is printed out. Thus, in processing, items can be aggregated and related to each other. Eventually, it will be possible to compare two sets of data and show changes.

Several styles of presentation of data have been developed, both for black and white and colour presentation. The styles are variously appropriate for particular types of subject matter, and differing geographical scales. Thus cheering progress is now being made toward automatic storage, retrieval and processing of data, including mapping. It is clearly desirable to learn as much as possible from experience obtained in developing such systems elsewhere. Sweden, for example, has had for some time a compehensive national information system.[17] (See Figure 4.2.) In the USA, data banks have been operated by various agencies with land use planning functions. From an examination of the US experience, three kinds of deficiency commonly encountered were specified by Lindberg.[18] First, where the data within the system refers only to the area of the particular local authority it is hardly likely to shed new light on problems, and may be considered an expensive filing system.

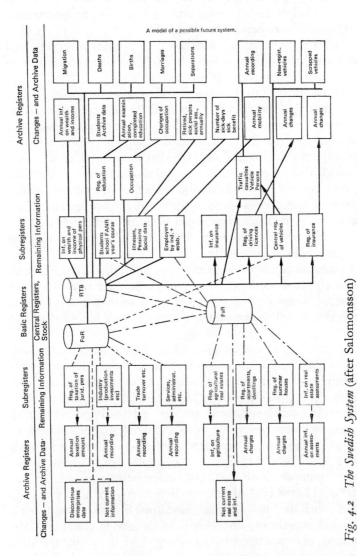

Fig. 4.2 The Swedish System (after Salomonsson)

SOURCE 'Data banking systems for urban planning', *Information and Urban Planning*, CES IP 8, **2** (1969)

Secondly, it is too often assumed that one computer system can meet the needs of day-to-day management and of long-term planning. The result is so much 'governmental housekeeping' work that analysis of information for strategic planning becomes a luxury.

Thirdly, the statistical expertise required for interpretation and manipulation of data is grossly under-estimated, data collected is of inadequate quality, analytical techniques are misused, and complex mathematical models are created regardless of whether they can be satisfactorily tested or supplied with information that is reliable.

Finally, perhaps I should explain the purpose of an information system that is not fundamentally a numerical one. Much information needed by planners is literary (as discussed further in Chapter 10, see page 185): reports, articles, product specifications and so forth. For such information, efficient systems of storage and retrieval are also required. Many of the same considerations apply as have already been discussed in relation to data banks. A fundamental problem is an appropriate classification basis. Possibilities are an alphabetical index—easy to set up, but quite arbitrary in relation to the subject matter; numeric and alphanumeric systems, such as the Dewey, Universal Decimal or SfB systems, but these are always to some extent subjective, with the possibility of communication failure between the person classifying the data for input to the system and the user; or a keyword system, which has its drawbacks, too.[19]

Non-statistical information

There are other categories of factual information for land use planners, and other ways of presenting statistics that commonly receive less attention. Maps are a 'stock in trade' of those with a geographical background and can provide information on one or more related subjects, from the geology, topography, soils, vegetation or climate of an area to settlement patterns, resource, economic and social factors. Indeed, anything with spatial variation can be presented in cartographic form, and the exciting range of computer mapping techniques has been mentioned earlier. Since the spatial dimension is of particular relevance to land use planners, the expression of information in a spatial form is often an essential part of a planning exercise. The next chapter will discuss the general development of spatial data processing techniques, which encompass the spatial dimension throughout, in contrast to many of the analytical techniques planners have traditionally used which have been borrowed from other disciplines and which relate poorly to the spatial dimension. Photographs and aerial photographs are another valuable source of information for land use planning, with a wide range of uses, for example, landscape analysis, housing surveys, checking numbers of caravans.[20]

Another more general category is records, which are kept by an organisation for its own purposes, but which may also be of interest to the land use planner. A few examples are the records of births and deaths kept by local registrars, attendance records—at a health centre or a swimming pool, sales—of specialised sports equipment or even of bread (used respectively in studies of angling and of tourism, see Chapter 15), motor licences, litter collected—physical evidence of seasonal variations in the use of beaches and so on. Records kept over time may also be relevant—parish registers, one of the historian's sources of information, or, more obviously, applications for planning permissions. In very specialised cases, written accounts—either factual, as in Engels' description of the condition of the working classes, or in fiction as in Dickens—may provide useful back-up 'pictures in words'. I have quoted two historical examples, but contemporary descriptions of, say, the teenagers who cannot find jobs, or the West Indian community of Brixton, as have appeared in recent issues of *New Society*, fall into the same category of descriptive information. The records of the deliberations of bodies of men who strongly influenced the development of land use planning in some way—the Reith Committee on New Towns, for example, might also be mentioned here.[21]

References

1 See, for example, views expressed by B. Benjamin, based on experience at the Greater London Council, in the Research and Intelligence Unit.

2 Harris, B., 'The future of models and data in urban analysis and design', in *Information and Urban Planning*, CES IP 8, **2**, Centre for Environmental Studies (1969).

3 Friedly, P., 'Welfare indicators for public facility investments in urban renewal areas', in *Socio-Economic Planning Sciences*, **3**, page 291 (1969);
Shonfeld, A. & Shaw S. (Eds.), *Social Indicators and Social Policy*, Heinemann, for the SSRC (1972).

4 Moser, P., *Survey Methods in Social Investigation*, Heinemann, see also Social and Community Research, 3 *Manuals—1. Postal Survey Methods*; 2. *Sample design and selection*; 3. *Interviewers Guidebook*, Research Publication Services Ltd., London (1972).

5 Phillipson, M., *Making Fuller Use of Survey Data*, PEP (1968).

6 Department of the Environment, *General Information Systems for Planning*, HMSO (1972).

7 The Hunt *Report on Intermediate Areas*, HMSO (1969), Cmnd. 3998;
The Redcliffe-Maud *Report on Local Government in England*, Cmnd. 4040, HMSO (1969).

8 Hammond, E., *An analysis of regional economic and social statsitics*, Rowntree Research Unit, University of Durham (1968).

9 Secretariat of the Standing Conference on London and South East Regional Planning, *Report on Sources of Regional Statistics*, see GLC Research and Intelligence Unit Quarterly Bulletin, **9**, December 1969.

10 Sillitoe, A., *Britain in Figures: A Handbook of Social Statistics*, Penguin (1971);
see also, *Facts in Focus*, by Central Statistical Office, Penguin (1972).

11 For example, the series of Working Papers published by the Department of Town Planning, Oxford Polytechnic.

12 Lee, C., 'Data banks for planning', in *Planning Outlook*, New Series, **10**, spring 1971;
see also Brindell, J. J., 'The functions and characteristics of data banks', in *Proceedings of the Town Planning Institute Computer Conference*, April 1969.

13 Lee, *op. cit.* (12) above.

14 Urban Planning Directorate, *The Principles of a Land Use Classification in a Computer Data Bank*, MHLG, (1968);
Town Planning Institute Research Committee, *The Use of the the Computer in Planning*, Town Planning Institute (1968).

15 Department of the Environment, *Point Referencing Properties and Parcels of Land,* HMSO (1971).
16 Department of the Environment, *Linmap and Colmap (a Brief Description): Techniques for Planning,* HMSO (1971).
17 Salomonssen, O., *Data Banking Systems for Urban Planning,* in Information and Urban Planning, CES IP8, **2,** Centre for Environmental Studies (1969);
Cripps, E. L., *A Comparative Study of Information Systems for Urban and Regional Planning: 1. Scandinavia,* Working Paper 7, Urban System Research Unit, University of Reading.
18 Lindberg, F. J., 'Urban information systems and data banks: better prospects with an environmental model', in *Threshold of Planning Information Systems,* Report of 1967 Conference of the American Society of Planning Officials, published by the Society, Chicago (1967), described in Fry, R. E. 'Urban information systems in the United States—a review and commentary', in G.L.C. Research and Intelligence Unit, *Quarterly Bulletin,* page 3, **3,** July 1968.
19 Pearce, D. M., 'Information retrieval—methods available', in GLC Research and Intelligence Unit, *Quarterly Bulletin,* page 12, **6,** March 1969.
20 Collins, W. G., *Aerial Surveying and its Potential in Urban Planning,* in Information and urban planning, CES IP 8, Centre for Environmental Studies, page 117, **1,** (1969).
21 Ministry of Town and Country Planning, *New Towns Committee: Final Report* (Reith Report), Cmd. 6876 (1946).

5 Preliminary Analysis

The subject of the last chapter was information; in particular, what I termed 'research' information, which is needed for a particular problem under study. In this chapter I shall discuss the next stage of dealing with that information—namely preliminary analysis. In the context of the overall land use planning process as commonly followed, this can be regarded as beginning to convert information into alternative possible futures. Indeed, the final section of this chapter concentrates on forecasting techniques. The following stage of the process—plan design or plan making— is the subject of the next chapter.

There is a very wide variety of approaches to the analysis of data, and I cannot pretend to a comprehensive coverage.[1] However, to illustrate the range of techniques available I shall pick out a selection. It has already been suggested that much of land use planning's data is statistical, dealing with quantitative spatial variations and their relationships, with each statistic 'tagged' by subject, area or time, or some combination of these. The techniques discussed first are, therefore, those that attempt to make progress in the understanding of spatial variations and relationships from given data.

Classifications

A simple approach is to sort data according to predetermined categories or classes. This is an example of imposing a subjective preconception of the world on to information, but the results are usually presented as objective statistics. Two examples of the use of classification in land use planning will suffice. Employment statistics are one of the key sets of data in a land use planner's analysis of an area. It is usual to look at the employment structure as given in central government statistics sorted according to the Standard Industrial Classification. These statistics are then used as the basis for sophisticated analyses of an area's present character and likely future. However, the deficiencies of the SIC are well known, particularly its weakness in treatment of the tertiary (mainly service) activities. Specific examples are cited of the misleadingness of this particular classification in a discussion of 'shift and share' analysis, in the chapter on employment (see page 240).

One more example of the classification approach is the attempt to agree on a clear set of categories for leisure activities, which preoccupies recreation land use planners. It is quite clear that the exercise is far from straightforward, but without such a categorisation, many analytical techniques used for establishment of causal relationships and for forecasting cannot be applied, and survey data is of limited usefulness. Thus a classification has to be established.

Statistical techniques of analysis

Many statistical techniques depend upon data already classified, but some techniques work on disaggregated information. The establishment of significant relationships through regression analysis is common in land use planning, and more complicated approaches, such as types of factor analysis are also now familiar.[2] Examples of the use of component analysis and cluster analysis may be found in the chapter on housing (see page 277) and on shopping (see page 323).

Since land use planning is concerned with spatial variations, the construction of 'surfaces', which indicate variations in the intensity of some element of interest from one place to another, are often useful. Such surfaces may be constructed from composite items of information as well as from very straightforward data. The Coventry-Solihull-Warwickshire Study's use of surfaces is described in Chapter 8 (see page 144).

Spatial data processing

The methods so far described could certainly be called processing of spatial data, but I wish to deal under this heading with advances currently being made. The advances I refer to are in the development of more integrated and automated methods of handling data, so that the elements of initial input of data, geographical referencing of it, analysis in various forms and output of either simple or composite statements of spatial characteristics in a graphical form can be handled together.

This involves the use of several items of electronic equipment, and standard computer programs are being worked out to handle the various component tasks needed within such an integrated process. Related elements are the co-ordinate referencing of basic data and computer mapping techniques, both of which were described in the last chapter (see page 74).

Graphical methods

Analysis of data may be carried out statistically, as discussed above, but often there are several other ways that the same analysis could be approached. It is traditional in land use planning —with its essential interest in the spatial dimension—to make considerable use of graphical methods. Thus the 'sieve map' technique carries out a form of selection based upon the comparison of various different sets of data referring to land characteristics. The same approach can be followed without the use of maps; indeed it is a form of linear programming.

Graphical methods have a great advantage in communication over tables of figures. It is thus possible for an analyst to perceive points of significance he might otherwise miss, and it is certainly very easy to convey information using such illustrative devices as graphs, histograms, bar charts, population pyramids and so on. They will undoubtedly continue to have value, perhaps not so much for analysis of information, which seems certain to become much more automated, but for communicating.

83

Analysis of sequences

Planning deals with the dimension of time, as well as space, thus techniques are needed to look at information in terms of relationships over time. The relevance tree technique, mentioned below, helps to analyse both the significance of activities and the priority sequences that are necessary (see page 89). Critical path analysis, which is discussed in the chapter on implementation (see page 168), is another technique for analysis of information to produce programmes of work and action.

Models

Models are given the following chapter to themselves, because they cut across almost every land use planning subject that is discussed. They must, however, be mentioned here as a powerful array of techniques for analysis of information in a preliminary stage of evolving plans, as well as in the later stages of the same process. Thus, for example, Ray Maw, in developing his leisure model, had as his initial purpose, greater understanding of demands for leisure. He sought to clarify the relationship between the leisure activities people actually carry out, their own characteristics and the characteristics of leisure facilities.[3]

Forecasting techniques

Since planning deals with the future, a most important category of techniques used in the stages of preliminary analysis of information are those for forecasting. The traditional forecasting techniques of land use planners were not very varied, but in recent years a considerable number of methods have been added to the armoury. This was partly in consequence of the development efforts of future forecasting agencies not concerned with land use planning, and partly because of the incorporation into the profession of land use planning of many people from non-traditional disciplines, who brought their familiar techniques with them. There has thus been a sudden great increase in the range of and sophistication of forecasting methods used in land use planning in the last ten, and particularly the last five, years. Let us consider first the objectives of future oriented research (based mainly on Kahn).[4] It is necessary to stimulate and stretch the imagination and improve the perspective, and hence to clarify, define, name, expound and argue major issues. Thus alternative policy contexts and 'packages' may be designed and studied. In the process, intellectual communication will be improved and co-operation stimulated, particularly by the use of historical analogies, metaphors, scenarios, analytic models, all trying to employ precise concepts and suitable language. Such future-oriented research increases the ability to identify new patterns and crises and to understand their character and significance. Appropriate methods are very varied, and perhaps most importantly include both 'linear' and 'non-linear' approaches, for example—a paradigm—which is a structured set of propositions—or a heuristic—which serves to discover, or to stimulate investigation, but not necessarily in a scholarly or rigorous way, or a propaedeutic exposition—which pertains to introductory instruction without oversimplification.

Such techniques are indispensable since creative integration of ideas must eventually take place in one mind, and so even the most sophisticated and knowledgeable policy maker, analyst, planner must absorb new ideas from unfamiliar fields.

Kahn has suggested some of the ways in which forecasting may go wrong—including criteria set too narrowly, inadequate thought given, inapproprate values used or models constructed, over or under discounting of uncertainty or of the future, decisions taken in the forecast at inappropriate points in the structure (for the end in view and with the consequences known). This is not to include the bad luck elements—unknown issues, unlikely events, a change in the actors involved, or the danger that the best may be the enemy of the good or vice versa.

Nevertheless, forecasting is indispensable. It can provide information about the types of future development that are possible, provide a probabilistic assessment of the likelihood of each development—'it is a way of charting the range of possible or alternative futures'—and it also influences the direction and pace of development, so is, to some extent, self-fulfilling. A distinction is generally made between two types of forecasting— extrapolation, which works forward logically from the present, and normative forecasting, which starts by identifying some

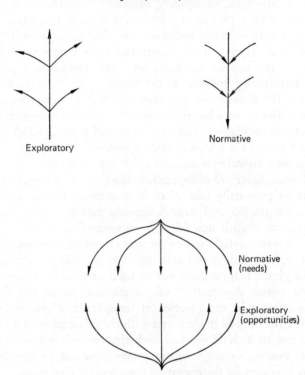

Technological
Forecasting — exploratory or normative

Exploratory

Normative

Normative
(needs)

Exploratory
(opportunities)

Fig. 5.1   Technological Forecasting: Exploring a normative (after Jantsch)

SOURCE Technological Forecasting in Perspective, by E. Jantsch OECD,
Paris, 1967

desirable state in the future then works back to discover the intermediate steps involved (see Figure 5.1). Techniques have been developed by governments, firms, and research agencies; it is commonly suggested that some classification is possible of the likely scope and time span of their various interests, which in turn, largely fixes which forecasting techniques are appropriate. This is illustrated in the following table, based on Jantsch:[5]

Agency	Forecast period of concern Formal	Informal
'look out' institutions, social technology, natural resources, etc.		Up to 50+ years
industry in social technology, e.g. communications	5–10	30–50
space programme	10–20	20–30+
defence	7–10	20–25+
national economy e.g. French plan	5	20–25
national goals e.g. US government	5– 6	10–30
innovating industry e.g. chemistry electronics	5–10	10–20
consumer type industry	3– 5	5–10

It is clear from such a table that land use planning has been, and still is, expected to forecast for a long period—formally for 20 years, and informally up to about 40 years. It is not surprising, therefore, that it proves difficult. What is more surprising is that the complexity is not intelligently acknowledged and more attention paid to the appropriate way to approach it, both conceptually and specifically in the techniques used, the outcomes expected and the way they are then employed. It has often been implied in land use planning that there is no difference in kind between making a forecast for the next five years, and making one for a five-year period 20 years ahead. A little thought will show that this is nonsense, since the measure of uncertainty has changed to cover a much greater portion of the relevant information. Therefore, techniques suitable for such an uncertain context must be used.

The following table sets out a few of the techniques which are used for forecasting; the more important of them are then discussed in greater detail. This table also is based on Jantsch's work.[6]

Let us start with those techniques most familiar and traditional in land use planning. *Trend extrapolation* has long been a method used by land use planners, particularly for population forecasts;

Forecasting has two main branches:

Extrapolation from present situation

Normative — working back from future hypotheses

Scenario writing — logical sequence of events in order to show how, starting from present (or any other given situation) a further state may evolve step by step. Primarily not to predict future, but systematically to explore branching points dependent upon critical choices

Normative Relevance Tree Technique — start from goals and objectives. 'Branches' — alternatives — are traced to a number of tips which represent deficiencies in existing state of science and technology

Systems Analysis

Morphological (study of form) *Research* — orderly way of looking at things, to achieve a systematic perspective over all possible solutions of a given large-scale problem

Feedback Schemes — to anticipate and evaluate 'possible futures'

Long-Range Forecasting using *Simulation Models* and *Future Models* whose basis may be one or combinations of Extrapolative, Goal seeking, Synthetic, Morphological, Intuitive or Theoretical

Delphi Technique — whereby a group of experts is asked to predict on certain aspects of human knowledge. Their resultant predictions are then sent to other members of the panel, who are asked to revise their own predictions. This can happen several times

Trend Extrapolation including *Envelope Curve Extrapolation* which permits forecasting of characteristics of future breakthroughs even before the possibilities of technical realization become visible. But beware high degree of uncertainty in parameters to be chosen and interpretation of empirical trends

Trend Extrapolation is a purely exploratory approach which works well only with pace setting data. It can be expected to become less accurate the more developments over time are influenced by normative thinking, and the more they depend on complex interactions

the above approaches come under the umbrellas of *Organisation Theory* (with its sub-branch of *Game Theory*) and *Epistemology* — branch of metaphysics dealing with nature and validity of knowledge it is not unfair to say that it has perhaps been over-used. As stated in the table, it is best seen as an exploratory approach, most useful for the short-term and for problems which are of a sufficiently large scale for minor variations not to be important; it is of least use where the subject of the extrapolation has complex interconnections and is likely to be the subject of normative thinking. Its place in land use planning today is probably for 'thumb-nail sketch' type forecasts, for illustrative exploration of options and for forecasts where minimal calculation and effort is appropriate. Trend extrapolation essentially shows what would happen if the past extended with very little change into the future, and, as we know, that does not happen very much.

Systems analysis has received much attention by land use planners in recent years, and has, indeed been extended into a theory of planning and a process that reflects the theory. I refer the reader to McLoughlin's exposition in *Urban and Regional Planning*.[7]

The *relevance tree* technique is a very valuable one. In essence, a relevance tree starts from goals or objectives, or a desired future state, and traces back (if appropriate with alternatives) to the necessary intervening stages, and thus illumines deficiencies and choices in the immediate future. It is possible to weight different goals, and to spot commonalities in the lower levels of the relevance tree, so that available resources can be concentrated with the best effect. Early development of relevance trees was for the US space programme, but it is now a widely used approach. Wilson suggested a structuring of the land use planning process in the form of a relevance tree (see Figure 5.2).[8] More recent applications in land use planning have used the relevance tree approach in conjunction with other techniques, for example, the goals achievement matrix and the potential surface approach (both discussed elsewhere, see page 144). The related concepts of tracing the hierarchical importance and connections of actions, events and decisions, of attaching relative value weightings to their implications, and exploring the implications, whether or not in spatial terms, seems one of the most promising of current approaches to planning, as it brings together fittingly the elements of ascertainable information, uncertainty and valuing possible outcomes.

89

Policy (action/decision, goal formulation, evaluation)

1 *Action*

implementation of (sub) plans	decision-taking

2 *Goals*

local groups	residents	workers	employers	shoppers

3 *Evaluation*

criteria ?	weight relating goals	derivation of goals	evaluation of alternative (sub) plans

Design

4 *Plan formulation*

decide (sub) plan structure	decide time horizon(s)	methods of contingency planning (treatment of uncertainty)	generation of alternative (sub) plans	system model manipulation

5 *Design techniques*

data requirements	system model requirements	imagination aids

6 *Problem formulation*

system malfunctions (misfits)

Understanding

7 *System models*

aggre-gate popula-tion	aggre-gate economic structure	residen-tial	work-place	economic activity	infra-structure	social services

8 *Techniques*

system identification	principles of model design	eclectic selection of techniques by discipline	data	computers

Fig. 5.2   A Relevance Tree for Planning

SOURCE: Wilson, A.G., 'Models in urban planning: a synoptic review of recent literature', in *Urban Studies,* page 249, **5,** 3, November 1968.

The next two techniques are apparently less rigorous, but they do properly imply considerable intellectual discipline. *Scenario writing* attempts to set up a logical sequence of events to demonstrate plausibly how a future state might evolve, step by step. Such scenarios most often start from the present situation and their purpose is not so much to predict the future as to explore systematically the branch points in the possibilities which are dependent on critical choices.

This technique was developed principally by Kahn at the Hudson Institute, and his early scenarios were the ones that brought the technique into general knowledge, such as *The Year 2000*, written with Wiener.[9]

The *Delphi technique*, too, is now well known. This method is an improvement on conventional panelling, developing largely at the Rand Corporation, and it is a form of specialised brain-storming. The idea is to sharpen expert consensus about the future through a succession of iterative rounds in which the participants are fed back each other's reactions. The reasoning behind the technique is that experts in a particular field may make a forecast on their own which they would modify, given a similar prediction from another expert about a connected field. In the normal course of research, the interactions may not take place, so a method has to be employed to guarantee the inter-action of the individual expert forecasts. The disadvantages are exhaustion of the expert through undue time and effort needed to follow through the various rounds of modifications to original opinions, but it would appear that, given a clear statement of the bases for the original forecasts, much of the subsequent modifica-tion might be carried out by others, or even by computer. In such a form, the essential approach seems a most valuable one, and applicable in land use planning.

The computer is of great relevance to the other two forecasting techniques which seem of most significance for land use planning, namely, morphological analysis and modelling. *Morphological analysis* can be briefly discussed. It has been defined as 'an orderly way of looking at things to achieve a systematic perspective over all possible solutions of a given large-scale problem'. The working method is to define all the basic parameters which apply to a situation, then to scrutinise every possible combination, without any intuitive preconceptions about what is and is not relevant. It is argued that we reject workable solutions and possibilities in the normal course of events through an inaccurate and premature feeling of what is irrelevant. Though the most celebrated demonstration of morphological analysis was for jet engine design, I do know of its use in student project work, if not in any actual land use planning. The computer seems necessary for a morphological analysis approach to problems, to remove the drudgery involved in a conscientious scrutiny of every permutation of possibilities. Harris has discussed combinatorial programming for land use planning—a relevant technique.[10] It could, however, be argued that a more productive form of scrutiny of possibilities is that embodied in linear programming approaches, which identify a solution to satisfy given constraints, of performance specification, resource use or whatever.

The final forecasting method to be mentioned here—modelling —cannot be covered so briefly; indeed, since it has various uses in land use planning apart from forecasting, it is dealt with separately in the next chapter.

References

1 See Moroney, M. J., *Facts from Figures*, Penguin 1965
   Duckworth, E., *A Guide to Operational Research*, Methuen (1962);
   Houlden, B., (Ed.), *Some Techniques of Operational Research*,
   English University Press (1962).
2 Rommel, *Applied Factor Analysis*, Northwestern University Press.
3 Maw, R., 'Construction of a Leisure Model', in *Official
   Architecture and Planning*, page 924, **32**, 8 (1969).
4 Kahn, H. & Wiener A. J., *The Year 2000* (Hudson Institute),
   Collier Macmillan, London (1967).
5 Jantsch, E., *Technological Forecasting in Perspective*, OECD,
   Paris (1967).
6 Jantsch, *op. cit.* (5) above.
7 McLoughlin, J. B., *Urban and Regional Planning: A Systems
   Approach*, Faber, London (1969).
8 Wilson, A., 'Models in urban planning: a synoptic view of the
   literature, in *Urban Studies*, page 249, **5**, 3, November 1968.
9 Kahn & Wiener, *op. cit.* (4) above.
10 Harris, B., 'Planning as a branch and bound process', in *Papers
   of the Regional Science Association* (forthcoming).

6 Models

Introduction

Mathematical models are increasingly used by land use planners, but many of their colleagues, as well as their clients, are still somewhat hazy both about the way models operate and the credibility of their results. The word 'model' has many meanings in everyday speech, but any model, whether a hydraulic engineer's small-scale harbour, an analytical model of a region's economy, or a toy aeroplane, is simulating and abstracting from reality. In some dimension, models simplify the real world. By so doing, models can assist understanding by revealing patterns of interaction among different aspects of the subject of study, which can contribute to the predictive and evaluative components of the planning process. The policy maker can call upon the model maker to assist in structuring the choices available in a systematic way that facilitates evaluation of costs and benefits, and models thus help to provide more rigour in the process of making land use planning decisions.

Models are cast in whatever language has been considered most appropriate by the model builder; some of the modelling languages—like mathematics—may not be universally understood, but, like any other language, it should always be possible for those fluent to translate into other people's vernacular. Since many land use planning exercises must deal with wide-ranging and complex subject matter, the advantages offered by a model are often very significant, since, as Shubik puts it, 'the model is amenable to manipulations which would be too expensive, impracticable or impossible to perform on the entity it portrays'.[1]

Since the model builder must try to understand and deal with great complexity he must develop simplified and generalised versions of the relationships observed. Mathematical models can take quite simple forms—their simplicity or complexity depends upon what is being represented. Since so many things affect land use planning, the mathematical models used for land use planning studies are usually complex in order to take account of all the necessary elements in the model. Thus, as discussed in Chapter 3, the observation and recognition of patterns is crucial. Lowry expressed this by saying that a model designer has 'to perceive repetitive temporal patterns in the processes of urban life, fixed spatial relationships in the kaleidoscope of urban form'.[2] Their conversion into a model depends on three components, 'named' variables embedded in mathematical formulae . . . numerical constants . . . and a computational method', and the pattern generated comprises a set of variables each 'tagged by geographical location and/or calendar date of occurrence'.[3]

Variables

'Models may be used to estimate unknown values of one variable, given a range of known values of other variables. To achieve this the model builder formulates a hypothesis about the way the selected variable will behave under certain conditions, and constructs his model to express this hypothesis.'[4] Land use planning has to deal with a complex set of interlocking phenomena—capital investment, population structure, transport networks, recreation habits and so on. Each such phenomenon can be viewed as a 'variable'. The future of some of them can be determined by land use planners, through the implementation of policies. These mostly relate to the use and development of land, and can be termed 'planning variables'. Two other kinds of variable must be defined—some, whose future will be determined largely independently of the land use planner, such as investment levels or climate, can be called 'exogenous'—which merely means externally determined. The third kind of variable is the 'endogenous' or internally produced type, which are consequent in some way upon the planning variables—for example, the population structure will be influenced by employment and housing policies. Although these types of variable are not rigidly distinct in practice, it is a useful conceptualisation, especially since it may be developed into a common mode of working of a land use planner—ascertaining as much as possible about exogenous variables, as 'constraining' future possibilities, then considering alternatives for the planning variables, taking into account what the effects would be on endogenous variables.

This scheme establishes a key place for forecasting in land use planning, both for assessment of the externally determined factors, and for exploration of alternative planning possibilities, and the technique of mathematical modelling may be used to assist forecasting in a wide range of contexts. It is important to remember that such models often represent a formalisation of the approaches previously taken by planners, and are in such cases, a 'technical' innovation, rather than a 'theoretical' one, since a base of theory is always required for model construction and operation. This is not to deny, however, that insights gained through using models may well help to advance theory.

Land use planners thus need models to provide them with a systematic representation of some relevant part of the real world. By so doing the models may throw new light on relationships and aspects of behaviour. If analysis of the variables in a system has been the principal motive for construction of a model, it is a 'descriptive' model. Obviously, though, any model which is to be used for forecasting, must also be descriptive.

Mathematical models and land use planning

Three broad categories of the use of mathematical models in land use planning are commonly differentiated:
the *descriptive* model, intended to express a set of relationships at one point in time
the *predictive* model, which carries a set of descriptive relationships into the future, by some treatment of the time factor
the *planning* model (also called *evaluative* or *prescriptive* models), which incorporate some criteria against which alternative futures are tested, to discover which should be preferred.

More specifically, mathematical models may be used in land use planning to help with analysis, as forecasting tools, to assist the process of design, or for 'control' (where comparison of actual developments with projections may show divergences from what was expected, and thus point to needed policy adjustments). The further use often suggested for models in land use planning literature is for optimum design, which incidentally has produced one of land use planning's best *bon mots*—Lowry, commenting on Harris' discussion of the difficulties of optimum design—'If God had been exposed to Professor Harris' instruction, He would have postponed the creation indefinitely and applied to the Ford foundation for a research grant.'[5]

Most of the mathematical models used in land use planning at the present time are 'partial', in that they focus on one—or a few —activities, which are known to be in fact only part of a much greater network of relationships. But efforts to develop more 'comprehensive' models have been made too. As explained elsewhere in this book, the everyday work done by land use planners is almost always 'partial', whatever the conceptualisation of the process of land use planning may be—so partial models—for employment, housing, shopping and transport—are found extremely useful. It has been pointed out that, 'recent research in land use modelling has been largely focused on the design of comprehensive urban and sub-regional models, yet many recent applications of models in a planning context have been partial in scope, simulating single activity systems.[6]

Loewenstein sketched a typology of models used in 'city planning':

1 Micro versus macro models—
   an easily understood distinction, which concerns the area scale of the model, micro models being expressed in terms of persons or groups, within neighbourhoods, while macro models deal with cities or regions. Any precise demarcation would be artificial—the order of difference in practice may be illustrated by referring to the chapter on shopping—in which Bacon's work on the individual consumer is referred to, in contrast to the model of retailing developed for the West Midlands.

2   Static versus dynamic models—
    static models describe inter-relationships at one moment in
    time, but a dynamic model requires an iterative or 'step by
    step' solution, where the output from one step forms the
    input to the next step. A cohort survival model for population
    projection is an example.

3   Descriptive versus behaviouristic models—
    a descriptive model offers some 'portrait'—such as the central
    place theory 'nested hexagonals' distribution of central
    places. The contrasting type—behaviouristic models are now
    discussed;

4   Predictive versus prescriptive models—
    in a predictive model, the value of the dependent variable is
    established through its relationship with independent vari-
    ables, which are enumerated within the model—a gravity
    model, as used often for shopping studies, predicts the
    amount and distribution of retailing (usually in a comparative
    static sense). A prescriptive model is one that has been
    formulated to behave normatively, for example, to optimise.
    Linear and non-linear programming models are of this
    prescriptive type.

5   Deterministic versus stochastic models—
    Whereas deterministic models, like the gravity model alluded
    to, depend on fixed relationships, a stochastic model is
    probabilistic. Such models 'indicate the degree of probability
    of the occurrence of a certain event by specifying the statistical
    probability that a certain number of events will take place in
    a given area and/or time interval'.[7] An example is a migration
    model, which states a percentage probability that a certain
    number of migrants will move from one area to another.
    Stochastic models are the type most used in planning now.

Simulation models

Any model is, of course, a simulation. The particular term
simulation model is used for models which deal with a particularly large number of variables, where relationships are non-linear,
where the process is dynamic with long time lags, or where the

97

process may be probabilistic; these circumstances may occur jointly.[8]

Stages in a modelling forecasting exercise

I shall illustrate the stages in a modelling forecasting exercise by referring to interaction models. Such models are concerned with the interactions of different urban land uses and, in fact, quantify the movements that result from people crossing space—to go to work, or shopping, or to an airport and so on.

The three fundamental components of such models of spatial interaction are *generators, attractors* and *deterrents.* In the example of shopping, the generators might be taken as population, or spending power, attractors might be shopping centres, or shopping floor space, or retail turnover, the deterrent might be distance, or travel cost in money or time. In the simplest possible terms, it is suggested that the number of shopping journeys between any two areas will be the larger the more shoppers there are in the generating area and the more shops there are in the attracting area and the closer together the two areas are.

The basic description of the relationship between these three components bears a formal resemblance to Newton's law of gravity, and the generic term, *gravity models,* is normally used.

Essentially, the basic descriptive formula is—

$$T_{ij} = KG_iA_j \qquad f(C_{ij})$$

where T_{ij} is the number of trips between i and j

G_i is the generator at i

A_j is the attractor at j

C_{ij} is the deterrent of distance between i and j

and K is a constant, that is a parameter.

T_{ij} is the dependent variable in the equation—the determination of which the model is seeking to explain—and G_i and A_j and C_{ij} are all independent variables. The relationship of the dependent variable to the other variables is expressed in the form of the equation—in the case a direct positive and multiplicative relationship—and the constant gives more precision to it. The equation, to be useful, must specify both the nature and degree of the dependence of T_{ij} on the independent variables

98

—that is both the direction and the amount of change in T_{ij} that would result from change in the independent variables.

The constants add further precision to the amount of change that would follow.

There are three main phases to a modelling exercise. The first is *design*. For a problem which is considered susceptible to treatment by a model, it is necessary initially to decide on a general mathematical formulation deemed relevant. This may be based on a theory of behaviour already existing (such as the use of central place theory for a shopping model) or on observation undertaken specifically to develop such a theory.

Once the basic theoretical approach is determined, it must be decided how the world is to be represented in the model. The precise study area must be defined and divided up at an appropriate level of detail. The criterion for this is that there must be sufficient homogeneity in each unit defined to ensure an adequate accuracy in results, but that the fewer the number of units, the less the calculation that will be involved. Although most mathematical models are operated with the aid of an electronic computer, the systems described in a model are often so complex that minimisation of units remains a valid consideration. This may be illustrated by a shopping gravity model, for which the study area is divided into zones—considering the generators, each zone should be reasonably homogeneous in terms of the relevant characteristics of the resident population and not so large that a sufficiently valid description of likely journeys by the model is prevented—and considering the attractors, so that the shopping centres are each in one zone, and a different zone, as far as possible.

In order to model the behaviour across space of the generators moving to the attractors, it is then necessary to investigate the deterrence, the time and money costs involved, and an inter-zonal matrix can be produced containing this information.

The second phase in modelling is that of *calibration,* in which the generalised model developed in the design phase is made more specific to fit the real world and the particular area and time. This can only be done by the collection of a sufficient number of observations to guide a 'trial and error' process of adjustment of the elements of the model equation until it is considered acceptably accurate. There are, of course, techniques for carrying out

99

this part of the modelling exercise. Calibration is thus the procedure for finding parameters that will, with the rest of the formula, give values in the output of the model which are closest to the real world.

Once a model has been designed and calibrated, it is ready to be used and the third phase is thus *forecasting*. To use the model in this way, appropriate values for the date in time must be substituted into the formula, to be used with the values for the parameters that were established in calibration.

Model characteristics

Following the brief discussion of the modelling sequence above, I shall now consder in turn the key characteristics of such models.

Hypothesis about relationship between variables

All models must be founded on some hypothesis which expresses the relationship between variables in the real world. For land use planning, such theories range from descriptions of individual behaviour patterns to very generalised observations, such as the tendency for trips to decrease as distance increases. A theory may also simply be that things will occur in the future much as they have in the past. Thus the theories on which models are based vary with respect to the degree of causal relationship which can be empirically demonstrated to support it.

Since any variable to be forecast exists in three dimensions—subject, space and time—theories may relate to any of these. Thus, theories based on continuation of historic trends relate to time, theories that postulate a relationship between one area and another (a ratio population forecast, say) are spatial, and most theories are concerned with relationships between one subject and another at the same spatial scale and time—for example, the relationship of car ownership to income.

Equation

An adjustment is involved in converting a theory of real world behaviour into a mathematical equation. Such adjustment often involves simplification and a narrowing of the factors considered relevant. It may also be necessary to devise acceptable proxies for things that are hard to measure. There is a fundamental distinction in practice between linear and non-linear relationships, which is important in the different assumptions that have to be made and in the means available for calibration of the model. Linear formulations are ratios and linear regression equations, and non-linear formulations are curvilinear equations and matrices.

Operation

The model is operated both for calibration and for prediction—if it is to be used for forecasting. Although the equation remains the same, there may well be adjustment to accommodate the different data that are to be used.

Levels of detail

The number and size of zones and categories for all the variables in a model must be determined in relation to the theory of the model and to input data available and output required. Severe distortions can result from unsuitable aggregation or disaggregation. (Disaggregation comprises breaking a whole down into its component parts—say, area zones, or population categories; aggregation is the converse.)

Time

The treatment of time in most models used in land use planning today is static—that is, values for a future date are substituted straight in to the model equation. A few models treat time dynamically, with an explicit representation in the model of the processes of change over time. This is done either by using lagged variables, which recognise that change in one variable will only affect another after a period of time, or by making the forecast in steps, with some adjustment to the model after each step, in which case the model is termed 'recursive'. Such recursive models have certain advantages. It is possible to observe the output of each step of the calculation; it is possible to treat non-linear relationships as though they were linear if the time period is short; the assumptions can be varied for different time periods.

Data requirements

Data are required at two stages of the modelling process—first for hypothesis testing and calibration, and secondly for forecasting. As with many other land use planning techniques, it is vital that the data to be used as input to a model are sufficiently accurate. The equation and the level of aggregation of the model must relate to input data available, although some compromises are inevitable. The use of published information is far less costly than the special collection of data and this will be an important consideration in most cases.

Where variables are not directly observable, some more accessible proxy may be chosen; residential density for income, say. Another distinction is between variables which have been directly observed, say Census data, and those which must be estimated—perhaps in a sub-model.

Assumptions

Since a model represents the real world by simplifications, there are always assumptions implicitly made, as well as those explicit in the theoretical base. It is important that these assumptions are acknowledged and that care is taken to see that the model truly is and remains relevant to the purposes for which it is developed and used.

Nature of the results

The output required of a model is obviously an important determinant of such matters as the levels of aggregation and the precise expression of the equation. The results of the model may explain the system's behaviour or make forecasts of its future. Predictive models either output totals at the forecast date, or changes over the forecasting period. One can be simply converted to the other.

Advantages and limitations of mathematical models

Among the advantages of mathematical models are:

1 they can accommodate complexity, and enable scrutiny and analysis of many variables and their relationships
2 with a computer, large numbers of bits of data can be accommodated, for input, calculation purposes and output
3 they facilitate the exploration of a range of possibilities
4 it is necessary to formalise and make explicit relationships—which aids communication, and encourages new insights which may be missed with intuitive methods
5 they can assist with keeping planning information up to date, and with implementation of continuous monitoring and adjustment of land use planning policies.

Their limitations include:

1 every relationship and parameter in a model must be defined unambiguously
2 they depend on the acquisition, storage and handling of large quantities of data
3 expense, mainly because of the labour involved in design and calibration and in assembly of data, as well as the cost of computation
4 the requirement for special expertise
5 the difficulty of using a cheaper exploratory prototype when developing a model to solve a particular problem
6 their potential for mystifying and alarming people
7 a danger, as with other mathematical techniques, of an improper concentration on items which are easy to enumerate and quantify, even if they are not the items on which land use planners should be focusing attention
8 the fact that many assumptions always have to be made for a mathematical model, which may not be based on sufficiently informed judgement (see, in this connection, a recent note by Batty and Saether on the design of shopping models[9])
9 the obscuring of variations in the reliability of data used.

A model example

References to mathematical models used in land use planning in recent years will be found in every chapter in Part 3. But to illustrate here the technique of modelling in somewhat more detail, the Garin-Lowry model has been selected. It deals with a key set of relationships in land use planning—people, work, and homes—and has been used more than any other planning model. Many variations have been developed, relating to different spatial scales and different functions within the planning process, including analysis, prediction, design and evaluation.

The simplest form of the relationships considered is:

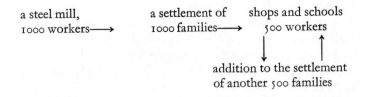

that is, a link between employment related to the world outside the area of study ('basic' employment) and population, which comprises the families of the workers, who then generate more employment, this time of the type that can be called service (or 'non-basic'), which again has a link with population, comprising the families of the service workers. Let us rewrite the relationship with an example:

a steel mill,   a settlement of   shops and schools
1000 workers⟶   1000 families⟶   500 workers

                           addition to the settlement
                           of another 500 families

(the third link—that between service employment and population is an iterative one, and there will be an eventual total balance greater than the first round figures given in the example.)

Now the Lowry model builds on the simple relationship given above, adding a land use dimension to the essentially economic relationship. Thus the model takes the amount and location of basic employment as an input, and allocates the residents to their places of residence from the workplaces, and then the services from residents, according to gravity type

104

formulae. When used for the Notts-Derby Sub-regional Study, the logic of the Garin-Lowry model was expressed thus:

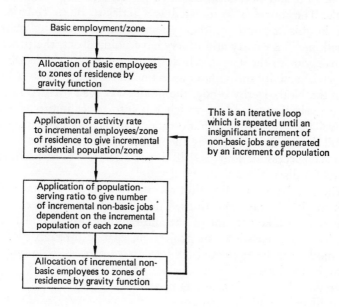

Basic employment/zone	
↓	
Allocation of basic employees to zones of residence by gravity function	
↓	
Application of activity rate to incremental employees/zone of residence to give incremental residential population/zone	This is an iterative loop which is repeated until an insignificant increment of non-basic jobs are generated by an increment of population
↓	
Application of population-serving ratio to give number of incremental non-basic jobs dependent on the incremental population of each zone	
↓	
Allocation of incremental non-basic employees to zones of residence by gravity function	

So the links in the process are:
the basic employment is distributed to residential areas by a 'journey to home' allocation rule
population is calculated from the activity rate (that is, the proportion of the population working)
a 'population serving' ratio then computes the 'non-basic' employment required to service the population
which is located at place of work by a 'journey to shop' allocation rule.

Michael Batty, who adapted and developed the model for the Notts-Derby Study, has summarised it thus:

'Briefly, the model allocates (to zones) population and non-basic employment, initially in relation to the distribution of basic employment. The generation of successive increments of population and non-basic employment is achieved by the use of multipliers—activity and population serving ratios. The process converges as additional increments of activity tend toward zero, and the values of these multipliers ensure that the increments of population and non-basic employment sum to their respective totals. The model is formulated as a series of linear equations, and in this application, the system is represented by matrix equations.'[10] As Batty and others have pointed out, the process is analagous to the way in which input-output models distribute industrial activity throughout an economic system.

In the Notts-Derby Study, the model was used for two stages of analysis the second of which put into effect improvements derived both from the calibration and from the first stage analysis. A full description of the way the model was used is to be found in several accessible sources.[11] In this chapter, it is more pertinent to restrict discussions to the model itself.

The data base for calibration was the Sub-region's Data Bank, plus special Census tabulations. The zones (62 in number) were delimited to take account of the sub-region's urban, nodal and physical characteristics. For projection, change through time in the model can be simulated by a recursive process. The output from the model was:

1 predicted non-basic workers per zone
2 predicted population per zone
3 a complete inter-zonal journey to work matrix
4 a complete inter-zonal journey to service matrix; this approximates to a 'journey to shop' pattern
5 internal migration components for population and non-basic jobs.

The 'learning' aspect of models

As Lowry wrote in the special models issue of the *Journal of the American Institute of Planners*, in May 1965:

'Above all, the process of model-building is educational. The participants invariably find their perceptions sharpened, their horizons expanded, their professional skills augmented. The mere necessity of framing questions carefully does much to dispel the fog of sloppy thinking that surrounds our efforts at civic betterment. My parting advice to the planning profession is: If you do sponsor a model, be sure your staff is deeply involved in its design and calibration. The most valuable function of the model will be lost if it is treated by the planners as a magic box which yields answers at the touch of a button.'[12]

Lowry stresses there the learning which is incidental to using a model *operationally*.

It would not be appropriate to conclude this chapter, however, without referring to a form of modelling where *learning* is the main purpose, namely the use of simulation models for gaming. As Shubik explains, 'Gaming is an experimental, operational and training technique, which may or may not make use of a simulated environment, but is invariably concerned with studying human behaviour or teaching individuals. In a simulation, the actual behaviour of the components is taken as given, and the actual presence of individuals is not necessary as it is to gaming.'[13]

Land use games are now a standard teaching method on land use planning courses and provide participants with valuable insights into the different groups involved with land use and into the interactions and repercussions of their decisions. It would seem quite possible to extend this particular use of models as an educational tool to involvement of the public, to put across some of the facets of decision making in land use planning.

References

1 Shubik, M., (Ed.), *Game Theory and Related Approaches to Social Behaviour,* see Introduction, Wiley (1964).
2 Lowry, I. S., 'A short course in model design', in *Journal of the American Institute of Planners,* **31**, May 1965.
3 Lowry, *op. cit.* (2) above.
4 NEDO, *Urban models in shopping studies,* Distributive Trades EDC, London (1970).
5 Lowry, I. S., 'Comments on Britton Harris', in *Regional Science Association Papers,* **19** (1967).
6 Batty, M. & Saether, A. 'A note on the design of shopping models', in *Journal of the Royal Town Planning Institute,* page 303, **58**, 7, July/August 1972.
7 Loewenstein, L. K., 'On the nature of analytical models', in *Urban Studies,* page 112, June 1966.
8 Loewenstein, *op. cit.* (7) above.
9 Batty & Saether, *op. cit.* (6) above.

10 Quoted in Steeley, G., 'Analysis by the Garin-Lowry method', in *Papers from the Seminar on the Process of the Notts-Derby Sub-Regional Study*, CES IP 11, Centre for Environmental Studies, page 63 (1970).

11 See, for example, CES IP 11, *op. cit.* (10) above.

12 Harris, B., 'Urban development models: new tools for planners', in *Journal of the American Institute of Planners*, **31**, May 1965.

13 Shubik, *op. cit.* (1) above.

See also Wilson, A. G., 'Models in urban planning: a synoptic review of recent literature', in *Urban Studies*, **5**, 3, November 1968.

7 Plan Design

It is perhaps artificial to draw any firm line between the stage of preliminary analysis of information, and the techniques used for it, which have been discussed above, and the next part of the sequence followed by a land use planner, which is plan design. Often, the plan design itself is a moment of truth since it must bring together a great deal of information which may well have been treated separately hitherto—including all the 'activities' a planner studies (as in Part 3), and elements of the planning process sequence—notably goals and objectives. Indeed, the whole conception implied here of 'planning' is debatable, and Batty's critique has been summarised in Chapter 3 (see page 53). But speaking more practically, in general the land use planner has some specification given to him of what must be considered in plan design; for example, the requirements for a Development Plan under the 1947 Act, or a structure plan as at present, or the model brief prepared by central government for recent sub-regional studies.[1]

I have described the 'strategic choice approach' already in Chapter 3 (see page 51), but will discuss here the specific technique—AIDA—associated with it. I shall also describe in some detail two recent exercises in plan design—the Notts-Derby Sub-Regional Study and the Coventry-Solihull-Warwickshire Study. In a concluding section, I refer to some other promising methods for plan design which are not yet well explored.

The AIDA technique

To structure a plan design problem in accordance with the strategic choice approach, described in Chapter 3, the technique known as AIDA has been developed. The account that follows is from a paper by Wedgwood-Oppenheim.[2]

1 Each decision may be regarded as the choice of one of a number of *options* within an area of decision. A planning problem can be structured by isolating its component *decision areas* and representing them symbolically, as in this *strategy graph*.

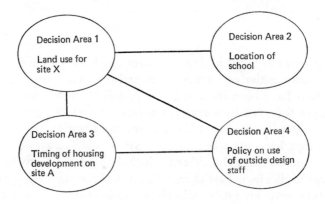

Decision Area 1 concerns the use of a particular plot of land; Decision Area 2 concerns the location of a particular facility; Decision Area 3 relates to the timing of the project; Decision Area 4 concerns the agency for part of the work. The links between decision areas in the strategy graph indicate that a decision cannot be taken in one decision area without reference to the decision taken in decision areas linked to it.

2 The strategy graph can be expanded into an *option graph* by making explicit the range of options possible in each decision area and the nature of the interdependencies, as illustrated below. The problem is so structured that a solution must consist of one option chosen from each decision area. The lines drawn between options, called *option bars* indicate that the combination of options so linked is unacceptable.

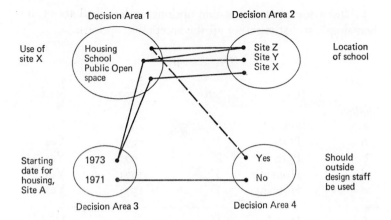

For instance, the link between the option of starting in 1971 the housing development on Site A (Decision Area 3) and the option of not making use of outside design staff (Decision Area 4) indicates that the early start for the housing could only take place if outside design staff are used.

An option bar may indicate a logically impossible combination (e.g. the Public Open Space on site X (Decision Area 1) and the option of site X for the school (Decision Area 2); but more commonly option bars indicate a statement of policy, for instance the bar between housing in Decision Area 1 and Site Z in Decision Area 2 might indicate that a school at Z would be considered too far away to serve housing at X.

The dashed link between Decision Areas 1 and 4 indicates a weak option bar, that might be removed by a change in policy.

Where decision areas are interconnected by many option bars, it may be clearer to represent the option graph in a series of tables; each table shows acceptable combinations of options by a * and unacceptable combinations by an †, as, for example:

Decision	Housing	†	*	†
Area 1	School	*	†	†
	POS	†	*	*
		Site	Site	Site
		X	Y	Z
		Decision Area 2		

3 After assessment of possible options, as described above, it is then simple to list together all the acceptable options:

	Decision Area			
	1	2	3	4
	Use	Site	Year	Staff
Solution				
a	School	X	1971	Yes
b	POS	Y	1971	Yes
c	POS	Z	1971	Yes
d	Housing	Y	1971	Yes
e	Housing	Y	1973	Yes
f	Housing	Y	1973	No

For a complicated problem, a computer would be used to carry out the search procedures needed to establish possible options.

Three elements of the decision problem are specifically recognised in the final overall strategic choice procedure, which incorporates the elements of AIDA discussed so far; these three elements are: evaluation, management of uncertainty and robustness.

Evaluation

In the context of the 'strategic choice' approach, less stress is placed on sophisticated measurement than in the analytical evaluation methods commonly in use in land use planning, but the choice of effects to include is of considerable importance. 'The need for the policy maker to strike a balance between a number of criteria introduces a degree of approximation which may often make a lack of accuracy in the measurement of effects quite unimportant.'[3] It is characteristic of land use planning problems that they impinge on several different interests and require evaluation in various dimensions. One approach is through the identification of agreed goals, another through identification of sectors of the community. But in either case, 'the aim must be to develop a set of effect measures which are both analytically useful, and "politically rich" in that they adequately reflect the diversity of costs and benefits which the policy makers will want to take into consideration'.[4] One method suggested to narrow the choice for policy makers is *dominance analysis,* which involves the elimination of any alternative that offers no advantage over others. To further assist policy makers, an attempt may be made to establish what values they place on competing criteria, so that *trade-off rates* can be constructed to express such relative weightings. Solutions may then be placed in order accordingly.

The management of uncertainty

The uncertainties which make it difficult to arrive at a preferred solution may be divided into three broad classes:

'Class UE: uncertainties in knowledge of the external planning *environment,* including all uncertainties relating to the structure of the world external to the decision-making system and also all uncertainties relating to expected patterns of future change in this environment, and to its expected responses to any possible future interventions by the decision-making system.

'Class UR: uncertainties as to future intentions in *related fields of choice* including all uncertainties relating to the choices which might in future be taken, within the decision making system itself, in respect of other fields of discretion beyond the limited problem which is currently under consideration.

'Class UV: uncertainties as to appropriate *value judgements* including all uncertainties relating to the relative degree of importance the decision makers ought to attach to any expected consequences of their choice which cannot be related to each other through an unambiguous common scale—either because the consequences are of a fundamentally different nature, or because they affect different sections of the community, or because they concern different periods of future time.'[5]

Actions may be taken to reduce such uncertainties—UE by further information gathering, perhaps, UR by extending the field of consideration and UV by obtaining policy guidance from decision makers and the public. It must always be assessed how much the reduction of particular uncertainties would actually assist and influence the final making of decisions before embarking on programmes of 'uncertainty reduction'. Examples of the use of *sensitivity analysis*, to place uncertainty in perspective, are given in 'Local Government and Strategic Choice'.

Robustness

The alternative to the approach to uncertainty just emphasised—that is, seeking to reduce it—is to behave in such a way that flexibility to respond appropriately in the future is retained. Sometimes, this may imply making no immediate decision, but more often it means selecting an immediate course of action that offers greater flexibility for future choice than do other options. The concept of *robustness analysis,* developed by Gupta and Rosenhead, is of relevance here.[6]

Analysis through AIDA may well lead not to a full immediate choice in all decision areas, but to the selection of a set of actions leaving open a range of alternative choices in other decision areas —a 'robust' decision, in other words. An example is the choice of location Y in Decision Area 2, which leaves open three or possibly four solutions, whereas the choice of either location X or Z would close options. The flexibility obtained would need to be evaluated against the other costs and benefits relevant to the decision.

The process of strategic choice

The main aspects of the AIDA approach, in relation to an overall view of the process of strategic choice, is now illustrated. It will be seen that the process is a cyclical one, where initial formulation of the problem suggests a number of possible choices; initial evaluation is likely to lead to attempts to reduce uncertainty before further evaluation. The areas for which early decisions are really necessary should be isolated, leaving useful options open wherever possible. Planning must be treated as a process without an end.

The AIDA technique was tested for local plan design in six case studies, in what is known as the LOGIMP experiment.[7] The Notts-Derby Sub-regional Study, which is described next, also paid serious attention to many of the points emphasised in the strategic choice approach.

Process of Strategic Choice

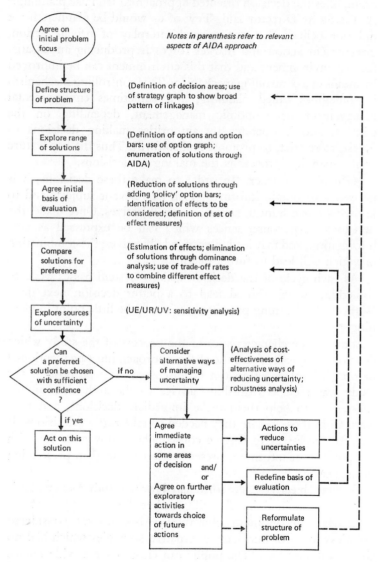

Notes *in parenthesis refer to relevant aspects of AIDA approach*

Agree on initial problem focus

Define structure of problem
(Definition of decision areas; use of strategy graph to show broad pattern of linkages)

Explore range of solutions
(Definition of options and option bars: use of option graph; enumeration of solutions through AIDA)

Agree initial basis of evaluation
(Reduction of solutions through adding 'policy' option bars; identification of effects to be considered; definition of set of effect measures)

Compare solutions for preference
(Estimation of effects; elimination of solutions through dominance analysis; use of trade-off rates to combine different effect measures)

Explore sources of uncertainty
(UE/UR/UV: sensitivity analysis)

Can a preferred solution be chosen with sufficient confidence?

if no → Consider alternative ways of managing uncertainty
(Analysis of cost-effectiveness of alternative ways of reducing uncertainty; robustness analysis)

if yes

Act on this solution

Agree immediate action in some areas of decision and/ or Agree on further exploratory activities towards choice of future actions

Actions to reduce uncertainties

Redefine basis of evaluation

Reformulate structure of problem

The Nottinghamshire and Derbyshire Sub-regional Study

It has already been suggested that this study, above all others, exemplifies the decision oriented approach to land use planning.[8] As the Study Director said, 'Few of us would be planners if we did not believe that the normal interplay of private action, government action and market forces is producing an unsatisfactory environment and that this environment can be improved by means of a controlling mechanism. This controlling mechanism is sometimes called planning, and sometimes environmental management or economic management, depending on the context, and it operates by authorities making decisions to invest, to restrict, to promote and so forth. Thus the key feature of the planning process is the making of decisions.'

He explains further, 'In order to make these decisions, it is necessary to obtain information on all relevant subjects and to know what we want to achieve—our objectives. Once made, the decisions have consequences which can be expressed as new information, and may lead to changed objectives, the combination of which will lead to futher decisions . . .

'As each cycle of the decision-making system passes we learn something which should lead to a better decision next time. Without this learning process there would be little point in planning.'[9]

Some of the characteristics of the process of the study which developed logically from the above approach must be mentioned before their plan design can be discussed. The purpose of the study was seen as furnishing advice to the authorities in the sub-region to help them make immediate decisions, and then learn from those before they needed to take further decisions. It was still necessary to foresee consequences, however, but with the purpose of informing present action rather than prescribing future action.

General objectives were formulated for the study, but emphasis was put on maintaining flexibility rather than attempting to get agreement on optimum objectives. Also, it was considered pointless to work out many alternative strategies which had no chance of adoption: 'The public can either have a wide choice now and little choice later because they have become committed to an inflexible plan, or they can have restricted choice now and keep plenty of options for later.'

Each stage of the study was viewed as its own 'decision making sub-system', and there were four such stages:

1 the first stage was preparatory, deciding what the study should be concerned with, which subjects should be surveyed, and which analysis technique developed
2 the second stage was the main survey stage which led to a decision on objectives for the plan and the data to be used for plan making
3 the third stage was plan-making, which brought information and objectives together and took them through four decision making and learning cycles
4 the fourth stage was deciding on the form in which to put forward advice.

The plan-making process was based on the use of 'parallel' methods—there was no cumulative elimination procedure, and the calculations were not input to the next stage. Needs and opportunities for each topic considered relevant to sub-regional planning, and objectives for them, had been produced from the survey analyses. The aim was to satisfise the objectives and two notions were used as guides—the variable control total, and the idea of multiple satisfaction. To explore the relations and conflicts of objectives spatially, two techniques were used—a potential surface technique and a sieve map of factors appearing in the objectives. The result of applying these techniques was the recognition of a 'mainstream' group of zones and sets of propositions which should be concentrated upon.

The evaluation needed finer examination, so the variable control totals were recalculated for smaller zones, ranges of assumptions on mobility being incorporated. Four techniques were used—the Garin-Lowry model to examine work—population—housing numerical and spatial relationships, a shopping model adapted from that used in the Leicester-Leicestershire Study, a synthetic transportation model, and an interrogation routine developed by the study team. The focus of evaluation shifted from preoccupation with consistency and sensitivity tests, multiple satisfaction and ranges of control totals, to more specific concerns including the upper and lower limits of site utilisation, road capacity, commuter flows, durable goods turnover and job mobility. The results from each of the four techniques were separately assessed and then brought together in a matrix form. The effects of this stage were to restrict further the mainstream area and the issues considered of special importance. At this stage it was possible to devise formulations of a sub-regional strategy which satisfised the objectives. Additional groups of tests were of an 'accounting' nature—checking the consistency of different totals.

The final part of the plan-making process produced three integrated strategies. It continued with the use of models, but brought together specific sites, routes and agencies to encompass the ranges of operational and locational factors that had been revealed to be viable. Thus projections with varying assumptions were run to isolate the items that were critical in terms of constraining future opportunities.

The final report was thus about the critical assumptions on which the strategy was based, and how these had been learned, and stressed the connectedness of things and the continuity of the problem. It is clear that the plan-making process adopted in the Notts-Derby study embodied a philosophy of what planning is and, therefore, what process is appropriate. The specific techniques used are really less significant than the *way* in which they were used to produce a plan.

The Coventry-Solihull-Warwickshire study

The approach to plan-making of the Coventry-Solihull-Warwickshire Study was quite different, although they made great use of a technique adopted from Notts-Derby, the potential surface analysis. The key to understanding their plan-making process is the desire they felt to improve 'the balance between the initial survey and forecasting stage of the study and the subsequent process of choosing the best strategy'.[10] They took the view that if objectives are worth expressing at all, then the Study must clearly relate to them throughout. Thus 'the alternative strategies were crystallised from the Study's surveys and forecasts by varying the relative significance placed on the various strategic objectives, and the tests applied to the final short-list of four alternatives came as the last stage in a steady narrowing of the range of variation and doubt about the strategic objectives and alternatives open to the sub-region.'[11]

The objectives were either *essential*—quantitative requirements relating fairly uncontroversially to population numbers—or discriminatory, which were qualitative, and derived as measureable operational objectives from the generalised goals for the study.

Requirements for inclusion in the strategies derived from the survey and forecasting stage, and alternatives were handled by means of the technique called Development Potential Analysis, which is a development of the Notts-Derby potential surface approach, but considers a much wider range of factors.

The sub-region was divided into a grid and *surfaces* were produced to represent the discriminatory objectives for the strategy, as illustrated in the following diagram (Figure 7.1).

Much attention was paid to developing a set of weights to be applied to the surfaces, in order to isolate the grid squares that should receive more detailed attention. As a result of this process, three strategies were detailed from the synthesis of the development potential data, plus a trend strategy. Finally, these alternatives were evaluated against the discriminatory objectives, using a technique which is essentially a form of 'goals-achievement' evaluation, plus some supplementary tests, and the 'best' strategy was chosen for a consistently satisfactory performance. The simplified flow diagram shows the relationship of the main stages of the study process.

Some other approaches to plan-making

Both the studies discussed above paid great attention to the integration of different conceptual stages of the plan-making process. This point was the focus of a recent paper by Batty (see page 53), which recommended three techniques for plan design.

The first is *linear programming,* which requires the statement of the criterion to be optimised, and of parameters to the solution. Although there are now highly efficient algorithms for solving various problems of a linear programming type, there are some difficulties in applying it to land use planning problems. Some work has been done on welfare maximisation models, for example, in connection with the US model cities programme, which made progress with the basic methodology, but concluded

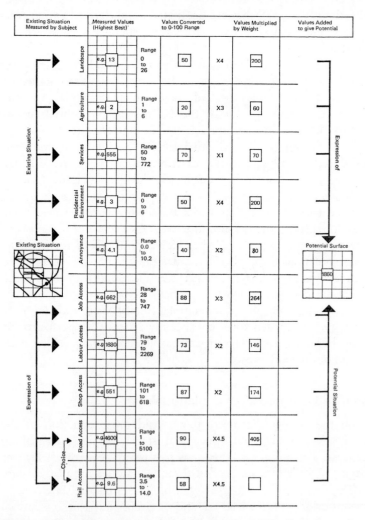

Fig. 7.1 Example of the Calculation of a Residential Development Potential Surface

that there was still quite still a way to go before such techniques could be used operationally for complex welfare problems.

However, linear programming has been used for problems of land use allocation, for example, by Schlager, in his Land Use Plan Design Model.[12] This particular modelling approach 'conceives of the urban complex as a subject for design', and thus 'design and not explanation and prediction becomes the primary problem for solution'. Schlager's method represents a fusion of Christopher Alexander's studies on design method and the use of the algorithms of linear programming.[13] Thus restraints are specified and the solution is then one of accommodating certain levels of land usage and design standards, subject to the constraints, whilst minimising costs.

To illustrate some of the elements of the model, restraints included limitations on density, the type of land uses that can exist simultaneously within a zone, and the need to provide schools within a certain distance of homes. Supporting land requirements—as for streets—were expressed as ratios to main land uses, such as agriculture, industry, housing, which were specifically dealt with. There were constraints on the maximum (or minimum) of land use in each zone, and on land use relationships within and between zones.

Four main classes of input data were needed:

1 costs—of unimproved land and land development by land use and type of soil
2 forecast total demand for each land use
3 design standards (e.g. densities) and inter- and intra-zonal limitations on land use relationships
4 the current land inventory including land uses and soil types.

The second method Batty suggested was *combinatorial programming,* appropriate for 'problems in which the variables are restricted to integers and an important class of such problems relates to situations where the variables take on binary values— zero or one'.[14] Thus the technique could be used in a planning context, where the only definite factor affecting a situation is the presence or absence of some variable.

Harris quotes the example of a problem in which a highway engineer must design a network where 40 links will connect

20 cities, so that benefits are maximised and the budget constraint is respected. Possible combinations total 2^{40}—about a million million. Thus any conventional method which examines a few alternatives is clearly ridiculously inadequate.[15] There is a whole range of relevant methods, which have received little consideration by planners.

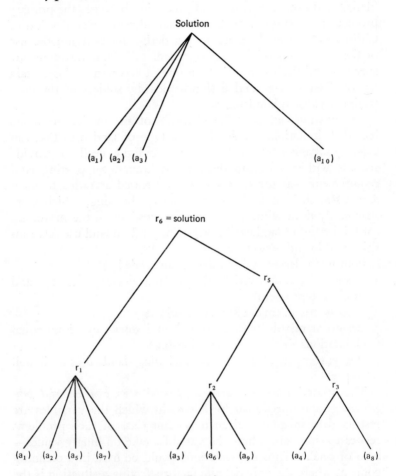

Fig 7.2   Graphical synthesis (after Batty)

SOURCE   An Introspective, but Scientific Approach to Plan Design and Evaluation, by M. Batty (1972)

Batty's third method for plan design was *graphical synthesis,* as proposed, for example, by Alexander.[16] The approach consists of decomposing a problem into its relative independent sub-problems, as indicated in Figure 7.2. It constrasts with, say, the sieve map technique, in that it recognises that problems have an internal structure.

As a final example for plan design, which relates to graphical synthesis, I shall mention *cluster analysis.* This technique is used a great deal now by land use planners for the analysis of information to structure relationships, but in the chapter on shopping (see page 323) I refer to its use to assist in production of a layout plan for the shopping centre of a new town.

It is perhaps fitting to conclude this chapter by saying that the next few years are certain to produce a considerable number of ideas for the improvement of the process of plan design, as many land use planners confront this problem in producing structure plans It is obviously a subject of crucial importance to land use planning, which I have only touched on; indeed, at least one book could well be devoted entirely to the subject.

References

1 See Jackson, J. N., *The Urban Future,* Chapter 3, Allen & Unwin (1972).
2 Wedgwood-Oppenheim, F., 'AIDA and the strategic choice approach', in *The LOGIMP Experiment,* page 15 CES IP 25, Centre for Environmental Studies (1970).
3 Wedgwood-Oppenheim, *op. cit.* (2) above, page 22.
4 Wedgwood-Oppenheim, *op. cit.* (2) above, page 22.
5 Friend, J. K. & Jessop, N. *Local Government and Strategic Choice,* Chapter 5, Tavistock (1969).
6 Gupta & Rosenhead, 'Robustness in sequential decisions', in *Management Science,* October 1968.
7 *The LOGIMP Experiment, op. cit.* (2) above, 'The Six Projects', page 37.
8 Notts-Derby Study Team, *The Nottinghamshire and Derbyshire Sub-regional Study,* Nottingham County Council (1969).
9 Thorburn, A., 'The decision orientated framework for the study', in *Papers from the Seminar on the Process of the Notts-Derby Sub-regional Study,* CES IP 11, Centre for Environmental Studies (1970);

see also Thorburn, A., 'Preparing a regional plan: how we set about the task in Nottinghamshire/Derbyshire', in the *Journal of the Royal Town Planning Institute*, May 1971, **57**, 5.

10 Wannop, U., 'An objective strategy: the Coventry-Solihull-Warwickshire Sub-regional Study', in the *Journal of the Royal Town Planning Institute*, page 159, **58**, 4 (1972).

11 Wannop, *op. cit.* (10) above.

12 Schlager, K., 'A Land-Use Plan-Design Model', in *Journal of the American Institute of Planners*, page 103, **31** (1965).

13 Alexander, C., *Notes on the synthesis of form*, Harvard University Press (1964).

14 Batty, M., 'An introspective, but scientific approach to plan-design and evaluation', paper given in Oxford (1972).

15 Harris, B., 'The city of the future: the problem of optimal design', in *Papers of the Regional Science Association*, page 185, **19** (1967).

16 Alexander, *op. cit.* (13) above.

8 Evaluation

Evaluation is the process of taking different possible courses of action, setting them side by side and drawing a conclusion as to their respective merits. From the discussion of decision theory in Chapter 3, it will be clear that the merits will depend both on the extent to which each alternative satisfies the values of the evaluator and the degree of certainty it possesses, since neither one is adequate for making a reasoned judgement without the other.

If it is a continuous planning context within which such judgements have to be made, then evaluation will not be a 'one shot' activity. The ideas of monitoring situations and adjusting planning action according to what is observed suggest a new interpretation for evaluation. However, in many instances, there is a need for a significant choice to be made at one moment in time— to provide a crude analogy—the latter type being whether to travel north or south, with subsequent decisions made only at forks in the road representing the 'adjustment' evaluations.

In this chapter I shall first discuss 'evaluation' in land use planning in general terms, then briefly mention partial techniques, including financial appraisal, before considering more fully the evaluation methods which have been most used for land use planning decisions, namely, cost-benefit analysis—with its best-known variant, the planning balance sheet, and the goals achievement matrix.

Evaluation in land use planning

At some point in the planning process, alternative courses of action will have been identified and these must be compared for their advantages and disadvantages There are significant merits in attempting to do this systematically, within some logical frame of reference. Thereby, the element of subjective judgement may be minimised and isolated from factual statements of the implications of different alternatives. Types of sensitivity analysis can allow the exploration of various different value systems and thus help to show which courses of action may best achieve which objectives. In general, communication between all those involved with making the choice is assisted and it is also easier subsequently to explain to others the reasons certain choices were made.

What evaluations do not do, of course, is make decisions. Nor, however, used with perception and honesty do they 'load' decisions It cannot be denied though, that, like all techniques, they can be used, if so desired, to blind the uninitiated with science. Again, like all techniques, they have their strengths and their weaknesses and whether or not these are properly allowed for in any particular usage must depend on the user. Thus evaluation is not decision making, but a supportive aid to decision making. Since most of the problems with which land use planners deal have complex and widespread repercussions such aids are indispensable. An important justification for the use of formal evaluation methods by decision makers in land use planning is that the various different interests in the decision have to be acknowledged (though as discussed below, one of the common deficiencies in evaluation exercises is too narrow a definition of the interests affected).

Although conceptually 'plan evaluation' follows on from 'formulation of alternatives' and precedes 'decision making', this sequence may be incorporated into a cyclical process with the consideration first of *coarse* alternatives and then, guided by the results of evaluation, *fine* alternatives. One such planning study—that of Coventry-Solihull-Warwickshire—will be discussed in some detail later.

It is inherent in the concept of evaluation that a *comparison* is being made—thus even if there was only one proposal, it should be assessed against a 'do nothing' approach. And if any individual (or group) would find himself in a different position in some aspect of his welfare as a result of the proposal, that should be taken into account by whoever is responsible for making the relevant choice. Thus any formal evaluation technique for land use planning decisions should take account of the proposals' consequences for the well-being of all individuals and groups affected. *Comprehensive* evaluation would attempt to do just this; the *partial* techniques discussed first below take account only of some of the consequences of action. In a classic article on cost-benefit analysis, the comprehensive approach is defined:

'Cost-benefit analysis is a practical way of assessing the desirability of projects, where it is important to take a long view (in the sense of looking at repercussions in the further, as well as the nearer, future) and a wide view (in the sense of allowing for side-effects of many kinds on many persons, industries, regions etc.), i.e. it implies the enumeration and evaluation of all the relevant costs and benefits.'[1]

It will be noted that the 'enumeration' of all effects is a preliminary stage to the evaluation of them. A major development in the use of evaluation techniques for land use planning decisions was the suggestion that the evaluation of effects could only properly take place within the framework of specified land use planning objectives. This concept marks a major departure from the early uses of evaluation techniques by land use planners where the traditional guide-lines of welfare economics (from which evaluation techniques originally derive) had been applied. Let us consider this change of emphasis further, as it is of some importance.

Each individual may be said to have his own system of values or preferences about the shaping of his future, although circumstances decide how much of his preference system he has thought about or defined. He will have ideas both about his attitude to single factors, such as traffic noise, and also about his preference 'trade-offs', that is how much he values one thing as against another—that he nevertheless prefers to have the noise of traffic outside his house to having the road turned into a pedestrian street, which would not allow him to drive his car right up to his house. It is clear that even for one individual it may sometimes be very difficult to decide on his 'trade-off' in certain situations. What has to be done in relation to a land use planning decision, however, is to establish the community's 'trade-offs'.

Welfare economics had an established body of theory relating to such problems, and these provided the original foundation for all current evaluation techniques. The simplest guide-line, the Pareto optimum (that no one should be made worse off) became modified to a Kaldor-Hicks optimum (that the sum of those made better off should exceed the sum of those made worse off). In any practical applications, the problems of enumeration of effects and their measurement are, of course, vast, but analysis of people's preferences as expressed in their behaviour and as illuminated by social surveys provide some guide.

Early uses of the 'planning balance sheet' provide an illustration of these approaches taken into land use planning evaluation methods.

However, various commentators, notably Hill, suggested that land use planning claimed to operate within a defined framework of goals to be aimed at and objectives to be achieved and that only these could provide the proper context for any evaluations undertaken. Thus the decision maker should be assessing which alternative is most effective in moving toward the land use planning goals, not in maximising overall community benefit in some 'objective' sense. The emphasis required shifting from generalised individual or group preference sets to the effects on groups in land use planning terms, that is, in relation to the specified land use planning objectives. Whitbread has examined these issues and emphasised that, because of the ways in which planning objectives are generally expressed, 'assessment of their achievement between plans presents special difficulties'.[2] An example he quotes is the preservation of a Green Belt, which is not a land use planning policy adopted for its own sake, but as a means to provide for recreation and agriculture, limit urban expansion, and so on. 'In order to obtain evidence as to the value to people of preserving part of the Green Belt it would be necessary to measure the achievement of these sectoral objectives by the implementation of such a planning policy.'[3]

The ways in which various land use planning evaluations have approached this key element has varied. Often, the members of the planning team or their technical advisers use their own assessment of how members of the public would value objectives, as in Lichfield's study of Edgware, the Roskill Research Team's work on airport sites, or Morris Hill on road proposals in Cambridge. Sometimes, an attempt is made to get the public to evaluate alternative aims, as in the recent South Hampshire Structure Plan Study. More examples of approaches taken in recent studies are contained in 'The Urban Future', as well as in the remainder of this chapter.[4]

I have now discussed at some length the matter of whose objectives should be considered and which of them should be regarded as relevant in a land use planning evaluation. There are three other aspects of evaluation methods which should be emphasised before talking about specific techniques. The first is that the most basic constraint on the choice finally made is what alternatives are considered for evaluation. This is a point simply made but it needs stating.

The second is the question of measurement, that is, converting the physical repercussions of planning proposals into common units of relative value. Some commentators have suggested that this is pretty well a hunt for the Holy Grail and that total comparability should be abandoned as unattainable. In practice this may mean one of two approaches—either adopting several scales and/or units of measurement, as suggested by Hill—or else converting some of the results to a common scale and leaving other elements unmeasured, as in some planning balance sheet applications. Where an effort is made to quantify all elements of the evaluation, some index must be constructed and often the £ is used. The suggestion that this implies a philistine approach is dealt with by Alan Williams, who points out what is involved in constructing any index:

'When you establish some scale of amenity, or accessibility or aesthetic beauty, and score points for various features, then "normalise" these scores by turning them all into numbers of points out of a hundred, and finally add them together to form a composite index, the process of scoring involves evaluation. The process of adding the scores together involves a statement about the relative value of one point on one scale compared with the value of one point on another scale. And the fact that the £

129

sign is absent from this calculation does not affect one bit the fact that such relative valuation is taking place.'[5]

He states furthermore that society already uses the £ as a day-to-day expression of many relative values, but that the real point at issue is that evaluation must focus on benefit obtained for resources (other opportunities) forgone and if indices obscure this trade-off relationship then they should be avoided. The only point I wish to add here is that sometimes an evaluator may wish to avoid using the £ index because it is, among other things, a reflection of the existing distribution of incomes.

The final aspect of evaluation techniques to mention is that the presentation of such exercises should always contain an explicit statement of how reliable and accurate the analysts consider their measurements to be. It might be argued that this is throwing the burden of judgement back at the decision maker, but that is where I consider it rightfully belongs. The role of the analyst is in saying 'if this is what *you* wish to see valued most highly, then *you* could adopt the following course of action' but he must be open about the inescapable uncertainties.

Partial evaluation techniques

Although land use planning is supposed to be comprehensive, in practice it is often far from it, and this is also true for evaluation of alternative investments. The justification for considering these techniques has been expressed by Barrell and Glasson as 'first, because in scarce resource situations funds may not be available for full evaluation and resort will be necessary to a coarse or second-best technique and, second, because these partial techniques are used in practice and their major limitations need to be understood'.[6] I would thoroughly endorse the second reason in particular.

The same authors define three broad categories of partial techniques:

1   those concerned with costs and revenues (benefits), but which fail to evaluate a sufficient range of factors
2   those which compare the effectiveness of schemes of equal cost

3 those which compare the costs of schemes regarded as of
   equal or sufficient effectiveness

Classification of such techniques and related terminology is far
from standardised, but they suggest 'financial appraisal' for the
first group, 'cost effectiveness analysis' for the second and 'cost
minimisation analysis' for the third, and each of the three groups
will now be briefly considered.

Financial Appraisal

Financial appraisal is concerned with the costs and revenues of a
scheme to agencies participating as investors.[7] It is thus appropriate for an individual firm's calculations about profit maximisation, but not for public sector projects in which the various
'externalities' should be considered. Such appraisals are commonly carried out for town centre redevelopments, but have
been used for other land use planning decisions, for example,
Lichfield's appraisal of Peterborough[8] (see Figure 8.1.)

Costs and Returns
Estimated Capital Costs and Returns of alternative Town Development Plans

	A Capital Costs	A Capital Returns	B Capital Costs	B Capital Returns	C Capital Costs	C Capital Returns	D Capital Costs	D Capital Returns
Revenue Producing Investments	50	60	50	60	50	65	50	65
Non Revenue Producing Investments	50	50	60	60	60	60	50	50
Totals	100	110	110	120	110	125	100	115
Proportionate return over cost	—	10%	—	9%	—	13.5%	—	15.0%

Fig. 8.1   Financial Appraisal (after Lean)

SOURCE   'Economic Studies and Assessment of Town Development' in
Journal of the Town Planning Institute, April 1967

It is quite possible to think of land use planning situations in
which financial appraisal is important as one of the evaluative
techniques used, but less easy to defend its exclusive use. There
would appear to be a lot of scope for incorporating such assessment into the early stages of formulating proposals rather than

reserve it until proposals have been hardened up, when categoric acceptance or rejection of the whole scheme or important elements of it may be based on the financial balance. I regard the typical use of financial appraisal as an excellent example of what is termed lexicographic decision making, which may rightly be described as taking things in the wrong order.[9]

Cost-effectiveness analysis

Cost-effectiveness methods compare the benefits of schemes which are roughly equal in costs. It may thus be regarded as a restricted form of cost-benefit analysis. If any money returns are involved, then financial appraisal will suffice. For other types of return measures of effectiveness will have to be devised.

In the chapter on housing, a description is given of a 'constrained cost-effectiveness method' used to assess possible housing programmes in the Tyne-Wear Study (see page 291). Forms of cost-effectiveness are also described in the section on Plan Programme Budgeting (see page 163), and on Welfare Maximisation Models (see page 153).

Cost-minimisation techniques

These techniques are properly used only when the benefits of different courses of action may safely be regarded as equivalent. In such circumstances, it is clearly legitimate to select the solution which offers the least costs. 'Costs' may be interpreted in financial, total resource, or wider terms as, say, they would be in a cost-benefit analysis. One particular technique of cost minimisation that at one time gained considerable currency in land use planning is threshold analysis. It has recently been suggested by one of the best known advocates of the technique in this country, Kozlowski, that it should properly be used in combination with other evaluative techniques, and this would allay much of the criticism that has been made of threshold analysis.[10] (See Figure 8.2.)

In essence the technique focuses on the various limitations encountered in the growth of towns, caused by topography, public utility systems or the existing distribution of land uses,

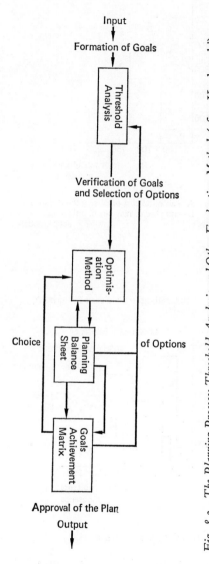

Fig. 8.2　The Planning Process: Threshold Analysis and Other Evaluation Methods (after Kozlowski)

SOURCE　'The Place and Role of Threshold Analysis in the 'Model' Planning Process' in Ekistics, November 1971

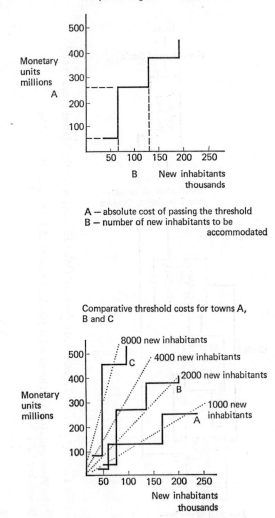

Simplified diagram of threshold costs.

A — absolute cost of passing the threshold
B — number of new inhabitants to be
    accommodated

Comparative threshold costs for towns A,
B and C

Fig. 8.3   Threshold Analysis (after Malisz)

SOURCE   'Implications of Threshold Theory for Urban and Regional Planning' in *Journal of the Town Planning Institute*, March 1969 notably town centres. These 'thresholds' to further development can be overcome only by a large investment of capital in addition to the normal costs incurred in development which relate more consistently to incremental numbers of population (see Figure 8.3). In least-cost terms, it is suggested that the particular patterns of development that minimise the combined costs incurred are to be preferred. The technique draws on economic theory, particularly the idea of 'fixed' and 'variable' costs in the 'theory of the firm' and is seen as a way of ensuring greater co-operation in the land use planning process of economists and physical planners. It has been widely used in its country of origin, Poland, and elsewhere abroad, as well as in this country, for example, in the Lothians Regional Survey and Plan, or the Grangemouh/Falkirk Regional Survey and Plan.[11]

Whilst I have already acknowledged the usefulness of this approach when properly used, its disadvantages appear to be:

1 difficulties in obtaining the necessary cost data for each application
2 its concentration on initial capital costs, and not subsequent running costs
3 its exclusive cost-orientation
4 its concentration on costs only to the investing agency.

However, as with all 'partial' techniques, it should be assessed for what it can do and not dismissed arbitrarily for what it cannot do.

Cost-benefit analysis

I have already quoted the description of cost-benefit analysis that emphasises its 'long-view' and its 'wide-view'; it is this perspective which distinguishes it from the partial techniques of evaluation described above. It can be argued that public investment decisions are particularly complicated by three factors, that there is often no direct revenue stream that can be accepted as a proxy for benefits, that often 'collective' goods are involved for which no direct payments can be estimated, such as defence, and that large and indivisible investments may be needed with far-ranging effects as with a motorway or airport.

In response to such methodological difficulties, techniques of cost benefit have developed—from early twentieth century American river and harbour projects, through to more recent usage in that country for multi-purpose water projects, and on to the next main category of land use decisions—transportation projects.[12] It was for transport decisions that cost-benefit analysis was first used in this country—the studies on the M1 and the Victoria Line, though restricted in the criteria used, aroused great interest among land use planners and in the last decade or so there have been many applications of cost-benefit analysis to land use planning problems.[13]

The technique leapt to the attention of the general public with its use for controversial choice studies that were given wide coverage by the media, notably the siting of the third London airport, which unfortunately tended to polarise advocates and opponents of c.b.a. in a quite artificial way.[14] Thus criticisms of its unrealism, undue concentration on tangibles and things easily quantified, and arbitrary identification of interests affected, have been manifold. But it is only fair to say that shortcomings in particular applications, or undue reliance on excessive aggregations do not, of themselves, condemn the approach if used properly—that is as a well understood and controlled *aid* to decision making by those with that responsibility. As has been said, 'At its theoretical best, the technique can provide conclusive and comprehensive assessment of the relative merits of different possibilities; at its practical worst, it provides a rationalised list of considerations to assist the decision maker in his deliberations, which is usually of considerable value.'

Before considering some developments of cost-benefit analysis specifically for land use planning decisions, it is of value to outline the basic methodology of cost-benefit analysis. Five stages can be differentiated:

1 *Project definition*

The basis for the analysis is a precise definition of the project or projects to be evaluated. I have already pointed out that this stage—often extremely arbitrary—is the most basic determinant of any outcome of the evaluation.

136

2 Identification and enumeration of costs and benefits

This stage involves the most work. For each alternative being considered the various costs and benefits must first be identified and then enumerated. Some of the difficulties of this process will be made clear in the example discussed later.

3 Evaluation of costs and benefits

The most common procedure is to evaluate in money terms wherever possible and to treat intangibles as a minor balancing factor. It is unfortunate that the varying marginal utility of money is rarely taken into account—studies assume that money has the same value to all members of the community, which is regrettably far from the case. (In our society old age pensioners are beneficently offered sums that would be regarded as derisory in most wage negotiations).

4 Discounting

Once the factors involved have been evaluated a discounting procedure must be used to make comparable the flows of costs and benefits over the life span of the project. There are various methods for doing this and, like the choice of interest rate to be used, they will produce widely differing results. These aspects of cost-benefit analysis are explained in a paper by Glasson.[15]

5 Presentation

The final stage in a cost-benefit analysis is the presentation of results and it is very important that there should be no over-simplification on the part of the analyst, whatever the pressures in this direction from decision makers. All the alternative assumptions that may be made and which affect the 'net benefit' result should be explained. It is arguable that cost-benefit analysis might often most properly be regarded as a tool for 'sensitivity analysis' rather than for indicating a single best solution.

The planning balance sheet

An adaptation of cost-benefit analysis intended for planning problems is Lichfield's *Planning Balance Sheet*.[16] In this, a plan is regarded as a series of interrelated development projects. For each project a list is produced of all parties (public and private) concerned with producing and operating the services, and of all those who will consume them, whether through buying them in the market or collectively with rates and taxes. For each producing or consuming party, a list is made of the costs and benefits that will accrue, each item being measured in money or physical terms as far as possible, otherwise noted as intangible. Thus a complete set of 'social accounts' is produced, normally in a descriptive table, which shows all the significant costs and benefits arising from the plan as a whole. The accounts are 'reduced' by eliminating double counting, transfer payments and common items. If alternative possibilities are being compared, the account reveals the differences. The final Planning Balance Sheet thus purports to be a summary of advantages and disadvantages to the public and to assist in more informed and rational policy decision making (see Figure 8.4).

Prest and Turvey made the following comments on the Planning Balance Sheet: 'Lichfield is primarily concerned to show how all the costs and benefits to all affected parties can be systematically recorded in a set of accounts. The arguments in favour of proceeding this way instead of by simply listing and evaluating the net amount of each type of cost or benefit are threefold. First, starting on an all-inclusive basis and then cancelling out to obtain net social benefits and costs ensures against omissions. Second the financial consequences of any project are sometimes important, and it may need to be redesigned in the light of the distribution of costs and benefits so as to compensate parties who would otherwise stand to lose from it. Third, whether or not financial transfers are used to affect the final distribution of net gains, that distribution will often be relevant to choice ... the attitude of a city council or similar body towards a scheme will depend upon who gains as well as upon how much they gain.'[17]

The Planning Balance Sheet was criticised by Hill, who disliked it particularly for ignoring the 'goal orientation' of planning.[18] He said that it failed to assess a project in terms of defined objectives, and relied on somewhat arbitrarily assumed universal values. Hill suggested an improvement—the Goals Achievement

	Plan A								Plan B							
	Benefits		Costs						Benefits		Costs					
	Capital	Annual	Capital	Annual					Capital	Annual	Capital	Annual				
Producers																
X	£a	£b	—	£d					—	—	£b	£c				
Y	i_1	i_2	—	—					i_3 M_3	i_4	—	—				
Z	M_1	—	M_2	—					—	—	M_4	—				
Consumers																
X'	—	£e	—	£f					—	£g	—	£h				
Y'	i_5	i_6	—	—					i_7 M_2	i_8	—	—				
Z'	M_1	—	M_3	—					—	—	M_4	—				

Fig. 8.4 The Planning Balance Sheet (after Hill)

SOURCE 'A goals-achievement Matrix for Evaluating Alternative Plans' in *Journal of the American Institute of Planners*, 1968

Matrix—which he prefers because it relates to the declared goals of a project and assesses how far they are achieved. The Goals Achievement Matrix, and its derivatives, will be discussed in the following section, but it should be explained here that the Planning Balance Sheet method has been modified somewhat in uses subsequent to Hill's comments, to attempt to meet the points he made.

The Edgware Study provides an example of the modified, more goal oriented version of the Planning Balance Sheet. This particular form of cost-benefit analysis of road proposals for a north-west London shopping centre has been fully described.[19] Planning studies showed that the fundamental choice to meet traffic problems was a relief road to the east of the main shopping street or one to the west of it. A relief road on the east would demolish few houses, but involve expense in bridging the railway; whereas a relief road on the west would save on construction but involve more property acquisition and disturbance. There were many variations possible to the basic routes and a Planning Balance Sheet was prepared to assist the local authority to make the choice. Four objectives were defined which related to removing traffic from the main shopping street, provision of rear service roads to shops, public car parking and a bus depot and expansion of the centre on to some adjacent undeveloped land. In the light of these, eight of the possible design solutions were selected and a ninth which was simpler and cheaper added as a comparative base.

The object of the technique was to produce a 'social account' which summarises the transactions taking place between the producers of services and the consumers. The actions that individual members and sectors of the community will perform in the completed project must be enumerated. Actions may comprise a wide range of things—providing a bus service or enjoying a view—but each one is defined and related to sector objectives. Objectives must, as far as possible, be precisely stated —for example, minimising cost for a given standard of service. These objectives are regarded as criteria, against which the values achieved in the plan can be measured.

As an interim product, for each sector the analysis ranks the schemes in terms of the objectives of that sector. Different types of measure were used for each entry—money, time or physical units of capital for tangibles, or an *I* to indicate that entry is not measurable. Where measurement was not feasible plusses and minuses indicated comparative differences between schemes. Then a points-scoring system was used to weight the various sectors and the different objectives.

The analysis was in fact carried out in two stages—first, of schemes which represented the major different alternatives available—and then of the possible variants of the alternative indicated.

The main conclusions were that three schemes merited consideration, each having different advantages and disadvantages, with one cheaper since it did not incorporate a relief road. The final choice thus rested on whether the cost differential for a relief road scheme was thought to be justified, and on the relative importance given by decision makers to the different sectors of the community. The analysts did make a specific recommendation, based on their own weighting.

It may be helpful to specify the assumptions and estimations that, in this particular application of the Planning Balance Sheet, were crucial in determining the final recommendations:

1 The alternative 'design solutions' considered
2 The identification of 'producers' and 'consumers'
3 The objectives they were deemed to have
4 Identification and measurement of 'costs' and 'benefits'
5 Procedures used for ranking, or otherwise weighting, sectors and objectives
6 A final balancing of financial against other factors. (In this study, no discounting decisions were involved.)

Goals achievement matrix

Hill's main point of quarrel with evaluative techniques hitherto used for land use planning considerations was the 'costs and benefits can be compared only if they can be related to a common objective', and that 'a criterion of maximising net benefits in the abstract is, therefore, meaningless'. He says, too, that 'benefits and costs are not necessarily additive or comparable' and are irrelevant if the objective to which they refer is of no value to the

Goal Description: Relative weight:	α 2			β 3			γ 5			δ 4		
Incidence	Relative Weight	Costs	Benefits	Relative Weight	Costs	Benefits	Relative Weight	Costs	Benefits	Relative Weight	Costs	Benefits
Group a	1	A	D	5	E	—	1		N	1	Q	R
Group b	3	H		4	—	R	2		—	2	S	T
Group c	1	L	J	3	—	S	3	M	—	1	V	W
Group d	2	—		2		—	4		—	2	—	—
Group e	1	—	K	1	T	U	5		P	1	—	—
		Σ	Σ					Σ	Σ			

Fig. 8.5 a The Goals Achievement Matrix (after Hill)

142

	Goal α : Weight = 2			Goal β : Weight = 1		
	Group Weight	Plan A	Plan B	Group Weight	Plan A	Plan B
Group a	3	+6	−6	3	−3	0
Group b	1	−2	+2	2	0	−2
		+4	−4		−3	−2

Plan A Score = +4 −3 = 1
Plan B Score = −4 −2 = −6
Therefore Plan A is preferable to Plan B

Fig. 8.5 b *The goals Achievement Matrix—scoring* (after Hill)

SOURCE 'A Goals Achievement Matrix For Evaluating Alternative Plans' in *Journal of the American Institute of Planners*, 1968 community. For these, and other, reasons he is highly critical both of what he terms the economic type of cost-benefit analysis and of the development balance sheet.

Hill proposes instead a 'goals achievement matrix', which would be constructed thus:

The first stage is to focus on the goals for the plan in question; the relative value to be attached to each goal must be established. Then each alternative course of action must be examined to see how far it satisfies each goal.

Thus the overall performance of each alternative in relation to all the goals can be seen.

In all cases 'benefits represent progress towards the desired objectives, while costs represent retrogression from desired objectives'.

Among the disadvantages of the suggested matrix are that it cannot be summed, and that interaction and interdependence between objectives is not registered. It also depends entirely on weighting—of 'objectives, activities, locations, groups or sectors in urban areas'—and it 'is not very useful if weights cannot be objectively determined or assumed'.

Hill illustrated his suggestion with a conceptualised matrix (see Figure 8.5), and also gave an example for the different types of measurement he envisages would be needed (see Table 8.1). His article has proved a valuable stimulant for development and discussion of evaluation techniques for land use planning. A recent study which was much influenced in its methodology by Hill's ideas was the Coventry-Solihull-Warwickshire Sub-regional Planning Study.[20] The terms of reference of the study required the team to look 20 years ahead to consider the need for land for homes, industry, commerce, recreation and other factors essential to the development of a robust economy and a satisfactory environment, the principal goal being to suggest a strategic planning framework to act as a bridge between regional considerations and the development plans of the local authorities in the area.

The study was the fourth in the present round of sub-regional studies, and its pedigree is out of Notts-Derby—from which they adopted and developed the 'potential surface' technique—by

Hill—who suggested the goals—achievement approach to evaluation.

The Coventry-Solihull-Warwickshire study's leader has stated that they were anxious to improve the balance between the initial survey and forecasting stage and the subsequent process of choosing the best strategy.[21] They therefore sought a procedure that emphasised a *progressive* shaping and evaluation of alternative strategies by reference to specified objectives. The view was taken that if objectives were worth expressing at all, the study must clearly relate to them throughout.

Table 8.1—Types of Measurement

The following outline is a possible set of objectives that would be affected by the plan for a new transportation route and a set of measures of these objectives. The objectives might be those of the entire community affected or sections of the community affected or of the users of the transportation system and are classified accordingly.

1 *Objectives measurable on a ratio scale*

User objectives

1 Increase of accessibility: measured in average travel time and, when valid, in monetary terms.
2 Accident reduction: measured in terms of numbers of fatalities and injuries. Injury costs and property damage measured in monetary terms.

Community objectives

1 Economic efficiency: measured in monetary terms.
2 Regional economic growth: measured in monetary terms.
3 Income distribution: measured in monetary terms.
4 Fiscal efficiency (defined as net returns to the fisc.): measured in monetary terms.
5 Reduction of air pollution: measured in terms of the amount of pollutants per unit volume of air.

Table 8.1—*continued*

2 *Objectives measurable on interval scale*
User and community objectives
Noise reduction: measured in decibels or sones.

3 *Objectives measurable on ordinal scale*
A. Objectives that can be measured on ratio or interval scales if suitable surrogates are employed
User objectives
1 Comfort of travel (defined as the absence of physical and mental strain):
  Surrogate measures are:
  a probability of standing in transit vehicles
  b probability of travelling on congested route.
2 Convenience of travel (defined as ease of performance):
  Surrogate measures are:
  a number of changes of mode of travel between origin and destination
  b aggregate amount of waiting time in changing mode of travel
  c aggregate amount of walking required, measured in time or distance in getting from origins to destinations
  d reliability of transit service, measured in probability of service being provided as scheduled.

Community objectives
1 Reduction of community disruption:
  Surrogate measures are:
  a Displacement of buildings and activities measured in numbers of buildings and people displaced and the monetary costs, direct and indirect, of relocation
  b Extent of interference with existing market areas and service areas of community services and businesses measured by number of intersections of trip origin and destination lines.
2 Preservation of open space:
  Surrogate measures are:

Table 8.1—*continued*

   a open space threatened as percentage of total community open
    space
   b accessibility to alternative open space serving similar
    purposes.

B. Objectives that can be measured only on ordinal scales even if surrogates are employed

User and community objective

Visual enhancement: a set of criteria can be postulated that can
enable the evaluation of a transport route from both the users'
point of view and the point of view of adjoining communities.
Such criteria can be employed with respect to the features of the
roadscape, the traveller's perception of space and motion, the
traveller's sense of orientation and location, the integration of the
facility into the surrounding area, the screening of traffic, and so
forth. The explicit and systematic use of such criteria as proposed
by analysts such as Appleyard, Lynch and Meyer or Tunnard
and Pushkarev, enables the measurement of the visual effects of
transportation improvements on an ordinal scale.

Community objectives

Preservation of historic sites and buildings: a set of criteria for
the comparative evaluation of historic sites and buildings along
the lines suggested by Tunnard and Pushkarev could be employed
when such sites or buildings are threatened by transportation
improvements.

    Effectively, evaluation began in a broad way as soon as the
range of surveys and forecasts had been decided—since alternatives were progressively refined as a battery of objective-
achievement tests were applied so that, finally, small differences in
advantage were being examined.
    The following summary may seem unduly lengthy, but I fear a
briefer description would be very confusing.

1 *Deriving the objectives*

The approach required careful definition of those objectives whose achievement could be influenced by the choice of a sub-regional planning strategy. The terms of reference suggested the broad scope of this study—from that starting point four goals were defined:

1 Social and economic:
   balance and prosperity in the sub-regional economy and the greatest social welfare;
2 Environmental:
   the best living and working environment throughout the sub-region;
3 Choice:
   the greatest choice of opportunities;
4 Flexibility:
   the ability to adapt to change while ensuring that social and economic advancement are maintained.

These goals are generalised statements to which no specific tests of achievement could be applied; therefore, operational objectives had to be defined—specific statements about the sub-region derived from the goals, for which a degree of attainment is measurable.

There were two groups of operational objectives:

1 essential objectives such as the quantity inputs to all strategies —numbers of houses, jobs, land and so forth
2 discriminatory objectives—whose attainment would vary between alternative strategies and are qualitative
   a To conserve areas of high landscape value
   b To keep the loss of good quality farm land to a minimum
   c To keep the cost of utilities and land development services to a minimum
   d To avoid the loss of workable mineral resources
   e To locate new housing areas in pleasant surroundings
   f To provide a choice of housing sites for residents seeking new homes
   g To avoid physical disturbance to existing development
   h To locate new development away from sources of noise and atmospheric pollution

i To promote the greatest possible choice of jobs for all workers

j To give particular assistance to those areas where existing industries are declining

k To provide the greatest possible choice of labour supply for all firms

l To provide the greatest possible opportunity for all residents to go out to work

m To provide the greatest possible accessibility to shopping centres for all residents

n To locate new roads so as to give the greatest possible benefit to all road users

o To provide the greatest possible opportunity for the operation of public transport services

p To provide the greatest possible choice of different types of transport

q To be able to cope with a faster or slower rate of growth

r To be able to cope with sudden or unexpected events

s To be responsive to changes in social values

t To be able to change to another strategy once implementation has begun.

The objectives were intended to be specific to the sub-region and its character and problems. At two stages in the Study, the objectives were redefined, and it was specified that they must be reconsidered as circumstances change.

2 *Generating alternative strategies*

The largest step in reaching the recommended strategy was taken when the alternatives open to the sub-region were identified. The best strategy was reached by progressive elimination to the final point where only a very detailed evaluation could choose from the final short list. They examined the process used in previous studies, and were particularly dissatisfied with the approach of examining 'patterns' of urban development. They wanted the recommended strategy to come from an understanding of economic, social and physical relationships—not to force such relationships into a predetermined conceptual envelope.

3 Development potential analysis

The technique used to crystallise alternatives relied on identifying the relative attractiveness of different parts of the sub-region for new development. It is essentially a systematic and comprehensive development|of traditional sieve map procedures, similar to that used in the Notts-Derby study, but with a much wider base of physical as well as social and economic factors used as a tool for generating alternative strategies and subsequently detailing those preferred, rather than only for evaluating previously defined alternatives as in Notts-Derby.

The data collection stage of the study produced a computer data file, related to the 1km National Grid, which enabled all factors influencing an area's suitability for development to be expressed quantitatively, and incorporated into a single composite factor diagram or surface of combined Development Potential. This represents an advance over the conventional sieve map in three ways:

1 It does not rely on using arbitrary cut-offs or thresholds to identify 'best' and 'worst' areas, but enables every factor to be graded throughout the area
2 Certain selected factors can be given greater emphasis by using a weighting system
3 By varying the weights, the effects of varying policy assumptions can be gauged.

The development potential of every part of the sub-region was examined; initially 93 5 × 5 km blocks, subsequently 23 161 1 × 1 km units.

Eleven factors were chosen to represent the discriminatory objectives, for the purpose of shaping the strategy—ten of these were represented as factor surfaces, i.e. contour maps, showing variations in development potential across the sub-region relative to each factor—the eleventh—choice of transport—was a combination of the road and rail surfaces:

a landscape
b agriculture
c services
d residential environment
e annoyance

f job access
g labour access
h shop access
i road access
j rail access
k choice of transport.

The main problem was how best to combine the scores for the factors. Most objectives were expressed in terms of minimising or maximising opportunities—the scores for each surface were put in the range 1–100, whatever the original units of measurement (e.g. hectares of farmland, miles to work).

The different weighting systems used were derived from:

1 a questionnaire to liaison officers in the three planning authorities

2 a short list of explicit policy alternatives intended to exaggerate weights.

In all 42 sets of weights were derived and, when multiplied by factor scores, these produced 42 different development potential surfaces, which were presented graphically. Two series were done —one including existing built-up areas, the other taking account only of land undeveloped at 1976.

An analysis was then made in several stages of the highest ranking squares from the 42 potential surfaces. Thirteen of the 5 × 5 squares merited close attention (forecasts had already shown 1976–91 development would require equivalent of four of the squares). At this stage, sensitivity tests were carried out to be sure that quite different results would not be produced with different weightings.

4 *The four alternatives*

The development potential data was synthesised into three major strategies, and a 'trend' strategy added, giving four.

The next stage was to explore changes in the weighting systems used and to refine the strategies.

So, to the weighting systems that had produced the three strategies, were added two more—one to give a landscape emphasis, the other applying to the 'trend' strategy.

A comparison between the five at both 5 × 5 and 1 × 1 km
level showed two to be so similar that they could be regarded
as one, leaving four to be detailed. A separate industrial development potential surface was carried out, as this was not well
enough taken into account—using factors—
    a landscape
    b land service constraints
    c private transport
    d choice of labour
    e flat land

5   *Detailing the strategies*

This process started with a common pattern of people, jobs and
highways projected to 1976, and on this base simulated four
alternative distributions to 1991, incorporating assumptions
about future residential and industrial densities, increases of
employment in town centres, areas of redevelopment, of obsolete
housing and factories, and costs of future roads. The 1 × 1 km
surfaces were used constantly in detailing. In fact, the land take
needed for new development up to 1991 varied only from 4 to 8%
of the total study area in different strategies.

6   *Testing the alternatives*

The alternatives were evaluated by measuing the promise of
each one against each of the discriminatory objectives for the
strategy. It was thus an objective-achievement procedure similar
to that proposed by Hill, which rationalises established evaluation
methods.

Again, the weights used are crucial; apart from the team's
views, the community was asked to weight objectives. Also, as a
check, a cost-based assessment was made to see whether it would
have produced a very different result. There was also a special
examination of strategies for flexibility.

The best strategy was selected because it scored consistently
high in all tests.

Another development of Hill's suggested matrix for evaluation—into a form of programming model—was presented by

Stuart, using an example related to the US Model Cities Programme.[22] Although his final conclusion accepts that it would not yet be possible to use a fully fledged model of the type he suggests in practice, the approach is nevertheless a promising one.

Stuart explains, 'The concept of a programs-objectives matrix can be more rigorously structured in the form of a mathematical programming problem. Such a mathematical model will require that we do establish a common unit of measurement for goal achievement, because the summing of matrix rows and columns is essential. The key feature of mathematical programming lies in the use of an *objective function,* a combination of program variables which we wish to optimise. In general, we will want either to minimise overall cost (given some specified minimum level of goal achievement) or to maximise goal achievement (given some maximum overall budget). In addition to an objective function, the basic programs-objectives matrix will usually be augmented by various constraints indicating minimum and maximum limits on certain programs and program combinations.'

Using the Model Cities Programme as an example, Stuart developed a simple linear programming model, built around a matrix of relative effectiveness coefficients, a set of performance standards and appropriate budget programmes (see Tables 8.2 and 8.3). Stuart concluded from his experiment that much work remains to be done before viable urban improvement programming models can actually be developed. The areas which first require more investigation include—identifying objectives, identifying alternative programmes of action, predicting and measuring effectiveness, and sensitivity analysis of all the elements that could be varied.

Stuart also mentioned previous work in this field, notably that by Schlager, Coughlin and Peterson.[23]

Table 8.2 Urban Improvement Programming Models

Hypothetical model neighbourhood: basic performance objectives

Type	Objective variable	Socio-economic condition	Reference group	Number present	% of reference group	Five-year performance standard	% of reference group
Housing	Y_1	Substandard housing units	Total housing units	6580	16	2060	5
	Y_2	Other deficient housing units	Total housing units	6170	15	2060	5
	Y_3	Inadequately housed L–I elderly households	HH 65 and over, income less than $3000	900	45	300	15
	Y_4	Inadequately housed L–I families	Family income less than $5000	7840	70	2240	20
	Y_5	Inadequately housed M–I families	Family income $5000–$8000	3200	38	1010	12
Employment-Income-Education	Y_6	Unemployed persons	14 and over, civilian labour force	4030	8	1510	3
	Y_7	Underemployed persons	14 and over, civilian labour force	5040	10	1510	3
	Y_8	Families with income less than $3000	Total families	5600	20	2240	8
	Y_9	ADC cases	Persons under 18	11130	30	2600	7
	Y_{10}	Annual high school dropouts	Persons age 14–17	1880	30	1250	20
	Y_{11}	Annual college or jr. college enrolment	Persons age 18–24	1300	15	2170	25
	Y_{12}	Adults with grade school education or less	Persons 25 and over	29620	44	20190	30
	Y_{13}	Net new industrial jobs lying within ¾-hr travel time via public transit	None	—	—	1000	—

Table 8.2 continued

Type	Objective variable	Socio-economic condition	Reference group	Number present	% of reference group	Five-year performance standard	% of reference group
Health-Safety-Environment	Y_{14}	Annual infant mortality	Live births	180	6	75	2·5
	Y_{15}	Annual new tuberculosis cases	Total population	700	0·7	70	0·07
	Y_{16}	Annual juvenile arrests	Persons under 18	2020	5	1010	2·5
	Y_{17}	Annual criminal arrests (excl. minor misdemeanours)	Total population	9000	9	2000	2
	Y_{18}	Persons unserved by adequate local recreation facilities	Total population	35 000	35	5000	5
	Y_{19}	Persons expressing satisfaction with general environmental living conditions (excl. housing)	5% sample survey	1000	20	2500	50
	Y_{20}	Persons attending, local community planning meetings (annual)	Total population	1000	1	2000	2

Note: total population   100 000   total families: 28 000   total housing units   41 150.

SOURCE: D. G. Stuart, 'Urban improvement programming models', in *Socio-Economic Planning Sciences*, **4** (1970).

Table 8.3 Urban Improvement Programming Models

Hypothetical model neighbourhood: basic improvement programmes

Type	Public improvement programme	Output unit	Cost/ unit ($) (000)	Output Units /$1000 expenditure	Assumptions
Housing	Clearance, existing housing	H.U.	5·0	0·20	
	Private redevelopment, new housing (clearance subsidy)	H.U.	4·0	0·25	
	Public housing, elderly	H.U.	3·5	0·29	Includes clearance of existing housing
	Public housing, family	H.U.	4·5	0·22	Includes clearance of existing housing
	Housing rehabilitation, substandard units	H.U.	1·8	0·55	
	Housing rehabilitation, other deficient units	H.U.	1·2	0·80	
	Moderate-income housing	H.U.	0·1	10·00	
	Receivership rehabilitation, substandard units	H.U.	1·3	0·75	
	Receivership rehabilitation, other deficient units	H.U.	0·8	1·25	
	Rent supplements (5-yr)	H.U.	3·5	0·29	
	Code enforcement, substandard units	H.U.	0·4	2·50	
	Code enforcement, other deficient units	H.U.	0·2	5·00	

Table 8.3 *continued*

Type	Public improvement programme	Output unit	Cost/ unit ($) (000)	Output Units /$1000 expenditure	Assumption
Employment-Income-Education	Community action job training, unemployed	Persons	4·2	0·24	$500/referral; ½ of referrals are placed; ⅓ of placements keep jobs
	Community action job training, underemployed	Persons	3·4	0·29	Somewhat better performance
	Manpower development and training, unemployed	Persons	5·2	0·19	$1300/referral; ½ of referrals are placed; ½ of placements keep jobs
	Manpower development and training, underemployed	Persons	4·0	·025	Somewhat better performance
	ADC job training, unemployed	Persons	3·0	0·33 ⎱	Similar to community action job training; somewhat lower referral costs
	ADC job training, underemployed	Persons	2·4	0·42 ⎰	
	Day care centres, reduce unemployment and underemployment	Persons	0·2	5·00	Partially self-supporting

Table 8.3 *continued*

Type	Public improvement programme	Output unit	Cost/unit ($) (000)	Output Units /$1000 expenditure	Assumption
Employment-Income-Employment	Industrial redevelopment, new jobs nearby	Persons	1·5	0·67	$90,000/acre; 60 jobs/acre
	Industrial redevelopment, reduce unemployment and under-employment	Persons	15·0	0·07	10% of new jobs for unemployed; 10% for underemployed
	Industrial promotion, private development, new jobs nearby	Persons	0·1	10·00	Highly variable, but costs/job would be low
	Industrial promotion, private development, reduce unemployment and underemployment	Persons	1·2	0·83	10% of new jobs for unemployed; 10% for underemployed
	Basic adult education, unemployed	Persons	13·8	0·07	$275/person; 2% gain employment who otherwise would not
	Basic adult education, underemployed	Persons	11·2	0·09	Somewhat better performance

SOURCE: D. G. Stuart, 'Urban improvement programming models' in *Socio-Economic Planning Sciences*, **4** (1970).

References

1 Prest, A. R. & R. Turvey, 'Cost-benefit analysis: a survey', in *The Economic Journal,* page 683 (1965).
2 Whitbread, M., *Evaluation in the Planning Process,* Working Paper 3, Planning Methodology Research Unit, University College, London.
3 See Whitbread, *op. cit.* (2) above, page 10.
4 Jackson, J. N., *The Urban Future,* Allen & Unwin, London (1972) see Chapter 9, 'Cost-benefit analysis and the planning balance sheet', page 233.
5 Williams, A., 'Cost-benefit analysis: a basic exposition of its intellectual foundations,' in a *Report of a Seminar on Recreation Cost/Benefit Analysis,* held by the Countryside Commission (1971).
6 Barrell, D. & J. Glasson, 'Partial Analysis', a paper given at a Course—*The Application of Evaluation Techniques in Urban Planning,* Department of Town Planning, Oxford Polytechnic (1972).
7 Ratcliffe, J., 'Financial Appraisal in Plan Evaluation', a paper given at a Course, see (6) above.
8 Lichfield, N., 'Cost-benefit analysis in urban expansion: a case study: Peterborough', in *Regional Studies,* 3 (1969).
9 White, D. J., *Decision Theory,* Centre for Business Research, University of Manchester, Allen & Unwin (1969).
10 Kozlowski, J., 'The place and role of threshold analysis in the 'model' planning process', in *Ekistics,* 32, 192, November 1971.
11 *Lothians Regional Survey and Plan,* HMSO, Edinburgh (1966); *Grangemouth/Falkirk Regional Survey and Plan,* 2 HMSO, Edinburgh (1968).
12 Prest and Turvey, *op. cit.* (1) above.
13 Coburn, T. M., Beesley, M. & Reynolds, D. *The London–Birmingham Motorway: Traffic and Economics;* Road Research Laboratory Technical Paper No. 46, HMSO (1960); Foster, C. D. & Beesley, M. 'Estimating the social benefit of constructing an underground railway in London', in *Journal of the Royal Statistical Society,* 126, part 1 (1963).
14 *Commission on the Third London Airport, Papers and Proceedings,* 3, part 2, HMSO, London (1970); see also, Frost, M. J., *Values for Money,* Gower Press (1971).
15 Glasson, J., 'Introduction to cost-benefit analysis', a paper given at a Course, see (6) above.
16 Lichfield, N., 'Cost-benefit analysis in city planning', in *Journal of the American Institute of Planners,* November 1960, page 273;

and *Cost-Benefit Analysis in Town Planning—A Case Study of Cambridge,* Cambridgeshire and the Isle of Ely Council (1968).

17 See Prest and Turvey, *op. cit.* (1) above.

18 Hill, M., *A Method for Evaluating Alternative Plans: The Goals Achievement Matrix Applied to Transportation Plans,* Ph.D. Dissertation, University of Pennsylvania (1966); also, 'A goals-achievement matrix for evaluating alternative plans', in *Journal of the American Institute of Planners,* page 19, **34** (1968).

19 Lichfield, & Associates, 'Cost-benefit analysis and road proposals for a shopping centre: a case study: Edgware', in *Journal of Transport Economics and Policy,* **2,** 3, September 1968.

20 *Coventry-Solihull-Warwickshire, A Strategy for the Sub-region,* Supplementary Report 4, Evaluation, May 1971.

21 Wannop, U. A., 'An objective strategy: The Coventry-Solihull-Warwickshire Sub-regional Study,' in *Journal of the Royal Town Planning Institute,* **58,** 4, page 159, April 1972.

22 Stuart, D. G., 'Urban improvement programming models', in *Socio-Economic Planning Sciences,* **4,** 1970, page 217; see also, Ben-Shahar, H., Mazor, A. & Pines D., 'Town planning and welfare maximisation: a methodological approach', in *Regional Studies,* page 105, **3** (1969).

23 Schlager, K. J., 'A land use plan design model', in *Journal of the American Institute of Planners,* page 103, **31,** May 1965; Coughlin, R. E. & Peterson G. L., *Complete Value Analysis: Highway Beautification and Environmental Quality,* Highway Research Record 182, 9–17, Highway Research Board, Washington (1967); see also, Coughlin, B. E. & Stevens B. H., 'Public facility programming and the achievement of developmental goals', a paper prepared for a *Seminar on Land Use Models,* Institute for Urban Studies, University of Pennsylvania, October 1964.

9 Implementation

Introduction

It is a familiar, but still valid, criticism of land use planning that it fails to place enough emphasis on 'the quality of the action'. A look at the literature of planning, the allocation of research funds or the content of planning courses would give the impression that much more effort, time and money goes into the production of land use plans on paper than into the achievement of those plans in reality. However, in most land use planning departments in local authorities, the majority of the staff are employed in implementation, and it is that part of planning which impinges directly on the public. It is difficult, then, to over-emphasise the importance to land use planning of implementation.

Statutory structure planning now requires the land use planning authority to promote, encourage and influence all the individuals and agencies within its area, so that in the detailed planning and implementation of their own activities they fit in with the overall wider strategies. That fits into the traditional view of implementation, which comprised three types of activity:

1 organisation and co-ordination
2 control
3 stimulation.

To these should be added a fourth, which is the 'observing and learning' element, now recognised as an essential part of land use planning:

4 monitoring, to provide information, needed as feedback to the overall land use planning process.

These four aspects of implementation will be discussed in turn, with the techniques appropriate to them.

Organisation and co-ordination

Once a policy or plan has gained the necessary authorisations, implementation begins, and some framework for organisation and co-ordination is needed. I shall discuss three illustrative approaches to this task, which vary considerably in the range of activities they encompass, and in how far they reach out to embrace other parts of the planning process. It may well be felt that all three of them could have been discussed under headings other than 'implementation'. Indeed, they could, but I have stressed elsewhere that the divisions of the planning process are conceptual and do not retain complete validity in practice.

PPBS

The first approach to be discussed is the most comprehensive—it covers not merely implementation, or even the land use planning process, but all the functions of an organisation. It is, in fact, expressing the 'corporate planning' concept. The initials PPBS stand for Planning, Programming and Budgeting Systems, which is an approach to organisation and decision making that embraces a whole host of changes in approach and in operational procedures from those which are traditional. Its purpose is to make an organisation more systematic and thus more efficient in achieving whatever it exists to achieve.

Essentially it involves:

1 a clear and explicit definition of the overall *purposes* of the organisation, and then of any specific actions it proposes
2 This will generally involve a shedding of historically determined and now obsolete organisation structures
3 Priorities for action, spending, staff time and so forth must be intelligently arrived at
4 An effort must be made to assess the returns for any resources expended.

It can be seen from these points that several concepts of organisation theory and decision making are involved. PPBS includes 'management by objectives'—that is, deploying staff and resources quite consciously and explicitly to meet the declared goals of the organisation. It involves efforts at assessment of 'cost-effectiveness' of alternative claims on the organisation's resources. This, in the case of complicated multi-goal welfare objectives, such as those of a planning department, will almost certainly require the use of cost-benefit techniques. Since PPBS also includes the preparation of capital budgets for a period ahead, usually with a rolling programme regularly reviewed, it involves too the different parts of the organisation competing with each other for funds, on the basis of the contribution their effort will make to the achievements of the overall objectives of the whole organisation.

Clearly then, with the PPBS approach, the measurement of the cost-effectiveness of the use of resources on alternative possibilities becomes quite crucial in determining the pattern of activity of the organisation. PPBS certainly has its critics, who foresee an effort to rationalise all processes, regardless of the complexity of the objectives, and the difficulty of assessing their achievement in cost-effectiveness terms. They think the quality of planning will suffer from a quite unrealistic striving after 'the rational ideal'—'The historical convenience of economic and statistical decision models has been the plausibility to those who accept the rational ideal and utilitarian postulates (witness, for example, the rush of acceptance of PPBS, an operational formulation of the rational model.')[1] It is rather early yet to attempt to assess the working of PPBS, since it is still in the early stages of implementation and use even by those planning authorities who were the first in the country to adopt it.

The following description of the process of using PPBS is derived from a paper given by Amos in 1970, which had the main title—Systematic Local Government.[2] Amos' authority—Liverpool—was among the earliest in the country to take up PPBS.

1. The first operation for an authority which has adopted PPBS is to define its objectives. This is not a once and for all operation since the system is cyclical (see Figure 9.1), and the redefinition of objectives will occur at the beginning of each cycle. The

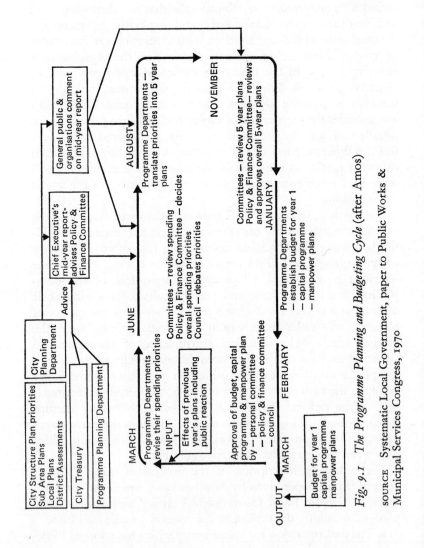

Fig. 9.1 The Programme Planning and Budgeting Cycle (after Amos)

SOURCE Systematic Local Government, paper to Public Works & Municipal Services Congress, 1970

164

purpose of defining objectives is so that an authority shall have some criteria against which it can assess the usefulness of current or intended action. It is hence important that objectives be expressed in quantifiable terms, so that achievement can be compared with targets.

2. The second operation is to group existing or possible activities of the authority, according to the objectives they will help to achieve. Programme is the term usually applied to these groups of activities, and there may be one or more programmes related to each objective (see Figure 9.2).

3. The third operation is for each programme structure to be examined separately to establish which activities within it are the most useful for achieving the relevant objective. This usefulness may be determined by the type and quantity of resources needed, the standard to be achieved, and any side effects. This examination is termed *programme analysis*.

4. The fourth operation is for the authority to take all the useful activities in each programme, and to rearrange them into a plan of activities and a budget. At this stage the resources available must be taken into account and allocated according to the importance attached to each programme. The budget should be prepared for several years ahead and should group expenditure according to objectives to be achieved. The end of this stage is thus the production of the programme plan and the programme budget.

5. The fifth operation is for the authority to review performance and achievement, assessing whether the intended progress towards objectives has been attained and whether the costs and effectiveness originally estimated for activities were correct. In the course of this review—which is the key to the success of the whole system—new or modified objectives may emerge. The review is thus a feedback process leading to the redefinition of objectives and the start of a new cycle.

Amos stresses that the total policy plan, which is in effect, a large number of sub-plans, is plan *plus* budget; there is no value in having a plan which is not realistic in budget terms, or vice versa, and the budget is a plan of expenditure (not an estimate of outgoings).

The adoption of PPBS at Milton Keynes has been described by one of those involved. After outlining their feasibility study, and the factors relevant to the introduction of PPBS, Welfare says, 'In conclusion, it must be said that although it appears that programme budgeting may prove to be an extremely

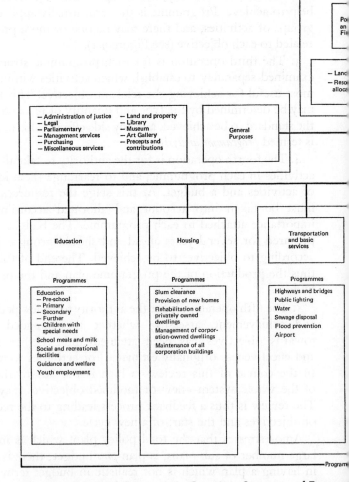

Fig. 9.2 Liverpool Corporation's Committee Structure and Programme Areas (after Amos)

valuable tool, it should not be regarded as a universal panacea since its prime function is as an aid, and not the complete answer, to management and the decision making process in planning. American experience has proved that an over-hasty adoption of the system, unsupported by an initial programme of research

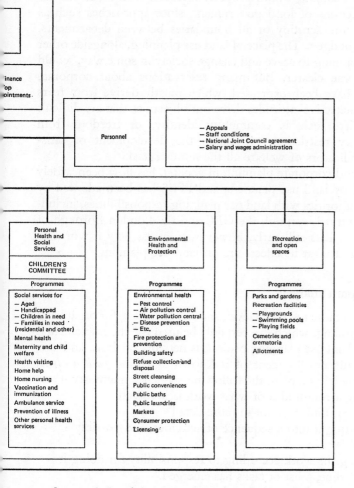

inance
'op
ointments.

Personnel

— Appeals
— Staff conditions
— National Joint Council agreement
— Salary and wages administration

Personal Health and Social Services	Environmental Health and Protection	Recreation and open spaces
CHILDREN'S COMMITTEE		
Programmes	Programmes	Programmes
Social services for	Environmental health	Parks and gardens
— Aged	— Pest control	Recreation facilities
— Handicapped	— Air pollution control	— Playgrounds
— Children in need	— Water pollution central	— Swimming pools
— Families in need (residential and other)	— Disease prevention	— Playing fields
Mental health	— Etc.	Cemetries and crematoria
Maternity and child welfare	Fire protection and prevention	Allotments
Health visiting	Building safety	
Home help	Refuse collection and disposal	
Home nursing	Street cleansing	
Vaccination and immunization	Public conveniences	
Ambulance service	Public baths	
Prevention of illness	Public laundries	
Other personal health services	Markets	
	Consumer protection	
	Licensing	

SOURCE Systematic Local Government, paper to Public Works & Municipal Services Congress, 1970 and feasibility studies, can present formidable problems on implementation.'[3]

It is widely assumed that the new units of local government, which will come into being in 1974, will adopt new methods of organisation, particularly the corporate planning approach. Apart from making land use planning itself more systematic, corporate planning would properly integrate it into the various other functions of local government, since approaches such as PPBS require scrutiny of all boundaries between departments, staffs and budgets. The place of land use planning, alongside other activities aiming to serve and change society in some way, would thus become clearer. But many reservations about corporate planning have been expressed, which mostly derive from fears that 'cost-effective' attitudes drive out objectives that are difficult to quantify, such as community identity, or freedom from unnecessary restrictions. It makes the development of satisfactory indicators of welfare all the more crucial.

PPBS and corporate planning in general, has now been widely discussed by land use planners, and PPBS has been adopted by several authorities with land use planning responsibilities, including Coventry, Liverpool, the GLC and the London Borough of Greenwich. It is still early, however, to assess how it works in practice and what its effects are on land use planning.

Critical path analysis

On a much more restricted level, another technique for organising and controlling, which can certainly be used for the implementation of a land use planning project, is network analysis, and particularly the development of it known as *critical path analysis*. In implementing a plan, the following sequence might occur:
1 Having a rough idea of what work is involved
2 trying to think this out in more detail
3 converting it into a sequence of activities, and possibly a timetable
4 dividing the work according to responsibility for doing it
5 by this time, a list of tasks has emerged.
This might be drawn up as a bar chart, in an attempt to show the job more clearly.

Those steps, which form the conventional approach to setting about a job, are all useful, but there is an important deficiency—it is not possible to tell the extent to which different parts of the work are interrelated, or indeed interdependent. This is essential knowledge for efficient organisation and control, for a delay in completing certain tasks may not be significant, whereas the project as a whole may be affected if some parts of the work are held up.

On a small project, the organiser can carry all the links between the different activities involved in his head; on large projects, this is not possible. Further, there is often a need to assess at the start of a job how long it will take to complete, or alternatively what resources must be devoted to the work to complete it by a certain date, and to do this the whole sequence of the work must be clear.

The theoretical development of what is now known as critical path analysis took place during the 1950's in the United States and in this country. There are many variants of the technique, particularly as computer companies offer their own packages under different names. One name often encountered is PERT—Programme Evaluation and Review Technique.

In essence CPA has three distinct but interdependent phases—

1 Planning
2 Analysing and Scheduling
3 Controlling

Planning

In this phase, the major activities involved in the project are defined and listed. The project is then represented graphically by a diagram, which is conventionally built up from circles representing events, and arrows representing activities. The arrows lead up to, or emerge from, the circles. An event is, in fact, the completion of an activity, and its completion usually permits the start of another activity.

At this stage, the time consideration can be introduced—the time each activity takes can be written on to the activity arrows.

Analysing and scheduling

Now analysis can be undertaken. First, the question—how long will the whole project take? This is clearly decided by the sequence of events which takes the longest—in early writing on network analysis, called *the longest irreducible sequence of events*. It will be evident that some activities possess 'float'—that is, they do not occupy a critical role in the completion of the entire project in the shortest time, and there is, therefore, some flexibility as to when they are undertaken. Those activities which have no float are on the *critical path,* that is, they must be undertaken at the earliest time possible (once the activities on which they are dependent are completed), in order to keep the project as a whole to schedule. Hence the name—critical path analysis.

From this analysis, actual start and finish times can be assigned to the various activities—this is called *scheduling*. These times will obviously be based on the resources known to be available to carry out the project.

Controlling

As the project progresses, a note of the actual performances can show whether the over-all project time is going to be achieved. Any delays may be made up, if it seems desirable, by starting certain activities earlier or allocating additional resources to the completion of critical activities.

This form of network analysis thus offers the following advantages—it helps think out the work involved in a project, and to communicate this clearly to co-workers or clients. It is possible to allocate definite responsibilities, and to have a clear workable timetable, which can be used to keep work up to schedule. These are all necessary components of plan implementation.

Threshold analysis

Threshold analysis is usually discussed as an evaluation technique, and, indeed, it is in that chapter that the method itself is outlined (see page 132). But it does offer assistance with the detailing and with the programming of a development project, and focuses on the investments necessary from different agencies, which all assist implementation. Thus is has been used for sub-regional planning, when an overall strategy for the sub-region had been agreed, but the most effective specific locations for development and the most suitable programming had to be established. It therefore seems appropriate to mention the technique in the context of implementation, and to point out its relevance to this part of the land use planning process.

Control techniques

Land use planning as practised in this country depends more than anything else upon its techniques of control to implement preferred policies. This part of planning employs great numbers of staff, and impinges most directly on the public, yet it is given very little attention in comparison with other aspects of the process. The profession invests hardly any effort in improving the techniques of control, both those in use now and possible new methods.

There are two technical devices used in the control process—land use zoning, and standards. It is true that some countries, for example Canada, depend even more than we do on land use zoning, but it plays a crucial part in planning from day to day here too. In theory its significance has diminished with the various recent changes in planning thought and legislation, which seek to put a more positive gloss on land use planning. But the eventual implementation of the great majority of land use planning's strategic policies and plans remains dependent on the zoning based controls over permissible uses of land.

Planning standards

In considering applications for development, local authority planners depend heavily upon planning standards. There are two categories of these—'prescriptive', for example, national standards for new house building, and 'regulatory', which relate to individual development projects, and mainly to the quantifiable aspects of site development. The standards to be discussed here fall mainly into the latter category. Planning standards have long been used both in the preparation of plans, where they function as specifications, helping to define acceptable quantities of various uses of land, and in the operation of development control, which is the continuous regulation of all changes to the urban fabric, which together determine its future character.

Among the standards operated in development control by each local authority planning department are certain key standards, which, in practice, give considerable comparability throughout the country. In London, the Boroughs inherited several such standards from the London County Council.[4] Such key standards include guide-lines on the following:

1 *Residential density*

   that is, persons per unit area of land; it involves constituent decisions on the definition of a habitable room, acceptable occupancy rates, and methods of application of residential plot ratios.

2 *Plot ratio*

   that is, the relationship between a building and its site. The general purpose of plot ratio control was summarised in *Planning Bulletin* 1, of the Ministry of Housing and Local Government:

   'In general over the town centre as a whole, the aim should be to fix building densities in a way which provides opportunities for achieving a desirable height and massing of buildings and strikes a balance between the street and car parking capacities and the traffic attracted by the buildings'.

   Plot ratio has been used for two main purposes, as a control over employment floor space, and as a means of controlling building bulk. It is not entirely satisfactory for either of these. In relation to employment, the local authority has no effective control over the number of employees in a building (except in enforcing minimum acceptable working conditions, under the 1963 Offices, Shops and Railway Premises Act). In relation to building bulk, control over floorspace is not at all the same thing as control over building volume. It would thus be better to operate through separate standards, defined explicitly to meet the various purposes for which plot ratio is now used.

3 *Daylighting and sunlighting*

in relation to these aspects of building, there are, in fact, nationally defined standards. Indicators are used to help analyse whether proposed development meets the standards laid down, but an element of judgement has to be used. The relevant codes have recently been revised by the Department of the Environment.[5]

4 *Car parking control standards*

5 *Highway standards*

relating to minimum carriageway widths, and to visibility triangles.

In addition to these, supplementary controls are used, which relate to the local area characteristics, and therefore its planning problems, for example, standards concerning rear extensions to existing residential property, or to control of non-retail uses in shopping parades.

Forward looking planning authorities are aware of the need to add to their existing mechanisms with other standards, and the following are becoming increasingly widely recognised as necessary:

provision for access and other needs of the chronically sick and disabled in all public buildings;
visual privacy in residential development;
protection of buildings and spaces from traffic noise;[6]
provision of communal play space and amenity space;[7]
segregation of pedestrians from traffic.

There exist also 'special' standards, for example the Greater London Council 'high buildings' policy, based on powers defined in the 1963 Local Government Act. The general policy and criteria are set out in the *Greater London Development Plan Written Statement*.[8] Land in London is allocated to three categories, which in effect are areas where high buildings are inappropriate, areas where they are undesirable, because they are likely to have a considerable impact, and areas where they are possible in principle.

The way in which planning standards have been used for development control has been unduly rigid. Flexibility is essential, so that local circumstances, which may preclude the attainment

173

of rigid standards, can be allowed for (for example, the inability of inner city areas to reach the traditional open space standards). Standards have tended, too, to be based on past experience rather than values appropriate to the planned future. It is increasingly recognised in particular that standards relating to physical criteria alone are not enough, and that socio-economic indicators reflecting access to facilities and opportunities must be incorporated into the development control mechanism if they are to attain any real meaning in the land use planning process as a whole.

In 1967, the Management Study of development control found that there were no uniform procedures, and that hardly any authorities had a true intelligence system, or data and information handling, adequate for the policy analysis and monitoring that is supposed to underlie development control decisions.[9] Two more recent studies concluded that the rather variable and loosely defined codes of practice (relating to daylight and sunlight, for example) and standards (say, for residential density or site coverage) which are used with the zoning of land to guide control decisions are working less than satisfactorily.

McLoughlin and Webster found that, 'a decision is frequently derived from standards weighted more in favour of physical and visual terms, than the social and economic considerations underlying them'.[10] Harrison emphasised the key point, which is development control's separateness from the rest of land use planning—a 'policing activity with a heavy reliance upon rather rigid requirements'. It has essentially a 'paternalistic approach that relies heavily upon standards and denies consumer choice'.[11]

Stimulation

The other side of the implementation coin—positive encouragement and stimulation of activity to implement land use plans—is even less well charted than the control of development. The activities of analysis of the existing situation in an area and its possible futures, the presentation of such information and the involvement of members of the public and other organisations in assessing options can all be seen as 'stimulating' activity. An example is the publication and travelling exhibition, called the Camden Scene, organised by the London Borough of Camden.

174

More specific are the 'pump-priming' activities carried out by departments of local government, which ought to be co-ordinated, or even initiated by the land use planners. Thus the building of housing, social services, schools, roads, can all be made part of a more comprehensive change in land use—though not, I hasten to say, necessarily redevelopment. The Buchanan study of North East London followed this line of argument in relation to road investment, trying to demonstrate how it could be handled to 'spin-off' other land use benefits.[12]

The local authority also has the power to assemble sites for public or private development. It can be argued that much more positive use could be made of many of the existing functions of local government to secure the implementation of land use planning objectives. It is clear that many techniques of decision making and evaluation can assist with this type of implementation, for example, the Edgware study, which is discussed in the chapter on evaluation (see page 140). Land use planners have been obtaining considerable experience with the process of implementation in connection with the designation of General Improvement Areas. Other forms of local plan, which bring with them the need for 'stimulation' implementation techniques, must largely depend upon prior production of strategic structure plans, apart from those special projects of the action area type, which cannot wait for the production of the structure plan.

Thus, to summarise, the land use planner's involvement with implementation arises in three contexts:

1 Special *ad hoc* plans—which may be for areas wider than one local planning authority's area—the recent sub-regional studies, for example, where implementation consists largely of explaining and persuading other agencies to continue with and execute the strategies developed; or for areas within one planning authority, notably, at present, special action areas, including GIA's, where techniques both of persuasion and of compulsion and action by the public sector are used.

2 The statutory processes of plan production, presently concentrating on the structure plan stage, which stress the requirement for the land use planning authority to give evidence of the plan's economic and financial viability, and to promote,

encourage and influence the implementation of the plan within their area, by whatever means are appropriate.

3 The day-to-day process of development control, which continues whatever the state of the authority's plans or strategies may be for its area overall or for constituent parts of it. Those planners who have to man the enquiry counters in offices throughout the country are the implementation shock troops, who receive very little assistance from the researchers, and theoreticians of land use planning, who apparently prefer to focus on the intellectual challenge of plan design.

Monitoring and feedback

It is in conjunction with implementation of a plan that monitoring and feedback of results to modify the planning process must be carried out. Evaluation thus ceases to be a one point in time operation—which was usually of the plan on paper, rather than in bricks and mortar at that. It must instead become a continuing process with re-examination and redefinition of the objectives in the light of whether the plan is actually achieving what was hoped for. As Dyckman said, 'we have been reluctant to try direct output measurement and have frequently judged the 'goodness' of professional practice by quality of inputs. City planners concluded that the best results must be achieved in those situations where most money is spent, the greatest number of methodological innovations introduced and the most distinguished staff assembled.'[13]

We now accept theoretically that assessment of results should be on 'outputs' from planners, not on 'inputs', but techniques for monitoring are as yet embryonic. They depend upon the clarification of what to look for—indicators of success or failure. I have suggested in the outline of the land use planning process in Chapter 2, that these 'objective measures' should be applied both in the assessment of alternative possible strategies, and then in measuring the performance of the chosen strategy in action. A system for assembling the necessary information is a vital component of effective monitoring. In the chapter on housing, a description is given of the monitoring system for housing that Cullingworth proposed for Winchester (see page 288). If the

176

requisite feedback of what is discovered through the monitoring process is to take place, the land use planning agency must have effective communication throughout—a situation rarely found in the average planning office.

Furthermore, the plan or strategy will need to have been designed from the first with sufficient flexibility for modification to be possible. The concepts of monitoring and feedback thus relate to a conception both of the land use planning process and of the organisation of a planning agency, which does not yet exist throughout the country. In consequence the learning part of implementation does not take place as it should. The learning approach is certain to gain ground, however, particularly if the new authorities in 1974 do organise themselves with some form of corporate planning.

One cannot help having fears, though, about the range of considerations that will be covered in monitoring of plans. It is difficult to see how a local authority planning committee, or the public, would react to being told that a plan was totally failing to achieve its objectives, and that radical changes must be made. The answer, of course, lies in a 'strategic choice' approach, where only the commitments that are strictly necessary are made, and future decisions are left until the right stage of the learning process has been reached—which depends on observation of the plan in action.

References

1 Dyckman, J. W., 'Guest Editor's Introduction to the practical uses of planning theory', in *Journal of the American Institute of Planners,* page 298, September 1969.

2 Amos, F. J., *Systematic Local Government—Some implications of Programme Planning and Budgeting Systems for Local Government,* paper given at Public Works and Municipal Services Congress (1970).

3 Welfare, J., 'Programme Budgeting: the experience at Milton Keynes', in *Journal of the Royal Town Planning Institute,* page 361, **57,** 8, September/October 1971.

4 See, for example, Section 13 of the *Greater London Development Plan, Written Statement.*

5 Department of the Environment, *Sunlight and Daylight—Planning Criteria and Design of Buildings,* HMSO (1971); see also, Ministry of Housing and Local Government, *Sunlighting,* Planning Bulletin No. 5.
6 For example, the standards recommended by the Wilson Committee, Command Paper 2056, HMSO (1963).
7 As suggested in the Parker Morris Report (1961).
8 See Section 6 (iv) of the *Greater London Development Plan, Written Statement.*
9 Ministry of Housing and Local Government, *Management Study of Development Control* (1967); see also, *Comment,* by Pragma, in *Journal of the Royal Town Planning Institute,* page 442, **58**, 10, December 1972.
10 McLoughlin, J. B. & Webster J., *Development Control in Britain,* undated.
11 Harrison, M. L., *Development Control* (1972).
12 Buchanan, C. & Partners, *North East London: Some Implications of the Greater London Development Plan,* a report to the Greater London Council (1970).
13 See Dyckman, *op. cit.* (1) above.

10   Communication

In view of the vital part played in the land use planning process by communication, it is remarkable how little explicit attention is given to it. Communication is essential both to the internal working of a land use planning agency and to its relationships with the public and other organisations outside. Communication embraces the seeking of information and knowledge, conveying information, and stimulation through exchange of ideas. The short-term purpose—relating to a particular job in hand—blends into the longer-term function of education. This aspect has been touched on in Chapter 3, in the section titled 'the way we think', (see page 43). Much communication in land use planning is obligatory; the rest is also in fact essential if formulation and implementation of proposals are to take place at all effectively.

The subject of communication has received some attention in the last few years as part of the debate on public participation. However, that discussion has focused mostly on how much to communicate and when to communicate, rather than on how to do it. There is, of course, a wide variety of means of communication, both of the formal and the more informal type. Thus we use speech, writing, pictures, models, films, TV, radio for communication in our society, with a great range of purposes. The significance of the method we use was raised in the minds of many people who had previously given the matter little thought by the writings of Macluhan, crystallised in the phrase, 'The medium is the message'. Land use planners, however, in the

179

main go on using their traditional and narrow range of communication techniques, regardless of what they are trying to achieve and who they are trying to reach.

This chapter falls into three sections; the first deals with the need of a planner to communicate as part of getting his everyday work done. The second section is on communication as it relates to participation by the public. The third section is about planners communicating to each other in the continuous development of professional ideas.

Communication as part of the everyday work of planners

Communication is an integral part of the everyday work of the land use planner, since he is never in a position to carry through any job entirely on his own. Six different types of everyday communication can be distinguished:

1. from one planner to another hierarchically—that is, from the land use planner in charge of a particular job to those working for him or vice versa
2. from one planner to another laterally—communication between a land use planner carrying out research into housing need and those implementing General Improvement Areas in the same local authority, for example
3. planners communicating to others working for the same local authority but in other departments, and who are not themselves planners
4. planners and the elected politicians for their area, notably those on the relevant committees of the authority
5. planners communicating with the general public, in relation to specific planning proposals
6. dealings with those outside the authority, for example central government.

Where communication is between land use planners, or with allied professionals, it is likely to follow fairly formalised patterns —the minute or discussion document, the formal report, the minuted meeting. The same is true for communication to the local government committees. All these methods are, of course, supplemented and reinforced by informal contacts, face to face or by telephone. The chance conversation in the lift often achieves something that would require much effort by official methods. As well as communication in writing or speech, the land use planner has always made considerable use of illustrative material—maps, diagrams, models and so on.

These illustrative devices are important, too, in communication with the public, but it is often underestimated how much practice is needed for their effective interpretation. A wider variety of techniques, and desirably less formal ones, should also be used. For example, Ed Berman (well known for street theatre) offered passers-by a large painting of Piccadilly Circus on which to express their ideas about its proper future. I have mentioned elsewhere the possibilities of forms of gaming for involving the public in land use planning (see page 107). The potential of television and radio have not yet been well exploited either, nor those of the planner going out into the community, to schools, clubs, factories and so on, to meet people, explain and listen.

Planners are resentful of the criticisms they receive from the public, which they attribute largely to a lack of understanding of the land use planning process, and indeed of the overall organisation of society. The inclusion of more subjects related to these matters in school curricula is one way of remedying this situation in the long-term. But it is also necessary for land use planners to put more effort into informing the public, and to use more effective ways of doing so than those generally employed at present.

Participation

Participation implies far more than a communication process. Indeed, as Figure 10.1 shows, if participation is conceived only as the right to be informed and to comment, it is a minimal interpretation of involvement in the decision making process. However, effective communication is a fundamental component of participation, and it is in that sence that it is included here.

The awakening interest in public participation in land use planning reflected a much more widespread debate about the organisation of society, and particularly of public sector enterprises. The conception of the land use planning process expressed in the 1947 Act, allowed only very limited opportunities for participation by the public; notably when a Development Plan had been formulated, or by those immediately affected by an application for planning permission. There existed, too, of course, the general right to participation through election of central and local government, supposedly then accountable to the public.

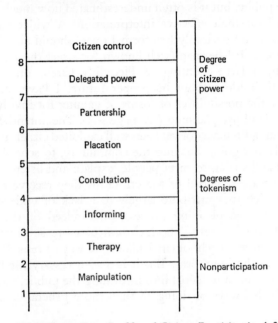

Fig. *10.1* *Eight Rungs On a Ladder of Citizen Participation* (after Arnstein)

SOURCE 'A Ladder of Citizen Participation in the USA', in *Journal of the Town Planning Institute*, April 1971

As part of the re-examination of planning that has occurred since the 1960's, and indeed still continues (see page 28), the Skeffington Committee was appointed in 1968 'to consider and report on the best methods including publicity of securing the participation of the public at the formative stage in the making of development plans for their area'. That Committee concluded that 'there will be full participation only when the public are able to take an active part throughout the plan making process'. Their specific recommendations included community forums, and community development officers, which were also a recommendation of the Seebohm Report.[1] Participation was made a statutory obligation in the 1968 Town and Country Planning Act and the 1969 Housing Act.[2]

However, the nature of participation, its relationship to established institutions and processes of government, and the closely related issue of the role, aims and values of the individual planner, remain extremely ill-defined. The shortcomings of the established land use planning process have been emphasised in recent years, both by major controversies, such as the selection of a site for the Third London Airport, and by the multitude of local schemes for slum clearance, renewal and urban motorways, which have activated communities previously indifferent to planning. At the same time, analyses of the role of the social services have helped to illuminate some of the fundamental issues which underlie action by government.[3] The results of these influences have been some modification of attitudes by land use planning agencies, and considerable growth of action groups.

The planning authorities, now obliged to attempt to secure the participation of the public, are exploring a whole spectrum of techniques for doing so. These embrace the 'informing' side of participation—news letters, reports on an area's characteristics and on future options, and exhibitions, such as those on proposals for Covent Garden and Piccadilly. Associated with these communications are usually formal opportunities for the public to express views. This conception of participation may be extended to an attempt to explain the reasoning of planning—particularly the fact of 'opportunity cost' (if you do one thing, you can't do another), as in the use of the 'planner's fruit machine', more properly called the priority evaluator, at the Camden Scene exhibition. It is a game, which requires the trading off of various improvements to housing and related facilities, and demonstrates, for example, that living in a house with a garden implies a longer walk to shops and buses than a flat over a main street store.

Other recent planning exercises have sought the involvement of the public in goal selection, and in evaluation of alternative proposals, for example, the recent South Hampshire Structure Plan, and the Coventry-Solihull-Warwickshire Study. At a local level, the initiation of General Improvement Areas depends on consultation with those living in the area, and explanatory leaflets, public meetings and exhibitions (including the Department of the Environment's touring caravan) are used. It should be obvious that the writing styles suitable for this type of contact with the public are different from those used for formal reports for professionals and committees. For the Thamesmead Draft Plan, in 1967, three quite different sets of material were prepared, which varied in the amount of content, and even more in the form of presentation. The ways in which various recent studies have presented their proposals is compared in The Urban Future.[4]

The second result of the influences listed above has been the growth of action groups—both those representing interests, such as the Civic Trust and the Claimants Union—and those based in a certain area—the many community groups. These, too, need effective communication methods. Journals such as *Community Action* help to provide a wider communication channel for local groups throughout the country many of which run their own newspapers. Additionally, local radio and television are certain to become more used. The BBC is offering a facility for any group to put out a programme on television expressing its views. A manual for the guidance of action groups has been produced— *The Householder's Guide to Community Defence Against Bureaucratic Aggression.*[5]

Many of the local action groups do not merely react to the official process, but initiate their own projects. Community Action recently published an excellent guide to the requirements for designation of a GIA, for example. The implications of community action and community development have been better examined in other fields, for example social work, than in land use planning, but are now receiving increasing attention by planners. The ways in which the individual planner can take part, whilst retaining a place in the profession and in local government, have been much discussed recently too. Many planners are already involved with tenants' or squatters' groups, or Citizens' Rights. Planning surgeries, to provide free advice and help, similar to Citizens Advice Bureaux, are one mechanism that has been suggested.

The formal interpretation of participation will become much clearer over the next few years, as more local planning authorities

184

make progress with their structure plans. Meantime, both the theoretical analysis of participation, and the actual means of securing it from the public's side, are undergoing very rapid development. Several recent books have focused attention on aspects of this subject, for example, Reich's *The Greening of America*, Goodman's *After the Planners*, and Davies' *The Evangelistic Bureaucrat*.[6] There have also been more dispassionately argued analyses, such as those of the Fabian Society.[7] Much of the material published, particularly the accounts of experience abroad, make clear the dangers that lie in a simplistic view of participation.[8]

Planners' continuous communication with each other

In Chapter 4, when talking about information, I drew a distinction between information with a specific focus, which I termed research, and the more general information which served to keep a planner generally well informed, which I called 'intelligence'. This intelligence information derives from the continuous communication of land use planners with their fellows, and with individuals and groups holding related interests. This communication includes research workers with those in practice, teachers with their students and so on. There is much to be learned about keeping well informed without a costly investment of time, money and effort. It is a large subject, and I provide only some guide-lines in the discussion that follows.

Periodicals are a good starting point. Depending upon its particular slant, a periodical may contain any of the following—articles that report results of research, ranging from extremely theoretical to totally practical case studies; description or assessment of individual projects; survey articles collecting together information on one subject, which may form part of a related series; reports on relevant activities and pronouncements of government and other agencies; news of the profession(s); notes on current practice; correspondence; book reviews; announcement of new publications and events. They thus both provide information and offer many leads to further sources of information. The reader can have a journal delivered to his own home or office if he decides it proffers enough of the particular information he seeks, but journals relating to land use planning have a very wide range of characteristics, reflecting all the different strands to the discipline. Without attempting to be comprehensive, the range can be illustrated as follows.

Some publications concentrate on offering news—for example, the *Planning Bulletin,* or the more recently formed news sheet, *Planning.* The Countryside Commission produces a specialised news sheet on planning for leisure—*Recreation News.* Professional journals have a clear orientation, and the conveying news is a large part of their function too. The *Journal of the Royal Town Planning Institute* is the obvious mainstream periodical for land use planners, but since there are so many different emphases to planning, there are a variety of other publications which are also basically professional that an individual land use planner might prefer—the *Architect's Journal, Architectural Design, Built Environment* and a number of others at the architectural end of the spectrum, journals such as *Ekistics* for a particular conception of land use planning, journals on applied economics or demography of futurology for those who are most interested in some special facet of land use planning. Some journals concentrate on one sphere of activity—*Community Action* as its name implies or *Town and Country Planning* on new towns.

For many people, the most satisfactory use of journals is, in fact, not subscribing regularly but visiting a library which stocks a good selection so that what is relevant to the reader's particular interests can be selected from among several journals. The facility of photocopying an individual article that is important enough to keep reinforces a selective use. Often, land use planners have access to a sufficiently specialised library at their place of work or study; such libraries can often also be used by interested outsiders. In London, the offices of the professional institutes have libraries, which may also run a postal service.

Once access to a suitable library is obtained, it is necessary to learn how it works. An understanding of the subjects it aims to cover, the system of classification used, and best of all the establishment of good relations with the library staff are prerequisites to best service from the material. The larger the library, the more important these principles are, and there is often a printed guide to using a large library.

Additionally, there are various bibliographies and guides published, some of which include abstracts, that can help to lead a reader to the information he seeks, and which the librarian can recommend. For land use planning, Brenda White's recent source book on the literature is an obvious starting point in many cases, although it cannot provide any help with the right up to date material so often needed.[9] I am not attempting here to deal properly with books, but will mention another one or two that relate to this subject of information:

Jackson—*Surveys for Town and Country Planning*; Cherry and Burton—*Social Research Techniques for Planners*; and Cherry—*Urban Change and Planning*.[10]

There are bibliographies and abstracts produced for limited circulation by libraries that are excellent—for example, the DOE'S and the GLC's. Sometimes it is helpful to maintain contact with a friend who is able to see these regularly, even if you cannot read them in person. Incidentally, groups of people can help to keep each other informed in various ways—by compiling brief summaries of what they read, holding lunch-time seminars and so forth. On a grander scale, people with a similar interest or conviction may form themselves into associations to carry out a wide variety of functions, amongst which keeping informed often figures. Conferences and short courses often produce reports which are valuable summaries of thinking on one subject—notably those of the Centre for Environmental Studies (CES), Planning and Transport Research and Computation (PTRC), and the Town Planning Summer School.

The discussion so far has related on the whole to 'professional' information, but I should not neglect to mention somewhat broader sources of written material—periodicals such as *New Society, New Statesman, The Economist, New Scientist*, and newspapers, both national and local. For an increasing number of people there is now local radio, as well as the nationally available radio and TV. (Digestion of complicated subjects of interest on radio may prove easier from *The Listener*.) If this seems to be extending the scope of what provides information for land use planning unduly, I may say that one of the best lectures I ever received was on landscape design and incorporated art, poetry and fiction in tracing the development of the English tradition.

It has been suggested that proliferation of 'facts' is a sign of immaturity in a science, and there is no doubt that much of the 'information' offered to land use planners is totally dispensable to all but a very few individuals. The difficulty, however, is for each person to sort out for himself how to maintain access to the information he actually wants. It is wasteful and frustrating only to know *after* reading a book or article that the time could have been better spent. Therefore, it is well worth while paying some attention to working out the easiest way of seeing the information that suits your own particular needs as a land use planner.

References

1 Ministry of Housing and Local Government, Report of the Committee on Public Participation, *People and Planning* (The Skeffington Report), HMSO, London (1969); *Report of the Committee on Local Authority and Allied Personal Social Services* (The Seebohm Report), HMSO (1968).
2 See, Cullingworth, J. B., *Town and Country Planning in England and Wales,* Revised 3rd Edition, Allen & Unwin (1970).
3 See, for example, Robson, W. A. & Crick, B. *The Future of the Social Services,* Penguin (1970); The Gulbenkian Report, *Community Work and Social Change* (1969).
4 Jackson, J. N., *The Urban Future,* Allen & Unwin (1972).
5 Jay, A., *The Householder's Guide to Community Defence Against Bureaucratic Aggression,* Jonathan Cape (1972).
6 Reich, C. A., *The Greening of America,* Penguin (1971); Goodman, R., *After the Planners,* Penguin (1972); Davies, J. G., *The Evangelistic Bureaucrat,* Tavistock (1972).
7 Fabian Society, *Community Action,* Fabian Tract 400, London (1970); Fabian Society, *People, Participation and Government,* Fabian Research Series 293, London (1971).
8 See, for example, Repo, M., 'The fallacy of community control', in *Transformation,* page 11, 1, 1, February 1971.
9 White, B., *A Source Book of Planning Information,* Clive Bingley, London (1971).
10 Jackson, J. N., *Surveys for Town and Country Planning,* Hutchinson (1963); Cherry, G. E. & Burton T. L., *Social Research Techniques for Planners,* Allen & Unwin (1970); Cherry, G. E., *Urban Change and Planning* (1972).

PART THREE
Land Using Activities

11 Population

Introduction

Behind almost every planning decision lie some assumptions about population. Whilst land use planners may often need to consult or rely on demographers and other experts for their population information, it is important for them to know something of the techniques of population analysis and forecasting, whether to use them, request others to use them, or simply to understand the value of results obtained. The factors land use planners need to know about population concern the present and the future and, as a guide, the past.

Analysis of existing population

The size and composition of a population are decisive factors in deciding what institutions and facilities require to be planned—that is, what needs of the population the planner should be concerned with meeting. Often, of course, it is not within the scope of the land use planner himself to make decisions about the priorities to be awarded to different needs—other members or groups in society have the power to make such decisions and merely look to the planner to guide them about the existing and future population and then to assist with the physical accommodation of their needs.

Since different people have very different needs, the characteristics of the population of any area—age, sex, family structure, socio-economic class, level of education and skills, ethnic characteristics or religious beliefs—are crucial, as well as their total numbers and geographical distribution.[1] Let us briefly consider the significance of each of these characteristics.

Age—Age is an obvious determinant of need—babies require clinics, small children benefit from nursery schools, teenagers need playing fields, young couples require suitable living accommodation, old people need specialised welfare services, and so forth. Many of the facilities with which planners deal are linked to an 'age-specific' standard—for example, so many maternity beds to be provided for every 1000 women of child-bearing age.

Sex—A second population characteristic which is of great significance is sex. Clearly, the needs of males and females are different, whether it be the provision of football pitches rather than netball courts, or trying to ensure that jobs are available for both the male and female work force. It is possible to formulate a 'normal' sex distribution for a given population, but usually the effects of natural and man-made events 'distort' the structure. Each sex is relatively prone to different diseases and the effects of two major wars on the sex structure of many European countries is well recognised. However, as a basis, it is known what ratio of male to female babies are born at any time (recently it was 6% more males), and what the mortality rates are likely to be for each sex at different ages. To make things difficult for the planners, however, such factors are not stable—for example, mortality rates change with advances in medicine and hygiene and varying life styles. The well-known graphical device—the population pyramid—helps to emphasise aspects of interest in the age and sex structure of a particular population.

Family structure—Together, the age and sex structure of the population influence (and then derive from) the family or household structure. This is of interest to the land use planner for two reasons:
1 many of the needs of the population have to be provided in relation to the groupings in which people choose to live, and, therefore, analysis of family structure is a prerequisite for many planning studies

2   estimations of future population are often based on the 'repro-
    ductive unit'—that is, the male/female unit including the
    female of child-bearing age—and thus the family/household
    structure of a population may be an important basis for future
    estimates.

Socio-economic group—What people do in their daily lives—their
purchasing habits, their hours and place of work, their forms of
recreation—is vital information for land use planners in their
task of helping to accommodate the physical 'clothing' for such
activities. Any fairly accurate method of generalising about the
behaviour of individuals is helpful, and it has been found that
behaviour patterns can be correlated to a certain extent with
socio-economic group. The basis for allocating a person to a
particular socio-economic group varies in practice, but is often
the type of employment of their head of household. The type of
employment is thus often taken to be a proxy for income level,
educational background and social needs and habits. Such
classifications have many imperfections but are still, on balance,
found to be helpful. A series in *New Society* on the significance of
'social indicators' discussed in much more detail why planners
are interested in these factors and what they can learn from such
information on the characteristics of a population under study.[2]

The idea of a 'balanced' population

Mention of population characteristics leads on to the notion of
a 'balanced' population. If this concept is used normatively, it
may cause controversy—a dispute as to whether or not people
should be encouraged by land use planners to live in a homogeneous mixture, or whether segregation according to characteristics of class, wealth, race or whatever should be permitted or
even facilitated. It is, however, sensible to recognise some of the
planning problems that can arise from a *demographic* imbalance in
a population—that is, a distorted age or sex structure.

   Where age structures are distorted it becomes difficult to ensure
continuous use of facilities. Two examples may suffice to illustrate
this. In the newspapers one sees reports of coastal towns, especially in the south and south-west, increasingly concerned at the

193

numbers of old people migrating there to retire. This places a considerable strain on medical and welfare services and it becomes a difficult problem for the community to finance adequate facilities.

The second example is the 'new town bulge'. It has generally been found that the people most attracted to new towns have been young couples in the relatively mobile phase of their household cycle. In consequence, the early years of a new town's development have generally seen a population structure dominated by young married couples and their small children, with consequent demands for houses of a certain size, maternity facilities, children's clinics and so forth. As time goes by, the two bulges in the population structure get older, thus creating heavy demands for different types of facilities—jobs for working mothers, youth centres for the teenage children.[3] Demographers have estimated that such 'bulges' take several generations to dampen down; meantime, there are considerable problems in ensuring that the facilities required by the population are adequate, without being subsequently much under-used. This introduces the idea of flexibility of provision, which is fully discussed in a paper, *Projecting Age Needs*.[4]

Trends

It is obvious that the study of population cannot be handled as a static thing—any individual is somewhat different this year from either last year or next year and, in consequence, is seen by the land use planner as a different 'unit' having different needs (of course, in the aggregate, population may be stable). Before discussing methods of estimating future population, it is necessary to assess the relevance of the past to a planner's study of population. In general, much of our expectations concerning the future are based on what we know to have occurred in the past. In population studies, existing trends must be given careful consideration to assess the likelihood of their continuance into the future.

In overall terms, the population may be changing in numbers—increasing or decreasing—which clearly has implications for land use planners in their co-ordination of the provision of facilities.

Within any area, the geographical distribution of the population may be altering, which can pose problems of maldistribution of facilities, even if they are adequate in total. Such trends, when identified, can be examined as to causes, and then the planner can attempt to assess whether or not they are likely to continue unchanged into the future, and whether their continuance should be accepted, encouraged or discouraged. Although it is not feasible for a land use planner to act directly on population changes, other policies—for housing, employment, schools or leisure facilities—can greatly influence the numbers, distribution, and characteristics of population in any particular area. Knowledge of the trends of change in population characteristics may also help the planner in his assessment of present and future population structure—information which is needed in deciding on appropriate provision of facilities.

One general trend, an increase in the number and proportion of old people in the population, has already been referred to. Other well-publicised trends in our society at the moment are towards more women working and longer full-time education, each of which has demographic influences on patterns of household formation and child-bearing and social influences on income levels and behaviour patterns.

Sources of information for population studies

A major producer of data for population studies is central government, and the outstanding basic source is the Census of Population. This is accepted by land use planners as reasonably reliable, but difficulties arise over definitions, unit boundaries and samples. The main deficiencies of the Census for planners have been that figures may not be published for the precise area of interest (although information more detailed than that published may be obtainable from the OPCS) or that there may have been no Census at the date required, in which case inter-censal estimates will have to be used. These deficiences are discussed further below.

The Census has evolved over a long period of time in response to matters of current interest and to improvements in demographic and social survey techniques. At one time it was a total count taken every ten years, and dominantly concerned with demographic and housing matters. In 1966, a mid-term Census was based on a 10% sample, and had more coverage of the socio-economic characteristics of the population. The 1971 Census is discussed below.

A full and interesting account of the development of the Census is given by Benjamin.[5] In addition to the Census, the Office of Population, Censuses and Surveys (which now incorporates the Office of the Registrar-General and the Government Social Survey) publishes statistics relating to births, deaths and marriages in various returns and reviews.[6] The most obvious deficiency in population information to date has been data on migration, and there are currently many pressures on central government to improve such data. The Registrar-General makes an annual estimate of *net* migration for all administrative areas, which is not published, but is used by his office for their annual estimates of population. It is possible to deduce net migration from these estimates, with some difficulty and considerable inaccuracy.

Planners frequently build up their own information on the population within their area, often as a by-product of other work, such as transportation studies.[7] In such a way, it may be possible to assemble a quite detailed picture of the characteristics of the population within the area of interest.

Limitation of Census data in practice

At a seminar of London planners and representatives of the OPCS, held as an exchange of views prior to the 1971 Census, Blake gave a paper on the limitations of the Census in relation to population studies.[8] He suggested that there are three main questions which planners continually ask about population:
What is the present population?
How has it changed in recent years?
What is likely to happen in the future?

The areal unit for which such questions are asked varies according to the responsibilities of the planner in question. Thus, in London, the GLC is concerned with Greater London as a whole, with individual London Boroughs and with traffic zones; on the other hand, the Boroughs often need such information for much smaller areas—individual enumeration districts or *ad hoc* groupings of them, like environmental areas. It is with the latter scale of concern that Blake deals.

The first question—regarding the *present* population—is quite well answered from the Census, using the data given on the size, age and sex structure of the population, their place of birth, their household composition, their place of residence one and five years previously, and a range of information relating to their housing conditions and socio-economic characteristics. However, there are limitations, notably those concerning area, time, sampling and definitions. Thus, the geographical units for which data are available may not be suitable for many planning studies, the information becomes seriously out of date as the publication of new Census results is awaited, the sampling errors are proportionately more worrying as smaller areas come under scrutiny and some key definitions, such as 'household' may receive such varied interpretation by enumerators that the information needed by land use planners is not provided. (Blake gives as an example the difficulty of assessing rehousing needs from Census information on 'households'; also the 'lack of precision in recording family relationships', which makes fertility studies almost impossible.)

In relation to the second question, concerning the *past*, problems are graver. Changes to enumeration district boundaries and alterations of key definitions make comparability of successive Censuses difficult. Added to these problems are the uncertainties resulting from under-enumeration and sampling error, which are not, of course, constant.

The third question, concerning the *future*, raised aspects where additional information would be helpful. Forecasts can be either demographic or based on some closely linked factor—often housing, which involves projecting housing capacities and occupancy rates. In this connection, more needs to be known about 'movers' and 'non-movers'.

How do these comments of Blake (made on the 1961 and 1966 Census information) look in the light of the recent 1971 Census? As Benjamin said at the seminar in 1969, 'Knowledge of the end use of the census data is extremely important to the census organisation. I have always argued (and it has always been practised at the General Register Office) that the only effective way of organising a census is to start from the end result in terms of the figures that you are actually going to use and to work back to the beginning. This is because the way in which you use the figures has a very important effect on the way in which the topics are actually handled in the census questionnaire. The way in which the figures are finally to appear determines the shape of the questions asked.'[9]

At the time of writing, information from the Census taken in April, 1971, is only beginning to be published. The form for private households to complete comprised three parts—Part *A* relating to accommodation; Part *B* for demographic, employment and educational details of each members of the household present; Part *C* for details regarding absent members.

More specifically, topics covered included:

Household questions (Part A)

*A*1	tenure of occupation
*A*2	whether sharing room, landing etc. with any other household
*A*3	number of rooms
*A*4	number of cars/vans per household
*A*5	use of amenities and whether shared.

Personal questions (Part B)

*B*1–6	name, date of birth, sex, usual address, relationship to head of household, marital status
*B*7–8	job status and whether student
*B*9–10	country of birth and year of entry into UK; country of each parent's birth
*B*11–12	address 1 year and 5 years ago
*B*13–14	qualifications
*B*15–22	for women ever married, questions concerning their children and first marriage

198

Persons absent (Part C)

A restricted selection of personal questions concerning those members of the household not present on Census night.

Key definitions

The 'household' was defined as persons living at the same address and sharing housekeeping, as in previous Censuses. However, 'dwelling'—previously based on structural separateness—was defined on the basis of 'reasonably separate dwelling space'. Within shared dwellings, there will be a distinction in classification according to whether or not a household's own actual living space is private.

Comparisons with previous censuses

In comparison with the 1961 and 1966 Censuses, the most important new question is that asking for place of birth for each parent. Other new questions are year of entry into UK if foreign born, and occupation one year ago. Information asked for in 1966 and now dropped includes details of place of birth, second jobs and garaging facilities. From the 1961 Census, questions on citizenship, terminal education age, duration of residence, and second marriages, have been dropped. Also, this time, the full range of information has not been sought from those absent from home on Census night. There have also been some innovations in sampling and processing. Sampling for the 1971 Census was not done in the field, but will be done in the course of processing. Thus, all households received the full questionnaire, though some data will only be processed for a 10% sample. Those topics to be handled on a 10% sample basis include: household composition, industry, workplace and means of transport to work, occupation now and one year ago, education, migration and fertility. For the first time, the place of enumeration of each household will be allocated a co-ordinate reference, based on the National Grid system. It will then be possible to produce statistics for any area, of whatever shape or size, subject only to restrictions of confidentiality. However, geocoding will have a low processing

199

priority compared with other Census work. (For a discussion of spatial data processing, including geocoding, see page 74.)

The geographical referencing of Census information opens up exciting possibilities for spatial data processing, and for automatic mapping.

Methods of population forecasting

Willis made the following distinctions in population forecasting: *direct or indirect approach*—in direct techniques, forecasts are based on past data and recognised trends which can be extrapolated. Indirect techniques relate forecasts to other indicators which are supplied to the model as independent predictions;

closed or open systems—for population, the ultimate closed system is the world, but areas such as nation states can be effectively treated as closed systems. Where movement between areas is free, for example with regions, the systems being dealt with are open;

macro or micro approach—a macro approach to population aggregates individuals, who are treated as though they had the same characteristics, whereas a micro approach disaggregates into cohorts with common characteristics, such as age group, sex, marital status, race or income. It is then considered that each cohort can be treated as subject to the same dynamics—that is, survival rate, fertility rate, propensity to move and so on.[10]

Trend projections

Trend projections exemplify the macro approach, where it is assumed that past relationships over time for the whole population will continue to hold good. Methods of trend projection can be expressed either mathematically by formulae, or graphically (see Figure 11.1).

Well-known forms of trend projection are—

$$P_t + o = P_1 + b_0$$

where P_1 is the base population at time t,

$P_t + o$ is the population after a time interval of o,

and b is a constant representing annual growth,
which is a polynomial curve, and an exponential curve:

$$P_t + \circ = P_t b^0$$

A special form of this is the compound interest curve:

$$P_t + \circ = P_t (1 + r)^0$$

where r is the average annual rate of change.

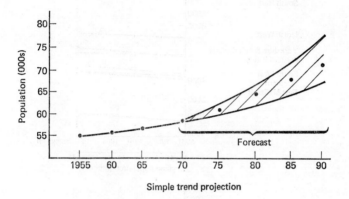

Fig. *11.1* *Simple Trend Projection*

Many of these curves have no limit and will approach infinity
unless modified. In general, curves are now used only for limited
purposes in population forecasting—for making speculative
projections about large 'open' areas, short-term predictions for
areas subject to little change in growth rate, and for illustrative
purposes.

Ratio methods

Ratio methods of population forecasting are used when some
inter-connection between growth in two areas can be established.
Once a projection has been made for the 'pattern' area, the population of the study area can be forecast as a ratio; at its crudest
this may be a constant ratio, or it may be modified to allow for

observed past behaviour or anticipated future influences. This method has been used for making projections for planning

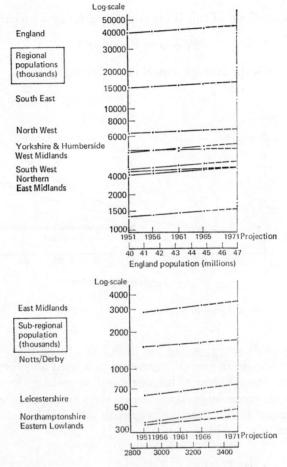

Fig. 11.2 (a) Ratio Method: areas

areas, notably regions, when national forecasts only are available (see Figure 11.2(a)).

Such methods can, of course, be terribly misleading if areas are erroneously regarded as 'closed' systems—thus at one time, local planning authorities in the South-east greatly over-estimated land needs through using population forecasts derived in a series of inaccurate ratios from a particularly high national projection.

Another common (and perhaps more valid) use of ratio forecasting is to assume that some particular element of the population will vary in constant proportion to the total—for example, school age children (see Figure 11.2(*b*)).

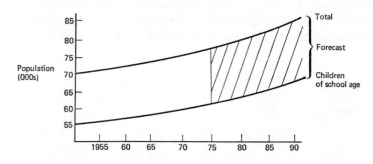

Fig. 11.2 (b) *Ratio Method: group within population* (after McLoughlin)

SOURCE *Urban and Regional Planning: A Systems Approach*, Faber & Faber, London (1969)

Regression methods

With regression methods, population is treated as a dependent variable related empirically to independent variables, such as employment. The model may assume either simultaneous or lagged variation. In the latter case, population responds after a time interval to a change in the independent variable. With a multiple regression model, the behaviour of the dependent variable is associated simultaneously with more than one independent variable—say a population forecast related to employment and housing factors. The difficulties with regression methods lie in prediction of the independent variables and in deciding whether past causal relationships will continue into the future. Such methods seem to be most useful when incorporated into a broader model which can provide the necessary information on the non-population elements. One such model with a population component, which has been used in several recent planning exercises, is a Lowry Model (in the version known as a Garin-Lowry model), which relates employment, population and their geographical distribution to produce both numerical and spatial forecasts as discussed on page 104.

Land use based projections

Particularly for areas already substantially developed, the most useful methods of population forecasting are not necessarily demographic ones, but methods related to land use capacities and

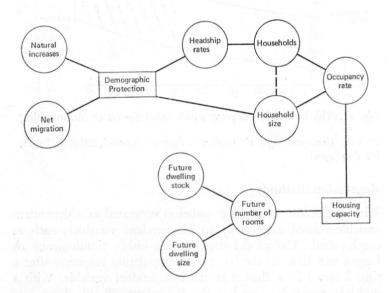

Fig. 11.3 Capacity Model

influences. For example, in their studies for the Greater London Development Plan, the GLC prepared a demographically based population projection, but also a forecast linked to housing capacity and policies[11] (see Figure 11.3). (This is discussed further, see page 289). Such methods have the particular advantage for land use planners of being directly policy oriented, rather than producing population data detached from any planning context.

At a local level, a similar method was developed by land use planners working for the London Borough of Lewisham—for application in an inner city area, with an ageing housing stock, considerable demand for accommodation and little space to provide it without redevelopment.[12]

The technique was designed to:

analyse the existing relationships between people and residential land as expressed in terms of residential density

assess the effect on population of proposed changes in land use, residential density and the amount of new building

estimate the actions which would be required to implement hypothetical policy decisions in terms of land allocation, density controls, and replacement and building rates

identify areas where change in the housing stock was occurring or likely to occur

provide a framework for programming the scale and location of redevelopment and improvement activities

Thus, as part of its output, the technique produced population forecasts likely to derive from different housing policies.

The technique tested four variable quantities, namely—

a total population

b residential density

c rate of new building

d rate of replacement of residential stock—

where any pair of variables can be taken as a control to assess the effects on the other two.

It was operated for three time periods, immediate future, short-term and long-term, and required the following inputs:

1 land use data

2 numbers of resident population

3 a grading of the residential stock, based on relative need for replacement

4 an estimate of the rate of population change in areas unaffected by redevelopment (for this, a formula was devised, which is given below)

5   estimates of future house building rates

6   information on all commitments, that is redevelopment schemes, planning permissions granted, improvement proposals.

The formula for the rate of population change in areas unaffected by redevelopment assumes only two factors can vary:

1   change in numbers of persons per household (household size)

2   change in numbers of households per dwelling (multi-occupancy), and is—

$$X = \left(D \times \frac{H}{D} \times \frac{P}{H} \right) - P^1 \times 100$$

where D is the fixed number of dwellings

H/D is the households/dwellings ratio at the end of the period

P/H is the household size at the end of the period

P^1 is the initial population in the dwelling stock.

The technique was thus easy to operate, had fairly simple data requirements, and is applicable at many area scales to assess changing trends and policies, for residential land use and their effects on population, and vice versa.

Growth composition analysis

This is now the most commonly used method of population forecast. It recognises the factors of change in population to be births, deaths and migration, and the magnitude of these factors is expressed in 'rates' which represent probabilities. Refinement is achieved by disaggregating the population into cohorts, with common age/sex characteristics to which 'specific' rates can then be applied. Properly extended, this becomes a 'cohort survival' population forecast technique (see Figure 11.4). It is generally applied to single sex five year age cohorts, although single year cohorts are sometimes used for the demographically more critical sections of the population (such as women of child-bearing age)

206

or for groups in which age is especially significant for provision of facilities (for example, school children).

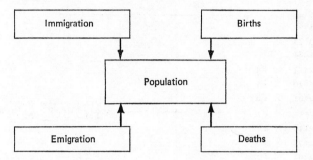

Fig. 11.4 Elements of Growth Composition Analysis Forecast

The method is as follows:
1   Population divided into cohorts—
First, the population under study is subdivided into appropriate cohorts—males separated from females, and each sex divided into age groups (usually five year or one year), to give a population structure for the base year of the forecast, as shown in Figure 11.5.
2   *a* Fertility rates applied to females of child-bearing age—
Forecasting calculation begins with the female population, and specifically the age groups of child-bearing age. The appropriate fertility rate is applied in turn to each of these cohorts (the fertility rate expresses the probability of each female in the cohort bearing a child during the calculation time period).
b Babies added up, and 'sexed'—
These separate calculations for each of the fertile cohorts are then totalled to give a total number of babies, which are then 'sexed' —divided into males and females—in the known proportion. If each of the forecasting periods is more than one year—say five years—the next step will be to apply survival rates to the babies, as explained below.
c These female and male babies will be the first cohort at the top of the matrix in the next round of calculations of the forecast.
3   *a* Females 'survived'—
Now the number of females who will survive the first forecast period have to be calculated, by applying to each cohort the

Age group	FP at year 0	× FR =	LB at years 0–5	× SR at years 0–5	= Sur.	× M/F =	$\dfrac{\text{F 0–4}}{\text{M 0–4}}$ at year 5
0–4	3180						
5–9	3173						
10–14	2681						
15–19	2512	× F4					
20–4	2826	× F5					
25–9	2361	× F6					
30–4	2332	× F7 =	——	× ——	= ——	× $\dfrac{fF}{fM}$ =	$3410\dfrac{F}{M}$ (to male table)
35–9	2152	× F8					
40–4	2271	× F9					
45–9	2393	× F10					
50–4	2145						
55–9	2248						
60–4	2179						
65–9	1947						
70–4	1597						
75–9	1117						
80–4	662						
85–9	301						
90	104						

Total FP at year 0	× SR years 0–5	= FP at year 5
3180	S(0–4) – S(5–9)	3410
3173	S(5–9) – S(10–14)	3174
2681	S(10–14) – S(15–19)	3169
2512	S(15–19) – S(20–4)	2678
.	.	.
.	.	.
.	.	.

(FP, female population; FR, fertility rate; LB, live birth; SR, survival rates; Sur., survivors; M, male; F, female)

Fig. 11.5 Cohort Survival Forecast

208

known survival rate (the survival rate expresses the known probability of females in the particular cohort living through the calculation period). Survival rates are generally used, rather than mortality rates, as it is easier to deal with positive rates than negative ones.

b Surviving females 'aged'—

The female population remaining after the application of the survival rates then must be 'aged'—that is, moved forward into the next cohort—before the forecast calculations can be carried out again for the next time period.

4 Male cohorts 'survived', then 'aged'—

The male cohorts in the population are then treated as explained in steps 3*a* and *b* above, that is, 'survived', and then 'aged'.

Those calculations complete one round of the forecast and the procedure is repeated as many times as may be required.

If migration of population is to be treated in the forecast, it becomes somewhat more complicated than the above outline, which treats only the demographic elements of population change.

The information required for this technique includes the initial numbers and age/sex structure of the population and appropriate survival, fertility and migration rates. The hazards lie in prediction of the rates. Changes in mortality rates, though complex, are less so than those of fertility, which depend on social influences and economic circumstances, as well as medical advances. Also, any incorrect estimation of births carries through the projection cumulatively, which is not so for deaths. The migration component is usually the most difficult factor of all to forecast confidently, particularly the age and sex structure of migrants. A cohort survival method is, therefore, most useful where the migration component is small. The technique does have the great advantage of producing not merely a forecast in total, but also the age and sex characteristics of the future population. It may, therefore, also be especially useful in any forecasts for demographically 'unbalanced' populations.[13] However, it says nothing directly about household structure and when such information is needed, as for housing policies, further calculations are necessary, as discussed in the chapter on housing (see page 271).

It will be noted that the cohort survival method as described above takes no direct account of any of the influences on fertility.

In the South Hampshire study, there were several improvements made on the basic technique in the handling of fertility—disaggregating the women of child-bearing age into cohorts based on age at marriage, duration of marriage and spacing of births of existing children. This involved the assessment of marriage rates. Mortality rates were also handled in that projection in a more sophisticated way than usual, by modification over time to take account of trends likely for each age group.[14]

A brief reference to an application of cohort survival methods will exemplify some of the complications inevitably encountered, even though the concept is so simple. It is a projection made for Greater London, described by Thompson.[15]

As he explained, 'Essentially any population projection operates on a base population which is assumed to be changed in four ways in each future period:

1 the population will be increased by births, the number of which is related to the female population at the start of the period
2 it will be decreased by deaths
3 it will be increased by the inflow of in-migrants,
4 it will be decreased by the outflow of out-migrants

He then discussed the process of fitting information to this simple methodological framework. The first difficulty is to fix a base for the projection—in this case, 1966 Census data were taken as the guide to numbers and age and sex structure, but had to be adjusted for under-enumeration. For births and deaths, the calculations started from the Government Actuary's Department's national assumptions given in the 1967 mid-year projections, but these were modified in the knowledge of Greater London's lower age-specific death rates. Differentials were also applied to the national age-specific birth rates, and these were then held to apply to the whole of the future population, including in-migrants. Six different migrant streams were incorporated into the projection, based on those revealed for the previous year in the 1966 Census, but modified pragmatically. The migrants are added and subtracted at yearly intervals in the program, with age and sex characteristics based on the Census.

Thompson stressed 'Like all projections, (they) are designed to examine the effects of a particular series of assumptions. They say what the population of London *would be* on the chosen assumptions, not what it *will be*—and much less what it *should be*.[16]

Matrix frameworks for forecasting

Techniques of matrices and matrix algebra are well suited to population projection, based on the same reasoning as the cohort survival method. Perhaps the best known work of this type is that of Andrei Rogers (see Figure 11.6).[17]

0	0	0	b_4	b_5	b_6	b_7	b_8	b_9	0	0	0	0	0	0	0	0	0
s_1	0	0	0	0	0	0	0	0	0	0	0	0	0	0	0	0	0
0	s_2	0	0	0	0	0	0	0	0	0	0	0	0	0	0	0	0
0	0	s_3	0	0	0	0	0	0	0	0	0	0	0	0	0	0	0
0	0	0	s_4	0	0	0	0	0	0	0	0	0	0	0	0	0	0
0	0	0	0	s_5	0	0	0	0	0	0	0	0	0	0	0	0	0
0	0	0	0	0	s_6	0	0	0	0	0	0	0	0	0	0	0	0
0	0	0	0	0	0	s_7	0	0	0	0	0	0	0	0	0	0	0
0	0	0	0	0	0	0	s_8	0	0	0	0	0	0	0	0	0	0
0	0	0	0	0	0	0	0	s_9	0	0	0	0	0	0	0	0	0
0	0	0	0	0	0	0	0	0	s_{10}	0	0	0	0	0	0	0	0
0	0	0	0	0	0	0	0	0	0	s_{11}	0	0	0	0	0	0	0
0	0	0	0	0	0	0	0	0	0	0	s_{12}	0	0	0	0	0	0
0	0	0	0	0	0	0	0	0	0	0	0	s_{13}	0	0	0	0	0
0	0	0	0	0	0	0	0	0	0	0	0	0	s_{14}	0	0	0	0
0	0	0	0	0	0	0	0	0	0	0	0	0	0	s_{15}	0	0	0
0	0	0	0	0	0	0	0	0	0	0	0	0	0	0	s_{16}	0	0
0	0	0	0	0	0	0	0	0	0	0	0	0	0	0	0	s_{17}	0

Fig. 11.6   A Survivorship Matrix

Household unit based forecasts

At one time, a much used method of forecasting population was based on the differentiation of household units and their stage in the 'family cycle'—for example, Ruth Glass' work. Thus, founding/expanding, stable and contracting units were distinguished (the details of the classification used have varied somewhat). This approach has been found especially useful where the forecast was required for the planning of some facility relating closely to households, such as assessing housing needs.[18]

Factors in population forecasting

Population forecasting is based on probabilities. Survival rates are estimates of the probability of any one individual surviving throughout the period covered by the forecast. If each person in a particular group has a 90% chance of survival, this individual probability can be translated into a survival rate for the group, say 90 per 100. However, such estimates of probability are always made in the knowledge that there are a multitude of influences at work that could, in the event, change and produce a different outcome. It is as well to be aware what these influences are:

Fertility—Fertility probabilities are usually applied as age/sex specific rates to cohorts within the range of women of child-bearing age. But fertility varies with factors that relate to the mother, the family unit, the geographical area and developments in society as a whole. Factors relating to the mother include her age and occupation, whether married and if so age at marriage. Number and age of existing children, social class of parents, their income and religion are family factors. Relevant aspects of the geographical area include whether urban or rural, and general standards of housing and environment. Developments in society include the extent of urbanisation, education and medical knowledge and fashions in family size.

Marriage—Fertility rates have a great deal to do with marriage; some forecasts include a direct estimate relating to marriage. Marriage rates will depend on the degree of urbanisation of a population, the prevailing social customs, availability of housing and real income levels. Important factors are also the age/sex structure of the population and the educational backgrounds and occupations of those unmarried.

The relationship of marriage, fertility and births is by no means easy to predict—at the time of writing the trend apparently is for decreasing numbers of illegitimate births, which may be associated with the rising number of divorces, as well as increasing abortion and use of contraception, but overall a slightly increasing birth rate (late 1971).

Mortality—Life expectancy tables tend to under-estimate survival, since they are based on the existing pattern of survival, not on improvements which will affect current age groups. Those things which influence survival (mortality) include an individual's age and sex, marital status, social class, occupation and life style. These in turn are affected by population density, general living standards and housing conditions, by the degree of urbanisation, standards of medical care and climate.

Migration—Migration taking place depends on individuals' ability and willingness to move. The forces behind migration act differently on the various age/sex groups in the population—for example, if a man is older, it is probable that moving will involve more of an upheaval—breaking ties with family and friends, possibly losing pension rights and encountering difficulties with a house mortgage (or loss of rent controlled property or giving up the chance of a council dwelling), disruption of children in school and so on.

In general, there are two types of move—a shorter distance for a change of house, further for a different job. A third, growing, factor is the move to areas pleasant for retirement.[19] There is a 'migratory elite' of white collar workers, who accept movement as necessary for career advancement, otherwise moves often reflect regional job availability and earning differentials, as well as the characteristics of the mover. For example, young single women are mobile but, predictably, married women generally follow their husbands' movements.

There is a shortage of data on migration in this country (in contrast, for example, with Sweden where every move is recorded). Any estimates made tend to be of *net* migration, which may well mask important differences in the composition of inward and outward flows. Various techniques have been developed relating to migration, including gravity models, intervening opportunity models, regression analysis and matrices.[20] There have also been attempts to use proxies or direct co-variables for example, Durham County Council have estimated out-migration from different areas on the basis of land available for new industry.

The uncoordinated state of both migration data and research was revealed by a recent appraisal of migration studies.[21] Ruth

Welch observed that in recent years there has been a rapid accumulation of information on migration and studies, particularly those recognising migration's role as a dynamic component of social and economic change and the contribution of different kinds of movement to the operation of the housing and labour markets. Unfortunately there has been great diversity in the scale, coverage and organisation of data collection—which has diminished its usefulness. She discussed two types of data source —national and local. Of the national sources the most important are the central government statistical services, notably the Migration Tables of the 1951 and 1961 Censuses and the two inter-censal sample surveys.

A number of local surveys—by planning authorities and independent research organisations—have provided information about aspects not adequately covered in the national surveys, especially household characteristics and reasons for moving. These local surveys vary greatly in size and scope, for example, from a series of special purpose studies in Northern England, relating to a wide range of planning problems,[22] to investigations by new town development corporations. There is also variety in approach—four types can be differentiated:

1 'area' studies, which often cover a wide range of topics, including migration
2 housing problem studies, which need migration data
3 labour market studies, which examine those movements which involve a change of workplace[23]
4 studies concerned with mobility as an element of social change[24]

In general, it is suggested that migration is rarely investigated as a coherent and unique field of research; separate 'types' of migration are looked at—for example, housing or labour—which have no real separate meaning.

I shall now mention briefly three recent studies dealing with different aspects of migration. The first is a study by Hart on the causes of inter-regional migration in England and Wales, which aimed to 'draw together various possible causal variables which are of interest both to the demographer and the economist.'[25]

The study revealed that the true migration pattern in England and Wales is different from the one which is popularly emphasised.

While there is certainly a fair degree of movement from under-employed to prosperous regions, by far the most significant degree of movement is taking place between prosperous and prosperous regions.

Over 40% of the variation in inter-regional gross migration was accounted for by a gravity factor; of course, this is revealed by the *gross* figures, 'the pattern of net gains and losses is more akin to popular belief'.[26] Hart's article contains a brief summary of previous work. Zipf in 1946 postulated the gravity relationship —depending on population sizes and inter-area distances,[27] which received widespread use in movement studies, e.g. by Isard in the USA.[28] Refinements were proposed by Stouffer, with his concept of 'intervening opportunity'[29] for example, Burford, in 1962, suggested the use of 'psychological' rather than geographical distance, by which he meant a 'feeling of remoteness'. Other analysts have tried to incorporate the gravity factor alongside others more overtly economic, for example Rogers' use of a modified Lowry model in California.[30]

In another study, applying a 'shift and share' type of analysis, Paris explains these two components as they relate to regional population studies.[31] 'Regional/structural analysis of population changes tries to identify some of the causes underlying inter-regional differences of growth. Differences between regional and national rates are explained by two components: the first reflects the structural capacity of a region to grow slowly or quickly (it is proved to be a relatively stable element in population changes); the second, the regional component, measures the ability of the region to perform in a manner which is different from the manner its structure would have implied (this element reveals the role of competitive migration among regions and shows much greater variations). Understanding these two components helps not only in historical analyses, but provides also a reasonable sounding board for checking population projections.'

A study by Craig explored methods of estimating the age and sex structure of a sub-region's net migration. He adapted survival rate methods to provide an analysis by sex and quinary age groups of total net migration, as estimated from births, deaths and population change. The various difficulties in doing this were also discussed.[32]

The procedure Craig used was essentially to apply survival rates to the quinary age groups in the population and then calculate the difference in the total number of deaths thus estimated and the actual number as recorded by the GRO. He concluded that 'Although the method involves many approximations . . . it appears, from what internal and external checks are possible, that the results are consistent and reliable.'[33]

Conclusion

To summarise, population analysis and forecasting is now increasingly treated by land use planners as a part of a more general model or analytical system. So a broad chronological development of techniques is discernible from the older methods of trend projection for a population in the aggregate, to growth composition analysis methods, which have the advantages of separating different components of the population and concentrating on the dynamics of change, to models which include among their variables the forces of population change. The shift has thus been from a 'black box' approach, to an emphasis on demographic factors alone, to a specific recognition of the multitude of non-demographic, socio-economic variables which are causative influences on population change.

The techniques that a land use planner or his advisers choose to use for any particular population study will depend on the time scale involved, the extent and nature of the study area, the desired end products of the study—which will determine what specific facts need to be estimated—but probably, above all, on the data available as input.

References

1 See, for example,
   Eversley & Sukdeo, *The Dependants of the Coloured Commonwealth Population of England and Wales,* Institute of Race Relations, 1969;
   Heraud, B. J., 'Social Class and the New Towns', in *Urban Studies,* February 1968;
   Reade, E., 'Community and the Rural–Urban Continuum', in *Journal of the Town Planning Institute,* November, 1968.

2 See series—Sociological Indicators, in *New Society,* weekly from 14 October, 1971, now also published as *A Sociological Portrait,* edited by P. Barker, Penguin (1972).

3 Burnett, F. T., 'A population record system for new towns', in *Journal of the Town Planning Institute,* November, 1968;
Cooke, R. L., 'An analysis of the age structure of immigrants to new and expanding towns', in *Journal of the Town Planning, Institute,* November, 1968;
Moss, J. A., 'New and expanded towns—a survey of demographic characteristics of newcomers', in *Town Planning Review,* July 1968.

4 Institut for Center Planlaegning, *Projecting Age Needs,* Copenhagen (1969)

5 'Censuses and Census Data—Their Interpretation and Use', in *GLC Research and Intelligence Unit Quarterly Bulletin,* 2 (1968), especially, 'The Population Census', by B. Benjamin.

6 See Hollingsworth, T. H., 'Population', Chapter 6 of *Regional and Urban Studies—A Social Science Approach,* edited by Orr and Cullingworth, Allen & Unwin, London (1969).

7 For example, Greater London Council, with Wilbur Smith, Freeman For and Partners, *London Transportation Study.*

8 Blake, J., 'Population Aspects', in *The Census of Population as a Source of Information for Local Authority Planning Departments,* GLC Research and Intelligence Unit, Occasional Paper 2, page 8 (1969).

9 See Benjamin, *op. cit.* (7) above—Seminar.

10 Willis, J., *Population Growth and Movement,* Centre for Environmental Studies, Working Paper 12, August 1968.

11 Grigson, of the GLC Planning Department, described the model in a paper at a Housing Seminar (1969).

12 Stanley, W. F. and Healey, P., 'A technique for assessing the effect of planning policies on residential land and population', in *GLC Research and Intelligence Unit Quarterly Bulletin,* 8, September 1969.

13 For discussion generally, see Hollingsworth, *op. cit.* (6) above.

14 Buchanan, C. and Partners, *South Hampshire Study,* HMSO (1966).

15 Thompson, E. J., 'A simple model for projecting the population of Greater London', in *Greater London Research,* 5, page 40, December 1968.

16 See Thompson, *op. cit.* (15) above.

17 Rogers, A., 'Matrix methods of population analysis', in *Journal of the American Institute of Planners,* January 1966, **32**;

also, 'Matrix analysis of inter-regional population growth and distribution', in *Regional Science Association Papers,* **18** (1967); also, *Matrix Analysis of Inter-regional Population Growth and Distribution,* University of California Press, Berkeley (1968).

18 See, for example, Glass, R. & Davidson, F. G., 'Household Structure and Housing Need', in *Population Studies,* **4** (1950–1); also, Glass, R. & Westergaard, J., *London's Housing Needs* (1965).

19 Centre for Urban and Regional Studies, Occasional Paper 4, *Retirement Migration,* University of Birmingham.

20 See a survey, *Distance and Human Interaction,* by G. Olsson, Regional Science Research Institute (1965).

21 Welch, R., 'Migration in Britain: An Appraisal of Research Findings', in *Greater London Research,* 7, July 1969; also, *Migration in Britain: Data Sources and Estimation Techniques,* Centre for Urban and Regional Studies, Occasional Paper 18, University of Birmingham (1971).

22 North Regional Planning Committee, *Mobility and the North* (4 volumes) (1967); also, *Papers on Migration and Mobility in North-East England,* commissioned by the Ministry of Labour from J. W. House, of Newcastle University; Economic Consultants Limited, *Central Lancashire New Town Proposal: Impact on North-east Lancashire,* Consultants' Appraisal (1967).

23 Including, Harris, A. I., *Labour Mobility in Great Britain, 1953–63,* Government Social Survey for the Ministry of Labour (1967); Hunter, L. C. & Reid, G. L., *Urban Worker Mobility,* OECD, Paris (1968); Heneman (Ed), *Employment Relations Research, A Summary and Appraisal* (1960).

24 For example, Pahl, R. E., *Urbs in Rure: The Metropolitan Fringe in Hertfordshire,* LSE Geographical Papers, 2 (1965).

25 Hart, R. A., 'A model of inter-regional migration in England and Wales', in *Regional Studies,* page 279, **4** (1970).

26 See Hart, *op. cit.* (25) above.

27 Zipf, G. K., 'The P1P2/D Hypothesis: on the Intercity Movement of Persons', in *American Sociological Review,* page 677, **11** (1946).

28 Isard, W., *Methods of Regional Analysis,* Regional Science Studies, Cambridge, Massachusetts (1963), see Chapter 11.

29 Stouffer, S. A., 'Intervening opportunities and competing migrants', in *Journal of Regional Science,* page 1, 2 (1960); also, 'Intervening opportunities, a theory relating mobility and distance', in *American Sociological Review,* page 845, 5 (1940).
30 Rogers, A., 'A regression model of inter-regional migration in California', in *Review of Economics and Statistics,* page 262 (1967); ter Heide, 'Migration models and their significance for population forecasts', in *Milbank Memorial Fund Quarterly,* page 56, 41 (1963).
31 Paris, J. D., 'Regional/structural analysis of population changes', in *Regional Studies,* page 425, 4 (1970).
32 Craig, J., 'Estimating the age and sex structure of net immigration from a sub-region—a case study: North and South Humberside, 1951–61', in *Regional Studies,* page 333, 4 (1970).
33 See Craig, *op. cit.* (32) above.

12   Employment

Introduction

The subject of this chapter is the economic structure of an area, and particularly one facet—namely, employment. Of all the complex inter-relationships with which land use planners must deal, perhaps the most fundamental involve employment—what work people do, where they do it, what incomes are generated for them and their families, and for the area as a whole. In particular, the relationship between people (population), their work (employment), and therefore where they live (housing), is at the core of many of planning's considerations; for example, the provision of services for people—such as shops, schools, recreational facilities.

Even dealt with as simply as possible, there is much to say about this subject, and the chapter, therefore, has several sections. After these introductory remarks, I deal first with the present overall policy framework within which the land use planner concerned with economic structure and employment must work, and then with sources of information. There follows a discussion of the techniques of analysis of such information, which leads on to a consideration of the economic system, and especially the *economic base* concept, and its extension into planning models. The next section is concerned with techniques that concentrate on *linkages*. After that is a brief discussion of the labour supply aspect of this broad subject. To draw some of the threads together, I then give an example of an employment forecasting exercise, with a final section on the translation of employment estimates into physical requirements, notably for land. Figure 12.1 attempts to provide a guide to the various elements with which this chapter is dealing.

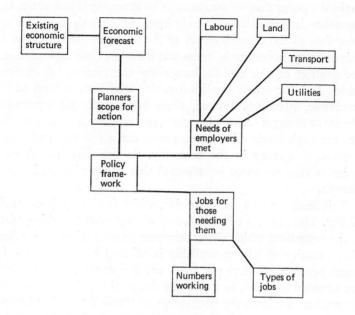

Fig. 12.1   Employment: General Policy Framework

Before embarking on the systematic discussion, however, there are four general introductory comments to be made. The first is a generalisation which may help to provide some overall perspective; it concerns the stages of evolution of economies. The first stage is dependence on primary activities, namely those directly utilising natural resources—such as farming, fishing, forestry and mining, which are often referred to as the *extractive* industries. The second stage of evolution is the development of secondary activities upon the primary base— essentially manufacturing industry. The third stage—of tertiary activities—comprises the growth of service industry; either of personal services, such as teaching or hairdressing, or services to industry, for example, insurance or accountancy. (Sometimes a distinction is made between these two groups of activities.)

Whilst it must not be supposed that this pattern will be followed in all economies, it is a helpful conceptualisation. It also serves to make the point that the structure of an economy is not static, and therefore information and techniques of analysis must be appropriate to the characteristics of the economy under study. In this country, for example, there was for some time an inadequate recognition of the rapidly increasing significance of services, which had important implications for land use, as well as for economic, planning. Indeed, there is certainly no agreement about the changes taking place now, and whether, for example, the present high levels of unemployment are a reflection of major 'structural' change in the economy. So the first introductory point is that we must be mindful that economies evolve and change.

This leads on to a second point, which is about labour availability. This, too, is not static, and changes can be taking place at the same time which either reinforce or act against each other. The quantity of labour available is affected by changes to the hours per day, the days per week and the weeks per year which are devoted to work, as well as by the total number of workers. At present, we have the beginnings of 'flexible working hours', and the prospect of longer vacations in the European Community. Changes are taking place, too, in relation to retirement age and the numbers staying on to further education, and political events determine the number of migrant workers allowed. All these matters impinge on the fundamental questions of whether there will be sufficient work for all, or, conversely, a need for all to work, and also whether a person can expect to base a working life on the same skills throughout, or will be expected to make 'mid-career changes'.

The third introductory point concerns geographical distribution of economic activities. This again, is the resultant of many forces and is never static. It is clearly, too, of central concern to the land use planner. A debate which illustrated well both the complexity of this subject, and how difficult it is to demonstrate incontrovertibly likely interactions and consequences, was the recent Greater London Development Plan inquiry. The economic position of Greater London was subjected to much analysis, as were the interactions between economic structure, availability of jobs and type of work, population numbers and socio-economic characteristics, housing stock and costs, the rateable base of local authorities and their responsibilities, and the overall income/expenses balance of an area and its local government. It was suggested by some land use planners that the move out of inner London of employment and population will have alarming consequences for the economic and social well-being of the capital and especially its inner areas. As will be amplified later in this chapter, it became clear that an effective and credible land use plan cannot be produced without a great deal of probing of the economic future of an area.

The fourth general point concerns the approach of a land use planner to this particular subject: it often seems as though planners working on economic structure and employment compile vast quantities of information, cross-tabulated in every conceivable permutation, which, of itself, generates no policy. Too often the methods of analysis depend on the categories by which the information happens to be available, rather than on functional relationships and the dynamics of the economic situation. Furthermore the information and its analysis is frequently completely unrelated to the scope of a planner has for *action* in this field. A planner does not exist only to understand the existing situation—he should, rather, identify and anticipate difficulties, and, so far as he is able, seek to remedy them.

Yet perhaps the planner should be forgiven some of the inadequacies, 'knowledge of economic interrelationships is imperfect and . . . by its nature economic progress is unpredictable. We are accustomed to living in an economy which provides us with an ever increasing standard of living. The essence of the economic growth which provides the increasing level of welfare is technological and organisational innovation, which makes economic projection a hazardous exercise.' To make matters more difficult, the time scale in land use planning decisions is a very extended one compared with that for industrial and economic planning—land use planners must look ahead for 20 years and more, whereas businessmen think of, say, a five-year forecast period.

Despite these difficulties, however, economic forecasting supplies information crucial for any plan—since 'Economic projections will carry implications for the formulation of aims in town and regional planning and will place constraints on the attainment of non-economic goals.'[1]

For example, 'The nature and structure of industry will have repercussions upon the size and the social structure of the population and will, therefore, influence the social behaviour, patterns of movement and expenditure decisions of that population; industry will, more directly, require sites, the location of which will be one of the main determinants of the transport network. Viewed dynamically, changes in the industrial structure will constitute powerful forces for change within an area.'[2]

Policy framework

This section discusses the fundamental matters of the policy framework for studies of economic structure and employment, and the scope that different planners have. A planner becomes involved in considerations of employment and economic structure from several different angles, and the techniques that he uses will clearly depend on the particular purposes of his work. Some typical aims for this part of a planner's work are:

1 to see that the demand for jobs corresponds with the supply, thus avoiding problems of under-employment or inappropriate employment
2 to ensure that the necessary labour is available to meet employers' needs
3 to make a suitable allocation of land and other services to meet the requirements of economic activity in the area
4 to ensure the overall 'economic well-being' of the area, with stable employment, high incomes and pleasant conditions
5 to make sure that planning policies for other matters co-ordinate with the economic circumstances
6 to provide data needed for other aspects of his work, e.g. future income levels will influence car ownership, which is an ingredient of transport planning studies.

In any work connected with the economy and employment in his area, the planner becomes very mindful of a wider policy framework within which he must operate. This wider framework —of central government controls and directives and regional co-ordinating and advisory bodies—alters constantly in detail, but is certain to persist in some form, and indeed seems likely to become more powerful as the need for broader handling of strategic issues in planning is increasingly recognised. Decisions relating to the planning of employment are thus operating on five levels at least—central government; regional, local planning authority; firms; individual worker. The first three levels are discussed in more detail below. We will shortly see another 'level' of course—the EEC.

1 Central government

At present, although this country does not have any explicit national plan, the direct and indirect controls and directives operated by central government departments largely determine the scope of the local authority planner. Examples are regional location policy, embracing controls and incentives to employers, Treasury controls over lending by the private sector and borrowing and spending in the public sector, communications decisions by the Department of the Environment. Also, of course, the Department of the Environment and the Department of Trade and Industry commission or approve the studies and decisions of regional and local authority planners. Opinions differ as to the effectiveness of central government policies and whether or not greater control is desirable. The 1965 National Plan declared— 'Some of the forecasts or projections for particular industries will inevitably turn out to be wrong. But this does not mean that it is useless to make them.' Others disagree: Jewkes said—'There are strong *a priori* reasons for supposing that failure will always be the fate of the kind of central planning that has been going on in Britain in recent years. First, it has no theoretical foundation; intellectually it is a vacuum.'[3]

Of great importance among central government economic and employment policies is that for the regions. The 1971 Town and Country Planning Summer School was told—'Since we know too little of the extent to which particular government measures influence the location decisions of individual firms, and less about the real costs of such measures, it is hardly surprising that they are constantly being changed.'[4] Townroe, in a discussion on regional policy, in which he asked—What alternatives?, suggested that 'In the eyes of the authorities, the main advantages of the present system are its comprehensiveness and its detail. Each proposal for development is scrutinised, individually and confidentially, by civil servants.' However, he says, 'Critics reply that the fact that each decision is reached independently is a weakness, and not a strength, when seen in terms of the need for positive regional planning. And many would-be refusals never reach the stage of formal decision.'[5]

2 Regional

The newest level in the hierarchy of economic and employment decision makers is the regional level. The last few years have seen the appearance of many studies and reports, including those by consultants, by regional economic councils and boards, by several sub-regional planning units, and now a new series sponsored by the Department of the Environment. These regional studies have not so far been in any way binding on local authority planners, but have been a powerful influence on subsequent proposals made. This seems likely to be increasingly true for the current regional studies, for example, the South-East Strategy, recently formally endorsed by central government.

3 Local planning authority

Every local authority finds itself concerned with trying, in so far as it is able, to ensure that its area has an appropriate economic structure and offers adequate employment opportunities and labour force. The dominance of this work among its other planning pre-occupations varies with the nature of the area, but it is true to say that it is of central concern to the majority of planning authorities, whether it be to attempt to control seemingly endless pressures on available office space or to attract industry to rural

226

areas losing population. The true powers of a local planning authority to *act on*, rather than *understand*, the economic forces at work within its area may be questioned. Fundamentally the land use planner has two 'controls': first, making land available to employment users; secondly, making land available for *other* uses which will help the direct employment uses, either at first hand, such as roads, or at one remove, like houses for workers. ('Land' here includes existing floor space.)

However, neither of these 'controls' can place a total ceiling on expansion of employment (if the forces are great enough, firms will squeeze more workers into a limited space) or induce employment where circumstances are not suitable (as witnessed by long empty land zoned for industry in rural areas).

In his commentary on that part of the Greater London Development Plan Inquiry dealing with employment, Blake concluded that much of the problem derived from responsibility without power:

'The GLC's employment policy was subject to a great deal of criticism at the public inquiry and much of it now lies in tatters. The economic objectives are still highly questionable, resting upon a number of untested and unproved hypotheses. Even if they were valid, the objectives would be incapable of realisation by means of the proposed floor-space controls. As for the idea of introducing selective economic criteria into the development control process, this has been shown to be quite impracticable at the present time.' Yet Blake concedes that the GLC is not wholly to blame for this situation. 'They were required to produce a "strategic" plan, but the area which they cover is not large enough, and the powers which they possess are not strong enough.'[6]

The GLDP is worthy of close attention—the first of the new style strategic plans, differing fundamentally from any previous development plan, as its objectives extend far beyond those of a physical land use/transportation structure plan, even though prepared by a local planning authority within a framework of planning legislation. As one of the GLC's officers said—'The objectives of the plan are social and economic more than anything else.' Blake suggests that one of the main lessons of the GLDP is that social and economic planning cannot be undertaken for towns or cities in isolation, even for a city as large as

London; it must essentially be carried out at a scale appropriate to contemporary social and economic life—namely, the region. It is also very clear that if social and economic planning is to have any effect, it must be backed up by strong physical and fiscal powers. 'However much time and effort has been put into its preparation, a plan is valueless if the means do not exist whereby it can be implemented. The powers at present available to local authorities are strictly limited. Local authorities can and do influence the type of pattern of physical development, but by themselves they are powerless to determine the pace and nature of social and economic change.'[7]

Information

In studying the economic structure of an area, a planner has three categories of information available to him: published information, local knowledge, and information specially collected.

1. *Published information*

Several departments of central government publish information relevant to economic structure. These include tables in the Census of Population reports, Department of Employment statistics of numbers employed in different industries and material from the Census of Production and Census of Distribution relating to manufacturing industry and retailing. The newly available floor space statistics, based on Inland Revenue rating surveys, but processed by the Department of Environment should also be mentioned.

However, despite the various sources of published information, it is impossible to establish a reliable, coherent and comprehensive picture of the employment in any area. Some of the difficulties are—that statistics are often not collected on a 100% basis; they are taken at different moments in time; some classify workers by end product and some by the type of work performed; some are concerned with place of residence and others with place of work. Finally, since they are collected by different agencies for their own specific purposes they *do not* complement each other's deficiencies as sources. The greatest gaps are in the coverage of offices and 'services', which are, of course, increasingly important. A recent paper centring on the use in this context of the Census of Population illustrates the drawbacks of published information.[8]

In his paper, Hoar considers the fundamental information required to formulate an employment or industrial policy for a local development plan, and the extent to which the Census of Population can supply it. He explained that within an area such as a London Borough, policies relating to work will need to take into account the existing location and distribution of offices, factories, shops and other buildings associated with the employment of people. The number of people employed in these places must be estimated and the particular skills or qualifications required by the firms concerned must be recognised. The next stage is to see where the people employed in the Borough live— do they live locally or do they commute? This is important, not only for understanding the journey-to-work pattern, but also to assess the desirable structure for population living in the Borough to support its industry. The location and movement of particular firms is important too, and also where the people working for a particular firm live.

His general conclusion about the information provided by the Census of Population is that it 'can only be a guide to further specialised investigations'.

2   Local knowledge

Any planner is extremely dependent on the knowledge he has himself, and can tap in others, relating to his area. Thus, any study of the economic structure of an area draws heavily on the experience of such officials as the factory inspector and the employment officers, whose daily involvement gives them much helpful information. Contact with industrialists, whether informally or in a more systematic way, as in an industrial survey, can be used to cross-check conclusions reached by other methods, or as a helpful indicator of the 'climate of opinion'.

3 Information specially collected

As with most other facets of his work, however skilfully a planner puts together and uses secondary sources of information, with economic studies he generally finds it essential to obtain particular information directly. The local authority *land use survey*, as well as providing information on buildings, generally includes data on employment. As land use surveys become more sophisticated, with computer processing of data giving greater ease of withdrawing and processing information, with continuous revisions and other refinements such as geo-coding and direct computer mapping, it will become an increasingly useful base for economic and employment planning.

In addition to the land use survey, planners may carry out surveys relating to one aspect of employment, such as offices, or to all types of employment, for example, the GLC Employment Survey, undertaken in 1966/7. Such surveys usually obtain data on a 100% or reliable sample basis, concerning numbers employed, type of labour, kind of work done, accommodation, future plans of the firm and so forth.

Another major source of data on employment collected by planning authorities may be in surveys conducted on other matters, which deal with employment as an influence, for example transportation or shopping surveys.

Employment statistics—classification and simple analysis

In order to assess which economic activities contribute significantly to the economy of any particular area, it is usual to assess available data for what they reveal about variations within the area, and how it compares with other areas. Several types of data might be used, for example, floor space, profit, value added, power used and so forth. In particular studies any one of these, or a combination, might be most helpful. The indicator used most often, however, at least in the UK, is employment. Some information on employment is readily obtained, and it is probably better as a single indicator for various types of economic activity than any other. Thus, typically employment statistics are analysed to reveal as much as possible about the relative significance of different employment categories. Tables 12.1 to 12.5 illustrate the

230

most conventional simple forms of analysis of employment data. They include the following:

Table 12.1: division of the total employed into the numbers and proportions in different industrial categories (classified by end product)

Table 12.1. *Employment by industry in a central business district, the rest of the city and in England and Wales*

Type of industry	Central business district	Rest of city	England & Wales
Agriculture	1	40	72 690
Mining	9	·250	63 590
Food	440	1 480	62 090
Chemicals	560	1 770	64 340
Electrical	650	5 650	267 640
Engineering	170	1 360	50 280
Paper	730	4 610	120 960
Other	4 320	6 540	54 830
Total Manufacturing and Extractive	6 880	21 700	738 420
Construction	620	4 920	142 570
Power	140	910	34 750
Transport	5 980	10 920	146 690
Distribution	5 590	15 510	287 110
Finance	12 170	5 005	52 940
Professional services	3 190	10 310	190 640
Public administration	960	10 570	130 570
Miscellaneous	2 280	19 360	211 240
Total Service	30 930	77 505	1 199 510
Industry inadequately described	130	390	6 960
Total All Industry	37 940	99 595	1 944 890

Table 12.2. *Employment in a central business district classified by occupation and industry*

Type of industry	Operational	Office	Transport	Sales	Other	Total
Agriculture	2	6	1	--	1	10
Manufacturing	2 734	3 700	191	378	475	7 478
Construction	395	203	4	7	17	626
Power	45	91	1	1	5	143
Transport	676	3 513	1 462	41	294	5 968
Distribution	751·	2 846	113	1 681	203	5 594
Finance	205	11 213	42	63·	655	12 178
Professional services	40	2 691	1	21	439	3 192
Public administration	138	1 390	36	596	722	2 882
Miscellaneous	40	724	5	2	197	908
TOTAL	5 026	26 377	1 856	2 790	3 008	38 979

Table 12.2: division of the total numbers working by occupation. This can be cross-classified by industry

Tables 12.3 and 12.4: comparison of the employment structure with other areas. The past growth records may also be compared. These tables then provide a picture of the *industrial mix*—that is,

Table 12.3. *Examples from tables of percentage of employment in central business district, rest of city and England and Wales in 1961 and growth of employment 1951–61*

| Industry | Areas | Percentage of employment 1961 | | | |
		Office workers	Other workers	Operatives	All workers
Manufacturing	CBD	9.5	2.7	7.0	19.2
	Rest of city	10.7	3.4	10.2	24.3
	England and Wales	7.6	3.7	31.8	43.1
Etc for other industries					
		Growth of employment 1951-1961 (1951 = 100)			
Manufacturing	CBD	110.5	156.1	101.6	115.5
	Rest of city	na	na	na	90.5
	England and Wales	129.1	171.7	89.0	98.5
Etc for other industries					

Table 12.4. *Simplified table of percentage distribution of employment in a central business district and comparisons with the employment in England and Wales and in the rest of the city using location quotients*

Type of industry	Percent employment in CBD 1961	Percent employment in England and Wales 1961	Location quotient of CBD of E & W	Percent employment in rest of city 1961	Location quotient of CBD of rest of city	Annual average rate of growth England and Wales 1951-1961
Fast growing industries	58.6	41.8	(1.4)	44.3	(1.3)	2.2
Slow growing industries	13.5	20.0	(0.7)	14.5	(0.9)	1.0
Declining industries	27.6	37.9	(0.7)	40.9	(0.7)	−1.1

Table 12.5. *Employees, classified by sex, age and level of skill*

	Skilled	Semi-skilled	Unskilled	(000's) Total
Juveniles				
Males	12	10	8	30
Females	14	11	7	32
Total Juveniles	26	21	15	62
Adults				
Males	109	86	70	265
Females	121	70	54	245
Total All Employees	256	177	139	572

whether the area's employment is mostly in a growing, stable or declining industry. This is highly significant for the likely future economic structure

Table 12.5: Division into type of worker, by sex and age, that is, male and female, adult and juvenile, and level of skill of training.

More complicated methods of analysis

Location quotient

Of the various techniques and indices that have been devised to carry somewhat further the analysis of the economic structure of an area, the simplest is the location quotient. This conventionally takes employment as a measure of economic activity and compares the proportion of an area's total labour force in one industry or industrial group with the proportion in a comparison area similarly employed. It may be calculated thus—

$$\frac{\dfrac{\text{Numbers employed in area } A \text{ in industry } X}{\text{Total numbers employed in area } A}}{\dfrac{\text{Numbers employed in area } B \text{ in industry } X}{\text{Total numbers employed in area } B}}$$

For example, if we hypothesise that Teesmouth has 40% of its total employment in the chemicals industry and the UK has only 10% of its work force in the chemicals industry, the location quotient of the chemicals industry in Teesmouth (compared with the UK) is 4, that is, it is four times as significant.

The location quotient thus provides a measure of the concentration of a particular industry in a particular area, by comparison with other areas. It has the advantages of being simple to calculate and understand and usable with data which are widely available. If calculated for all industries in a particular area, it may help to indicate which industries are most significant in that area as employers of labour, and how 'specialised' the area is overall—that is, how the location quotients differ from the comparison area (see Table 12.6).

Table 12.6. *Location quotients of central area activities in three different districts*

Activities	High Street	Castle Street	The Market
Finance	1.37	0.56	1.72
Markets	1.49	1.72	8.27
Professional services	1.77	0.21	1.85
Printing	5.49	0.34	0.20
Head offices	1.35	0.28	2.70
Transport	0.10	2.59	0.12
Others	4.48	8.51	1.30

The location quotient must be used with care, however, since geographical variations may be due to such things as older or less efficient plant, bad management, different industrial processes and so forth. It also ignores local variations in demand, so it must not be assumed that industries with a high location quotient are necessarily 'export' industries. It is used a great deal to indicate which industries deserve further investigation, and by incorporation into more complicated techniques.

Localisation curves

Localisation curves are another method of depicting the tendency of industries to concentrate in certain areas. In Figure 12.2 there are examples of localisation curves, to demonstrate some of the different inferences that may be drawn from them. (Based on examples used by Hughes.)

Thus in curve 1:

1   the shape of the curve represents the relative concentration of the industry in question (in particular regions)
2   the position of the region on the curve is determined by the degree of specialisation in that industry (in relation to the national standard)
3   the slope of the region's section of the curve is an alternative measure of the value of the location co-efficient for the industry.

In curve 2:

industry z represents the limiting case of an industry which is 'perfectly' distributed in all areas
industry w is a highly localised industry
industry y is less localised.

234

Curve 1 Localisation Curve for Industry

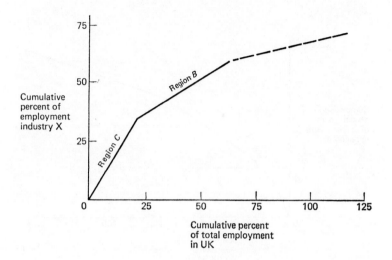

Curve 2 Localisation Curves for Industries w, y, z

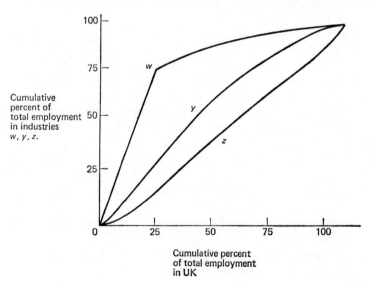

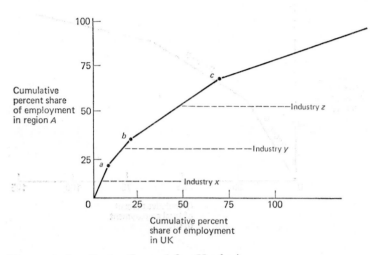

Fig. 12.2. Localisation Curves (after Hughes)

SOURCE *Employment projection and Urban Development, in Regional and Urban Studies—a social science approach,* edited by Orr & Cullingworth, Allen & Unwin, London (1969)

In curve 3:
the cumulative shares of the ranked industries in the regional and the national employment totals are plotted (ranking, for example, by means of a location co-efficient).

Two industries, x and y, are heavily concentrated in region A, but their importance is very much reduced by the fact that their total impact is small. Industry z has a relatively low location co-efficient but is an important industry in both the regional and the national economy. Thus this localisation curve demonstrates three points about the concentration of employment:

1   the extent to which the employment of the region is diversified
    will be measured by the deviation of the curve from the 45
    degree line

2   the slope of the curve over the industry sections will indicate
    the size of the location co-efficient

236

3 the relative importance of the industry in the region's employment is measured by the length of the industry's section.

Co-efficient of localisation

In a study of the *internal* variations in economic structure of an area, which has been divided up into sub-areas, location quotient analysis may be taken further to produce co-efficients of localisation. The co-efficient of localisation indicates in a single statistic the extent to which employment in a particular industry is localised or dispersed over all sub-areas. It is obtained by adding together all the positive (or negative) differences between the percentage share of a sub-area's employment in a given industry and that of its share of employment in the area as a whole, and then dividing by 100.

Complete industrial concentration (all employment in one sub-area) would give an index of 1·0, while completely even distribution would give an index of 0·0. Since the method does not take distance into account, the values depend on the pattern and number of units used (see Table 12.7).

Table 12.7. *Coefficients of localisation and relative dispersion indices of the leading activities in a central area*

Activities	Coefficients of localisation	Relative dispersion indices
Finance	0.43	0.73
Markets	0.50	0.30
Professional services	0.35	0.33
Printing	0.71	0.15
Head offices	0.53	0.28
Transport	0.55	0.54
Other	0.47	0.57

Index of relative dispersion

To overcome the problem just mentioned—that of distance—a technique may be used which attempts to measure the extent to which employment in a particular activity is concentrated and dispersed around its centre of gravity or mean centre.

237

The area under study must be imagined as a plane over which employed population is distributed—the centre of gravity would be the point on which the plane, differentially weighted by the workers, would balance. The different distribution of workers in each activity over the area would reveal itself in different balancing points. Once the centre of gravity has been statistically calculated for an activity, the spatial spread of employment in that activity around the mean centre can be assessed, and the measure of scatter is termed 'standard distance'.

The more dispersed the distribution of employment, the greater will be the value for standard distance. By comparing the standard distances of each activity with that for all employment, these can be expressed as an index of relative dispersion, ranging from o to 1·0 which indicates an activity as dispersed as the total employed population (see Table 12.7).

Co-efficient of specialisation

The co-efficient of specialisation examines the total structure of employment within an area, and indicates how specialised it is. It is calculated by taking the per cent share of total employment for each industry in the area, together with that in a comparison area (for example, the nation), and summing all the positive and negative differences between the percentages, then dividing by 100. The larger the number, the more specialised the area, regardless of sign.

Complete specialisation—that is, all the employment in the area being in one industry—would give a result of 1·0; if each industry were represented in the area of study in exactly the same proportions as in the comparison area, the result would be 0·0.

This technique may also be seen referred to as the Index of Regional Specialisation.

Minimum requirements technique

Another modification of the location quotient technique is minimum requirements analysis.[9] In order to determine which activities are most significant to the economy of an area, an

238

attempt is made to separate out that part of the economic activity which serves only the area itself. This is done by calculating the number of workers in particular industries who are surplus to those necessary to produce the goods and services in question for local consumption—this latter ratio is generally assumed to be the share of that activity in the total employment of the nation.

Alternatively, a number of places of similar population size may be examined in order to establish a *norm* of employment, or a *minimum requirement* for each industry. Any employment above the minimum requirement level is taken to be serving needs outside the area itself. Sometimes it may be decided to exclude a certain number of results from the bottom of the table, otherwise every area except one (the lowest) would appear to be exporting to some extent.

The formula used to compute 'surplus' worker in a particular industry in one area is thus:

$$S = e_i - \frac{e_t}{E_t} \times E_i$$

where e_i is employment in industry i in the area
  E_i is employment in industry i in the nation
  e_t is total employment in the area
  E_t is total employment in the nation.

Alexandersson used this approach to establish the locational character of different industries, calling the minimum requirement values K values. Those industries with a very low K value in relation to the average he recognised as 'foot loose', that is, with a considerable degree of freedom in location—and he termed them 'sporadic'; other industries, whose distribution did not vary so widely, he termed 'ubiquitous'.[10]

Shift and share

A method of analysis which is concerned with isolating the significance of local influences from the significance of the existing economic structure of an area is usually known as *shift and share* analysis. The technique is to look at the economic performance of the area under study over a period of time, usually through the indicator of employment statistics, and compare the growth performance of individual industries within the area with the growth performance of the same industries in some wider area— the region or the nation.

The *actual* performances are then compared with what *would have occurred* had the area followed the wider pattern, that is, with each industry performing in the area just as well as the same industry in the wider area. Any differences are then explained by two factors—a structural component relating to the existing mix of industries, whether dynamic, static, declining and so on— and a component which can be ascribed to locational (or, as generally expressed these days, infrastructural) factors.

It is accepted that this technique is best used for a fairly coarse level of analysis, and it has been most employed for studies at the regional level. Even so, however, it has been heavily criticised, for example, by Buck.[11] Its use has undoubtedly been influential. 'Despite frequent warnings, shift and share analyses have been employed by academics and Regional Economic Planning Councils as a guide to regional policy. Broadly it seems to have been assumed that a region may grow slowly in relation to other regions as a result of its "industrial mix" or of "locational disadvantages."

'It was once hoped that shift and share would prove more than a descriptive tool and provide the Regional Economic Planning Councils with a much needed, objective measure of regional performance.' Based on his own work on Merseyside and the North-west, he concludes, 'Dissatisfaction with the discrepancies introduced by the arbitrary choice of level of industrial disaggregation cast doubts on the value of the whole exercise.' This is because, 'Industries are composed of firms which do not have homogeneous products: in some establishments firms were making products with an income elasticity of demand very different from that for the products of "their" industry as a whole.' He quotes as examples, first, a printing firm which specialises in photogravure work, for which demand is faster growing than for the output of the printing industry in aggregate, and which alone has been responsible for the positive differential growth of employment in printing on Merseyside.

Secondly, the motor industry—'Almost by definition, motor manufacturers in the South-east and Midlands, short of capacity for new lines, are now producing new models using the most modern equipment available, on Merseyside. One can expect the market for these models to grow faster than for the output of the parent factories elsewhere, although Merseyside motor vehicle factories had a fairly long build-up period for employment which constrained employment growth for a while.'

Thirdly, a number of companies grouped on one site on Merseyside, each of which was the wholly owned subsidiary of the same rubber company, although they had fairly unrelated products. This meant that the labour force of the whole site was allocated to the rubber industry by DEP, but when the parent company decided to operate the companies as autonomous divisions DEP employment estimates showed a decline in Merseyside rubber industry employment.[12]

With such examples, Buck demonstrates the unreliability of conventional shift and share analysis as a policy guide, and ends his demonstration—'The sad lesson of this paper is to confirm a conclusion reached elsewhere (Mackay, 1968) that the regional problem is far more complicated than we once imagined, and that the difficulties of policy formulation have been underestimated.'

The economic system

Some understanding of the economic system, however crude, is necessary to understand the mechanics and significance of economic forecasting techniques. As we all know, in the production of goods and services to meet people's requirements, it is necessary to combine materials with the assistance of machinery and labour. For their contribution, the employees and providers of capital are paid, and then, as consumers, they use the money to buy goods and services (see Figure 12.3).

Any individual chooses to allocate the money at his disposal either to direct and immediate needs or for future use—savings. Apart from any savings, his money is passed on to others as

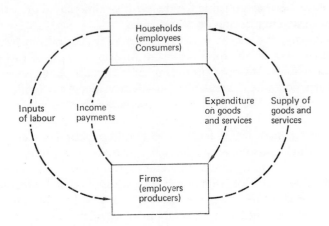

Fig. 12.3   Economic System

Addition of trade

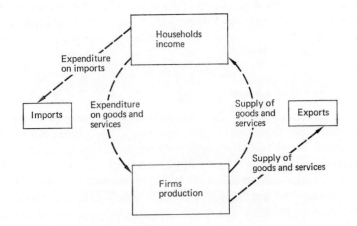

Fig. 12.4   Addition of Trade

payment for the goods and services he buys, thus generating further 'rounds' of spending. Every individual, or group of individuals such as a city, may be said to have a 'propensity to consume' a certain proportion of any money received additionally. (If the propensity to consume is 0·7, then of £10 received, £7 will be spent.) The eventual total effect of an additional sum of money coming into the community is greater, by a factor depending on the size of the propensity to consume, than the original sum. The relationship between the original sum and the eventual total additional spending is termed the 'multiplier' effect. If a community's multiplier is 2, then an additional £100 spent will generate new spending in total of £200.[13] Into this highly simplified discussion of the economic system, it is now necessary to add the complications of 'place', by recognising that not all the goods and services produced in an area are consumed locally, nor is all the money earned in an area spent on goods and services produced there. We therefore must include in the system, 'exports' and 'imports' (see Figure 12.4).

Economic base

The original idea of defining the economic base of an area has been adapted in various ways to serve the practical purposes of planning studies. As a result, it is now possible to find many different definitions of *basic* and *non-basic* employment, which do not correspond with each other. Indeed, this is not in any way surprising, since the sector of an area's economic activities that can be regarded as 'basic' varies with the character of the area's economy, the stage of its development and that of the nation, and the specific purposes of the study.[14]

However, the essence of the basic/non-basic division is to try to separate those jobs which are created only in response to *local* demands, from those which require *external* stimulus of some kind, and which then initiate further changes in the local economy—it is the latter group, which are linked to influences outside the local area, which are termed the 'basic' activities, (see Figure 12.5).

In economic theory, the external stimulus to economic activity in an area can come about in three ways—increase in export activities, increase in investment in the area, either through private activity or government intervention. The export activities can comprise tangible manufactured goods, services to customers outside the area such as insurance, or sales to people who come into the area as consumers, for example, tourists. For planning studies, where economic base analysis is used to assess the existing economic structure and future economic prospects of areas, a simplification is generally adopted, in which the base economic

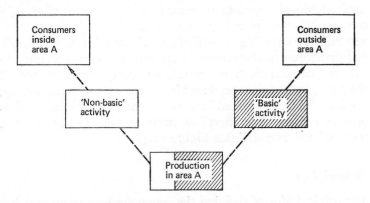

Fig. 12.5 *'Basic' and 'Non-basic' Activity*

activities are taken as extractive and manufacturing (sometimes with the addition of certain categories of services), and non-basic economic activities are taken to be services. Clearly, as the structure of the economy as a whole shifts towards an increasing proportion of employment in service activities of various kinds (many of which are not just personal services) such a crude distinction becomes increasingly invalid.

Nevertheless, the economic base concept remains a fundamental method of analysis used by planners, both in simple forms and as the point of departure for fairly elaborate models. It will usually be found that, however apparently sophisticated the construction built upon it, the initial division into basic and non-basic activities is very generalised, as it must be without a detailed knowledge of the geographical flows for consumption of products and services.

244

A formula for calculation of the economic base of an area, with its extension into an income model, is:

$$Y_i = (E_i - M_i) + X_i \qquad (1)$$

$$E_i = e_i Y_i \qquad (2)$$

$$M_i = m_i Y_i \qquad (3)$$

$$X_i = \bar{x}_i \qquad (4)$$

substituting (2), (3), and (4) into (1) gives

$$Y_i = e_i Y_i - m_i Y_i + \bar{x}_i$$

$$Y_i = \frac{\bar{x}_i}{1 - e_i + m_i}$$

That is, income in i is a multiplier of exports, provided marginal propensity to consume locally is less than unity.

This may be developed into an area income model: where income of area i is:

$$\frac{A_i + \sum_{j=1} m_{ij} Y_j (1 - t_j)}{1 - (c_i - \sum_{j=1} m_{ji})(1 - t_j)}$$

that is, a change in income can derive from

1 exports.
2 variation in autonomous spending in the area, for example, government investment
3 a change in income level in other areas
4 a shift in parameters, e.g. the marginal propensity to consume.

A variant of the economic base method of forecasting is to link non-basic industry by ratios to total population (or sometimes to basic industry) to derive the total future population, as well as the future number of workers, as for example in the Notts-Derby Study's use of a Lowry model.[15] In its simplest form, starting from a known distribution of basic employment, the model works out the amount of non-basic employment and hence population that will be supported by it. An input of basic employment will generate a succession of increments of non-basic employment and population and these are calculated by the use of multipliers, activity and population-serving-ratios. Totals are reached as the process converges, the increments coming nearer and nearer to zero. The model is formulated as a system of linear equations, and in the Notts-Derby application the system was represented by matrix equations. Once numbers of population have been worked out, the model distributes the people to residential areas, by using a journey-to-work function. The employees of basic industry, it is assumed, must live in residential areas within commuting distance of their work. Each residential area needs non-basic activity to serve it, and the population-serving ratio tells us how much. The non-basic employees (mostly shop-workers) are given a place of work by journey-to-shop allocation rules. The same series of steps is used to decide in which residential areas the non-basic workers live, then the amount of employment they will generate, and where those workers will live. The increments eventually become insignificant. Many refinements have been made in the model in its recent uses so that it can serve as a major plan generating or evaluation technique, (see page 105).

Linkages

There are several techniques of economic analysis and forecasting which emphasise the *inter-connections* of economic activities—the complex ways in which units of production are linked in the provision of goods and services for the eventual consumer.

Clearly, linkages vary greatly according to the nature of the economic activity. In manufacturing industry, the linkages comprise raw materials which pass through different processes from one plant to another before reaching the stage of completed manufactured goods. Incorporated are links with transport and other services which are indispensable to the process as a whole. In office work or retailing the linkages are less tangible and consist more of labour inputs.

Sargent Florence, who has written a great deal on linkages, differentiated four types:

1 *vertical*—for example, spinning—weaving—dyeing

2 *convergent*—such as the processes feeding the assembly line of a large plant
3 *diagonal*—that is, services to other industries, like plating
4 *indirect and social*—such as a pool of jobs, together ensuring a good labour supply[16]

It can be seen that in theory all the links of any particular firm could be traced and given a quantitative measure—either in weight of materials or, more usually, in money equivalents. This tracing of linkages for one particular firm can be extended to cover all firms in one industry, or, at its most ambitious, all economic activity within a certain area, which may be expressed in a form similar to national income accounts.

Although the discussion here will focus on linkages traced through money flows or employment, 'The fundamental linkages within regions can be traced from many sources: the distribution channels of retail or wholesale goods, and the locations from which consumers of centrally located social services, cultural and leisure facilities are drawn; intra-regional commodity flows, commuting patterns and migration flows; telephone and other communication densities; labour catchment areas and journey to work patterns.'

Input-output

One version of the tracing of linkages is termed 'input-output' analysis, because it reveals for each economic activity all the inputs required and outputs produced.[17] From such an analysis the influences of different demand sectors can be traced and useful conclusions drawn as to the effects of change in any one sector on all other sectors (see Figure 12.6). The input-output tables can also demonstrate how much of the input to an industry is derived from its own area and how much of its output is sold there or elsewhere. It may thus be used to define the basic economic activities of the area. Unfortunately there are considerable difficulties in constructing input-output tables, in that large quantities of data are required which are not generally obtainable.

The theoretical framework of a metropolitan input-output analysis, together with an application of the technique may be

247

found in Artle's work on Stockholm.[18] He was, however, fortunate in the availability of information about the Stockholm region, and it has been said that 'even the revised methodology outlined

Industry Producing	Industry Purchasing	East						South							West						
		1. Agriculture and extraction	2. Food Processing	...	9. Chemicals	...	21. Government	1. Agriculture	2. Extraction	3. Food Processing	...	9. Iron and Steel	...	2.1 Government	1. Agriculture and food processing	2. Extraction	...	9. Chemicals	...	21. Government	Total Gross Output
East	1. Agriculture and extraction																				
	2. Food processing																				
	⋮			⋮		⋮					⋮		⋮				⋮		⋮		
	9. Chemicals																				
	⋮			⋮		⋮					⋮		⋮				⋮		⋮		
	21. Government																				
South	1. Agriculture																				
	2. Extraction																				
	3. Food processing																				
	⋮			⋮		⋮					⋮		⋮				⋮		⋮		
	9. Iron and steel																				
	⋮			⋮		⋮					⋮		⋮				⋮		⋮		
	2.1 Government																				
West	1. Agriculture and food processing																				
	2. Extraction																				
	⋮			⋮		⋮					⋮		⋮				⋮		⋮		
	9. Chemicals																				
	⋮			⋮		⋮					⋮		⋮				⋮		⋮		
	21. Government																				
	Total Inputs																				

Fig. 12.6 Inter-regional Input-Output Flow Table (after Isard)

SOURCE *Methods of Regional Analysis*, M.I.T. Press

in his introduction to the American edition (of his work) requires a level of detailed information which would restrict the technique to very special cases in the UK'.

It is instructive to look at the work done on national input-output tables, notably at Cambridge.[19]

TAP

Since it is almost prohibitively complicated to draw up a complete input-output analysis for an area, it may be used in modified forms, as in the Technique for Area Planning (TAP), which identifies, by the use of location quotients, the major economic activities in an area and then traces the input-output linkages for these only.

Thus, TAP divides a region's industries into major sectors and minor sectors and records the full inter-industry transactions for the major sectors only (major sectors being defined by size and/or rapid growth or decline). All other transactions are classified within the household sector account. It works best for small, fairly specialised areas, when it is reckoned to be almost as effective as a full input-output study, although needing far less data. 'TAP is a mongrel technique, somewhat between an input-output model and an economic base study. It avoids the costliness of the former and the undue aggregation of the latter . . . TAP Study may be used either for projection or for evaluating the impact of alternative policies (e.g. the choice between promoting the growth of an existing firm, a new firm related to existing local activities and a firm in an industry new to the region) on local employment or income.'[20]

Industrial complex analysis

Also concerned with linkages is Industrial Complex Analysis. This focuses on the linkages of one particular industry or industry group, such as a steel works. Its purpose is to trace the linkages to other sectors of the area's economy through analysis of inputs and outputs. It is thus useful for various types of probe and impact study, for example:

1 To compare alternative locations for an industrial complex,
2 to estimate the effect within an area of changes to an existing industrial complex, such as expansion or closure.

Factor analysis

Another technique which can be used to assist in the clarification of economic linkages (as in many other statistical problems) is factor analysis. The purpose of this technique is to pick out from a large number of known relationships those which are of the greatest significance. A well explained use of this technique in relation to employment was in an economic study of the City of London.[21] A form of factor analysis—cluster analysis—was used as follows:

The first step was to establish and evaluate all the relationships which exist between activities. Then, statistical analysis isolated those factors which contribute the most to the explanation of the complex interrelationships observed. Thus the significant linkages were spotlighted. The results may be expressed statistically or diagramatically (see Figure 12.7) when the clusters of related activities stand out well. (This technique is more fully discussed in the chapter on housing.)

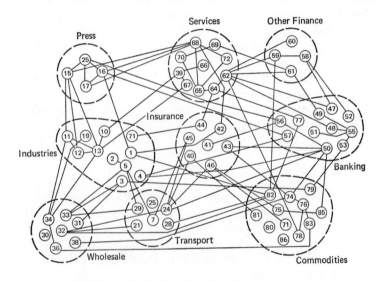

Fig. 12.7   Cluster Analysis (after Goddard)

SOURCE 'Multivariate Analysis of Office Location Patterns in the City Centre: a London example', in *Regional Studies*, 1968

Impact studies

We have said that the idea of linkages may be used in 'impact studies' of various kinds, which attempt to predict the eventual total effects on the economy of an area of an initial change. Interesting studies of this kind have, for example, been undertaken on the effects of a steel plant, an airport, a university.[22]

In practice, impact studies are usually required in one of two types of situation:

1 where a location must be found for something and alternative possibilities are being assessed, e.g. an aluminium smelting plant
2 where an area is recognised as deficient and alternative means of injecting economic activity are being explored, e.g. underdeveloped regions.

This may be an appropriate point to mention that many of the techniques relating to the planning of employment have been devised in connection with the development and implementation of policies for regional direction of employment.[23]

Growth poles

As a concomitant of such policies it has been necessary to assess existing local economies and the operation of various economic activities in order to try to use government subsidies to maximum effect. For example, techniques have been devised to assess the more favourable locations for new industries within larger areas (such as a development area).

A particular variant of such studies is the idea of growth points or growth *poles*. The modern development of growth point theory stems mainly from the work of French regional scientists, notably Perroux.[24] He has declared a growth pole to be 'A set of expanding industries located in an urban area and inducing further development of economic activity throughout its zone of influence.' Expansion depends on interaction between 'key industries' which form the nucleus of the development pole.

The 'key' industries are defined by characteristics such as:

1 a high degree of concentration
2 high income elasticity of demand for their products, which are usually sold to national markets

3 marked local multiplier and polarisation effects
4 advanced level of technology and managerial expertise.

It is suggested that the choice of key industries assures that the local multiplier effects are great, and the eventual increase in local income and employment as large as possible; also that by the force of example these characteristics are diffused through the area.

A recent article by Tolosa and Reiner discussed the economic programming of a system of planned poles, including pole selection and how to programme the allocation of investment among the chosen poles.[25]

Growth analysis of employment

In a recent article, Law suggested a technique of growth analysis that might be used to formulate employment location policies without the present almost exclusive concentration on unemployment rates as indicators. He attempts, 'to discuss employment changes in the same terms as those used in population studies. Jobs are created and disappear in the same way that people do. It is, therefore, reasonable to talk of a birth rate and death rate in jobs, and to use these terms to discuss the dynamics of change.'[26]

Thus, using data on the changes of jobs at each place of employment over a given period, and the origin of new places of employment so as to distinguish between indigenous development and that due to migration, the following rates could be calculated:
Birth Rate in Jobs

$$BR = \frac{X + Y}{T} \times 100$$

where X = sum of increases in employment in places of work existing at beginning of period
Y = sum of employment in new workplaces of local origin established since the beginning of the period
T = total employment at beginning of period.

Death Rate in Jobs

$$DR = \frac{Z}{T} \times 100$$

where Z = sum of declines of employment in workplaces during the period.

Migration Rate

$$MR = \frac{P - Q}{T} \times 100$$

where P = sum of employment at new workplaces in the area established by migration to the area

Q = sum of employment at new workplaces outside the area established by migration from the area;

The Migration Rate may be positive or negative.

Gross New Jobs in Area   = $X + Y + P$
Total Change in Jobs in Area   = $X + Y + P - Z$
Rate of Change of Jobs in Area = $BR - DR + MR$

Location theory

The early location theorists drew attention to the various influences on location of economic activity (a facet relatively neglected by conventional economic theory), and the implications this had for settlement patterns. Examples are von Thunen's well-known analysis of a Prussian estate and Weber's work on manufacturing industry and its cost structure. Their work has subsequently been extended by economists, such as Lösch, by geographers, and by regional scientists, notably Isard.[27]

Location theory, by definition, covers an extremely wide range of activities whose characteristics, both locational and other, vary greatly. Although the theories reflect the general economic structure of the time and place of writing (manufacturing activity has received more attention than services) they provide useful bases and insights for a great deal of practical work. We shall be discussing some elements of location theory in more detail in the chapter on shopping.

Labour—the 'supply' side

So far most of the discussion has been of elements affecting the 'demand' for employment, that is, by firms; obviously a planner

must be equally concerned with analysis of the 'supply' side—
the workers. In examining any existing situation, it is rather
difficult to separate the historical interactions of demand and
supply, but the two can be viewed to a large extent as independent
when forecasting the future. Supply of labour (or demand for
jobs) depends on various factors—demographic, socio-economic
and physical. The major determinants of the supply of labour to a
particular area are:

1 the size of the area from which its working population is
   drawn and the total number of people in that area
2 the proportion of the total population that is economically
   active—this depends principally on the demographic characteristics, but also on social ones
3 how many of the economically active wish to work—the main
   groups exercising choice are the young (who may prefer to
   remain in education), married women and the elderly[28]
4 the suitability of the work force for different occupations and
   industries—this will depend on the education, skills and
   training people have received
5 travel facilities and their effects on patterns of commuting.

Many of the above have been mentioned already in the chapter
on population.

In order to forecast labour supply, it is necessary to make:

1 forecasts of total population, including migration, with demographic characteristics
2 predictions regarding socio-economic habits and choices in
   the future
3 assumptions regarding travel facilities.

Activity rates and labour reserves

A recent paper by Gordon dealt with activity rates—particularly
their geographical variation—and with methods of estimating
local reserves of labour.[29]

'Activity rates are an expression of the proportion of the total
population or of a particular demographic section of it who are
engaged in economically productive activity. At the regional or
sub-regional level their significance derives from their close
relation to the average level of household or personal income . . .

and from their use as an index of the utilisation of possible labour supply and, conversely, the likely size of local labour reserves which could be mobilised.'

Gordon used data from the 1966 Census to show the variations in activity and inactivity rates by age group, region and sub-region within Great Britain and changes since 1961. Male inactivity was shown to be largely associated with unemployment, but female inactivity was equally linked with unemployment, lack of urbanisation and an unfavourable industrial structure.

Gordon used his results to produce revised 'armchair' regional and sub-regional estimates of labour reserves and to suggest an improved method for estimating local reserves, which combines the *armchair* and the *micro* approaches. These were terms used by Taylor, who in his study of female labour reserves in the North-west, pointed to:

1   the micro method—based on a sample survey of households
3   the *armchair* method—based on comparisons of actual and potential sub-regional activity rates.[30]

(For a discussion of activity and unemployment rates, see a recent article in *New Society*).[31]

Of course, there is a relationship between geographical variations in activity rates and migration. A paper by Hart referred to elsewhere (see page 214) investigated the causes of inter-regional migration, attempting to draw together economic and demographic causal variables.

Forecasting employment in an area

Forecasting has already been discussed in earlier chapters; many of the comments made there are relevant to forecasting employment. The process of predicting the employment of an area in the future is generally a composite one, which incorporates many of the techniques already mentioned. It may include a comparison with relevant national or regional forecasts and consultation regarding future plans with employers in the area. The predictions seek particularly to isolate growth and decline factors.

Although it is now several years old, the process used in the South Hampshire Study (1966) still provides a useful example of how statistical analysis, common sense and many forms of expertise may be combined to produce a forecast of future employment in an area.[32]

What follows is a simplified account of the method used.

1 The first step was to accept as a useful distinction the division into basic and non-basic industries—basic industry being that which is linked to an external market and hence to national factors, and non-basic being dependent on the growth of basic industry.

2 Industries were mostly allocated wholly to either the basic or the non-basic category, largely by location quotient methods. As an example, the basic (that is, nationally linked) industry included all manufacturing and primary industry except parts of food, drink, clothing and newspaper publishing, which were deemed to serve the local market. All employment that was not thought to be basic was classified non-basic.

3 For each industry, it was then necessary to establish the relationship between local and national employment trends; by combining this assessment with forecasts of national performance in that industry, a forecast of local employment was derived. Estimates of national employment trends were taken from the sources then available. In a technically sophisticated forecast, this part could be handled by an input-output analysis to gauge the multiplier effects of external demand. In a simple version, relatively straightforward projections can be made from past statistical trends, modified in the light of major national projections and specific knowledge about the prospects of local industry. At this stage then, estimates had been produced of future employment in the basic industries.

4 Predictions for the non-basic industries were made as follows —for each industry, the ratio of employment to total population was calculated (since it is reasoned that such industry exists to serve locally generated demand). Future changes in the ratios were allowed for by extrapolation of recent trends and comparison with expected national changes. Given the projected total population, it was then simple to calculate the employment in locally dependent industries for future years.

It may be useful to refer briefly to two comparable American studies. Both of them drew on the basic/non-basic concept and used limited input-output techniques. The first was undertaken in the *New York Metropolitan Region Study*.[33]

Industry was divided into two groups—*national market* firms and *local market* firms, the latter being those serving the local population and providing goods and services to the national market firms (i.e. non-basic). The national market firms were defined as those which 'export to other regions (or other nations) a considerable portion of their output, or which are subject to competition from firms in other parts of the country. The size of the output of such firms and their number depend not only on the national demand for their product, but on the relative advantages of a location in the New York Region as opposed to location elsewhere.'

The demand for the output of these industries was calculated by projecting the national demand for these industries, then New York's share in the output. Demand for 'local' goods and services was assessed through expenditure by three categories—business, private consumers and government. Regional estimates of both employment and output were made and intra-regional projections of employment to county level. However, the intra-regional projections were fairly pragmatic: 'How did we choose an appropriate degree and direction of redistribution for a particular activity? . . . By and large, the process was one of judiciously mixing all that we had learned about past trends and the forces underlying these trends with some speculations about the likely impact of foreseeable future developments on these forces. The precise quantitative figure which was used in each case was not generated by a model analogous to the model developed on the regional level, in which a lot of numbers were simultaneously determined.'

A similar methodology was used for the *Pittsburgh Regional Survey*, which produced four projections by varying assumptions about the competitive position of the Pittsburgh area in the US economy and the likely levels of employment (see Figure 12.8).[34]

A much more recent complex exercise in economic forecasting was that undertaken for the Greater London Development Plan, which well repays examination as an illustration of the process involved.[35]

257

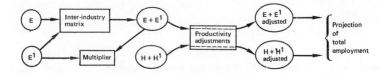

Fig. 12.8   Employment Projection: Pittsburgh Economic Study

Physical requirements

For the land use planner, the final outcome of his work on analysis and forecasting of the economic structure and employment of his area are bases for policy regarding physical facilities.

These comprise *land*, both for direct employment uses such as offices, industry and commerce, or to accommodate workers and their needs—housing, education, leisure.

Also, the other *services* required by industry, such as water, electricity, waste disposal.

Finally, of course, *transport* services, both for movement of goods and people. Thus it becomes necessary to make quantitative predictions about the amounts of land, floorspace, roads and so forth that will be required. Curiously enough, this stage of quantification has received much less technical attention than employment/income forecasting and is generally carried out by 'rule of thumb' estimates about future trends, based on present relationships.

In the South Hampshire Plan, for example, once employment projections by the conventional industrial sectors had been completed, jobs were reclassified into four 'land use types': manufacturing industry, attached offices (namely, those located with manufacturing industry), detached offices, and other (a very diverse residual group). These were examined to derive the future industrial land and office space requirements for use in structure plan preparation.[36]

In conclusion, the sequential interdependence of land use and economic planning should be stressed—'The decisions which follow a review of future economic prospects will often change many of the assumptions on which the propositions were based ... Given this complex interrelationship of cause and effect in a background of imperfect knowledge, it is important to set up a procedure which will review the changes in economic projections made likely by autonomous economic factors and by the implementation of development proposals.'[37]

References

1 Hughes, J. T., 'Employment projection and economic development', in *Regional and Urban Studies: A Social Science Approach,* edited by Orr and Cullingworth, page 213, Allen & Unwin, London (1969).

2 Hughes, *op. cit.* (1) above;
see also
Leven, C., 'Establishing goals for regional economic development', in *Journal of the American Institute of Planners,* page 100, 30 (1964).

3 Jewkes, J., *The New Ordeal by Planning,* Macmillan, London (1968).

4 Stewart, J. A., *Industrial Location: Great Britain and Europe,* paper to the Town and Country Planning Summer School (1971).

5 Townroe, P. M., 'Industrial development—what alternatives?' in *New Society,* page 269, 16 February 1971.

6 Blake, J., 'First aid for London's economy—some notes and reflections on the GLDP Inquiry', in *The Surveyor,* page 42, 16 April 1971.

7 See Blake, *op. cit.* (6) above.

8 Hoar, G., 'Employment aspects', in *The Census of Population as a Source of Information for Local Authority Planning Departments,* GLC Research & Intelligence Unit Occasional Paper 2, page 16, (1969).

9 Ullman, F. & Dacey, M. F., 'The minimum requirements approach to the urban economic base', in *Papers and Proceedings of the Regional Science Association,* page 175, 6 (1960).

10 Alexandersson, G., in *The Industrial Structure of American Cities,* edited by Almquist & Wiksell, Stockholm (1956).

11 Buck, T. W., 'Shift and share analysis—a guide to regional policy?', in *Regional Studies,* page 445, 4 (1970).

12 See Buck, *op. cit.* (11) above;
see also Stilwell, F. J. B., 'Location of industry and business efficiency', in *Business Ratios,* page 5, 2 (1968);
also 'Regional growth and structural adaptation', in *Urban Studies,* page 162, 6 (1969).

13 For fuller discussion, see
Beckerman, W., *An Introduction to National Income Analysis,*
Weidenfeld & Nicolson, London (1968);
Needleman, L. (Ed), *Regional Analysis,* Penguin (1968);
Nourse, H. O., *Regional Economics,* McGraw Hill, New York
(1968);
Richardson, H. W., *Regional Economics—A Reader,* Macmillan
(1970);
Steele, B. B., 'Regional multipliers in Great Britain', in *Oxford
Economic Papers,* **22,** 2, July 1969;
Weiss, S. J. & Gooding, E. C., 'Differential multipliers in a
small regional economy', in *Land Economics,* page 235, **44** (1968).
14 See Andrews, R. B., 'Mechanics of the urban economic base', ten
articles in *Land Economics,* **29–31** (1953–5);
Duncan, O. D., *Metropolis and Region,* Chapter 2, Johns Hopkins
(1960);
Jacobs, J., *The Economy of Cities,* Cape, London (1969);
Richardson, H. W., *Elements of Regional Economics,* Penguin (1969);
Tiebout, C. M., *The Community Economic Base Study,* Committee
for Economic Development, New York (1962).
15 See Notts/Derby Sub-Regional Planning Unit, *The Notts-Derby
Sub-Regional Study* (1969);
Centre for Environmental Studies, *Papers from the Seminar
on the Process of the Notts-Derby Sub-Regional Study,* IP 11 (1970);
Batty, M., 'An activity allocation model for the Nottinghamshire-
Derbyshire Sub-region', in *Regional Studies,* page 307, **4** (1970).
16 Sargent-Florence, P., *Investment, Location and Size of Plant,*
National Institute of Economic and Social Research—Economic
and Social Studies, 7 (1948).
17 See, for example,
Centre for Environmental Studies, *Seminar on the Construction
and Use of Small Area Input-Output Tables,* CP 1, June 1970;
Edwards, S. L. & Gordon, I. R., 'The application of input-
output methods to regional forecasting—the British
experience', in *Regional Forecasting,* edited by M. Chisholm,
Colston Papers, 22, Butterworths, London (1970);
Leontieff, W., *Input-Output Anaylsis,* Oxford University Press
(1967);
McCrone, G., 'The application of regional accounting in the
United Kingdom', in *Regional Studies,* page 39, **1** (1967).
18 Artle, R., *Studies in the Structure of the Stockholm Economy,* The
Business Research Institute of the Stockholm School of

Economics (1959), reissued Columbia University Press (1965); also 'On some methods and problems in the study of metropolitan economics', in *Regional Science Association Papers,* **8** (1961).

19 Stone, R., *Mathematics in the Social Sciences,* Chapman & Hall (1965).

20 see Richardson, *op. cit.* (14) above; also Regional Economic Development Institute of Pittsburgh, *Technique for Area Planning: A Manual for the Construction and Application of a Simplified Input-Output Table* (1967); and *Development of a Manual for Economic Impact Analysis in Urban Areas* (1967).

21 Described in the following:
Goddard, J., 'Multivariate analysis of office location patterns in the city centre: a London example', in *Regional Studies,* **2** (1968);
also published as London School of Economics, Department of Geography Discussion Paper 8;
and Greater London Development Plan Inquiry Document E11/10;
Economists Advisory Group, *An Economic Study of the City of London,* Allen & Unwin (1971);
Broadbent, T. A., *An Introduction to Factor Analysis and its Application in Regional Science,* CES WP 13, Centre for Environmental Studies.

22 Isard, W. & Kuenn, R., 'The impact of steel upon the Greater New York–Philadelphia industrial region', in *Review of Economics and Statistics,* page 289, **25** (1953);
Keeble, D. E., 'Airport location, exporting and industrial growth', in *Town and Country Planning,* page 209, **36,** April 1968.
Bonner, E. R., 'The economic impact of a university on its local community', in *Journal of the American Institute of Planners,* page 339, September 1968;
Grime, E. K. & Starkie, D. N. M., 'New jobs for old: an impact study of a new factory in Furness', in *Regional Studies,* page 57, **2** (1968).

23 See, for example, the following selection from the voluminous literature,
Britton, J. N. H., *Regional Analysis and Economic Geography,* Bell (1967);
Cameron, G. C. & Clark, B. D., *Industrial Movement and the Regional Problem,* University of Glasgow Social and Economic

Studies—Occasional Papers, 5, Oliver & Boyd, Edinburgh
(1966);
Dunn, E. S., 'A statistical and analytical technique for
regional analysis', in *Regional Science Association, Papers and
Proceedings,* page 97, **6** (1960);
Summary of Hunt Report, and Observations, in *Journal of
the Town Planning Institute,* page 392, November 1969;
Keeble, D. E., 'Industrial decentralisation and the metropolis:
the North-West London case', in *Transactions of the Institute of
British Geographers,* page 1, **44** (1968);
for a simple outline, see
Lee, D., *Regional Planning and Location of Industry,* Heinemann,
London (1969);
Law, C. M., 'Employment growth and regional policy in
N.W. England', in *Regional Studies,* page 359, **4** (1970);
Mackay, D. I., 'Industrial structure and regional growth: a
methodological problem', in *Scottish Journal of Political
Economy,* page 129, **15,** June 1968;
McCrone, G., *Regional Policy in Britain,* Allen & Unwin (1969);
Perloff, *et al., Regions, Resources and Economic Growth,* Part 3,
Johns Hopkins (1960);
Robinson, E. A. G. (Ed), *Backward Areas in Advanced Countries,*
see especially section on Location Theory, Regional Economics
and Backward Areas, page 3, Macmillan, London (1969);
Sant, M. E. C., 'Unemployment and industrial structure in
Great Britain', in *Regional Studies,* page 83, **1** (1968);
and 'Age and area in industrial location: a study of
manufacturing estates in East Anglia', in *Regional Studies,*
page 349, **4** (1970);
Townroe, P. M., 'Locational choice and the individual firm',
in *Regional Studies,* page 15, **3** (1969);
Tulpule, A. H., 'Dispersion of employment in the Greater
London area', in *Regional Studies,* page 25, **3** (1969);
24 Perroux, F., 'Note sur la notion de pôle de croissance', in
Economie Appliquée, page 307, **7** (1955).
25 Tolosa, H. & Reiner T. A., 'The economic programming of
a system of planned poles', in *Economic Geography,* page 449,
46, 3, July 1970;
see also

Darwent, D. F., 'Growth poles and growth centres in regional
planning—a review', in *Environment and Planning,* page 5,
1, 1 (1969);
Hansen, N. M., 'Development pole thoery in a regional context',
in *Kyklos,* page 709, 20 (1967);
Lasven, J. R., 'On growth poles', in *Urban Studies,* page 137,
6, 2, June 1969.
26 Law, C. M., 'Changing activity rates in N.W. England', in
Journal of the Town Planning Institute, November 1969.
27 Isard, W., *Methods of regional analysis,* M.I.T. Press
Chapter 7 New York (1960);
Losch, A., *Economics of Location,* New Haven (1954);
Christaller, W., *The Central Places of Southern Germany,*
Prentice Hall, (1966);
see also
Isard, W., & Smith T. E., 'Location games: with application
to classic location problems', in *Papers and Proceedings of the
Regional Science Association,* page 45, 19 (1967);
Stevens, B., 'An application of game theory to problems in
locational strategy', in *Papers and Proceedings of the Regional
Science Association,* page 143, 7 (1961);
bibliography by Townroe, *Industrial Location and Regional
Policy,* Birmingham University.
28 Rogers, H. B., 'Women and work in new and expanding
towns', in *Town and Country Planning,* January/February 1969.
29 Gordon, I. R., 'Activity rates: regional and sub-regional
differentials', in *Regional Studies,* page 411 4 (1970).
30 Taylor, J., 'Hidden female labour reserves', in *Regional Studies,*
page 221, 2 (1968).
31 Standing, G., 'Hidden workless', in *New Society,* 14 October 1971.
32 Buchanan, C. & Partners, *The South Hampshire Study* (1966). 1971.
33 New York Metropolitan Region Study, *Projection of a Metropolis,*
Harvard University Press (1961).
34 Pittsburgh Regional Planning Association, *Region with a Future,*
3 of the Economic Study of the Pittsburgh Region,
Pittsburgh (1963).
35 Greater London Council, *Greater London Development Plan—
Statement,* and *Report of Studies,*
also *Inquiry Papers,* especially 390 (1969–72).

36 South Hampshire Plan Technical Unit, *Study Report D1: Employment (1969)*, South Hampshire Plan Advisory Committee, Working Paper, 4;
see also
Kirkbridge, D. J., 'Employment demand projections and future land use requirements', in *Journal of the Town Planning Institute*, **56**, 6, June 1970.

37 see Hughes, *op. cit.* (1) above.

Della Nevitt has suggested that the term 'housing' should be used 'to cover all the socially accepted ways by which a man acquires a territory for his home, the procedures by which he retains that territory, the price he pays for it and the manner in which the

Need				Supply			
Numbers	Existing	House-holds	Dwell-ings	Minus	Demolitions	For housing reasons	Quantity indicators – age, condition, life, space, facilities, rateable value
Type							
Age/Sex						For other reasons	eg. roads
Socio-economic							
Cultural patterns				Kept	Unchanged	Concern for whole environment, not just individual dwellings. Provide parking, open space, a mixture of dwelling sizes	
Special needs	Projected				Improved		
eg. old people, young children, large families, disabled				Plus	New building	Who builds? What numbers? What tenure? What sizes? What characteristics? Which locations?	

Fig. 13.1   The Housing Planning Process

stock of houses is maintained and enlarged.'[1] Defined in this way, it is clear that the land use planner has powers to operate on only very restricted aspects of housing and, indeed, the fragmentation of responsibility is one of the many factors that work against providing satisfactory housing.

This chapter begins with a brief look at the present context for housing. The key to many of the difficulties is 'a real conflict between man's desire for security of tenure and the desire to exploit the economic potential of residential land.'[2]

The remainder of the chapter will deal first with techniques relating to housing need, then with assessment of housing stock, followed by a discussion of methods for the integration of these two halves of the equation into overall housing policies and programmes (see Figure 13.1). Finally, monitoring systems for housing will be discussed.

The present context

What then is the present context of housing within which a land use planner must work? It is said that with average living standards rising and increased personal mobility aspirations are great for space, adaptability and pleasant surroundings. The state now defines standards of fitness for dwellings and local authorities accept considerable responsibility for housing provision. However, the choices of tenure remain very limited, no family has a guarantee of housing and many find themselves without access to a home.[3] There has been considerable legislation concerning housing in recent years,[4] and central government is monotonously optimistic (see the tables below), whilst pressure groups and social commentators draw attention to the many existing deficiencies in the system. A report on existing housing throughout the country has estimated that 40% of dwellings are environmentally deficient.[5] The same report stated 'we noted the wide inequalities that are found in the present housing situation. To put the point briefly, these inequalities are firmly related to the pervasive levels of class in our society; the drab and deprived environment of older housing is inhabited by people who would describe themselves as working class; space, privacy and comfort appear to be the privileges of the wealthier middle class.'[6]

'Housing need'—as it is interpreted in the typical housing study

266

—is discussed in the next section but the major housing problems have recently been identified as follows:[7]

1 A conflict between current economic circumstances and the long period desire of the consumer of housing for stability in the market and security of tenure

3 a conflict between social policy—for example, toward low income families or the elderly—and the economic forces which allow the wealthy to outbid those poorer to secure accommodation

3 the dependence of the overall 'filtering process' of the whole housing market on a high effective demand for new houses; if this falters, there can be a slump in housing demand while the 'poor' remain very badly housed.

(The 'filtering process' here mentioned refers to the successive movements of households into the houses that become vacant in a chain effect, which is initiated by the building of a new house.)

These three problems are inherent in a housing market operating within the context of a price mechanism, but other problems are a result of social policies—for example, a desire to keep families together, without an adequate range of mechanisms to enable them to do so—though understanding of homelessness has greatly increased, policies to prevent it remain embryonic.[8]

Other difficulties arise from activities of government—worthy in themselves—that compete for land, e.g. construction of schools, or bring radical changes to areas, e.g. building a road, or restrict land supply, e.g. Green Belts. The government's policy statement 'Fair deal for housing' has been criticised as not facing squarely up to all these conflicts.[9]

How all these manifest themselves as 'housing need' in a particular area of study is the subject of the next section.

Measuring and forecasting housing need

Much has been written on the calculation of housing needs. Cullingworth stressed the distinction between 'demand' which implies consideration of market conditions as reflected in price, and 'need' which relates to a norm which society finds acceptable.[10] Thus, 'requirements' for housing in an area will be seen

267

quite differently by the local manager of a building society and by a charitable housing trust. The ideal goal would be to provide for every household a home of the right size, type, price and tenure, with all appropriate internal and external facilities in a suitable location. A land use planner working on housing, therefore, needs to be able to categorise his area's present and likely future resident population in terms of their needs in respect of all these various aspects of housing

A fundamental difficulty in analysis is that the assessment must be made not in terms of individuals but of *households*—that is, groupings of persons who wish to live together. The principal published source of information for planners assessing housing need is the Census of Population, which has traditionally been much concerned with housing.[11] For the Census, definitions must be very precise, and two terms are crucial—*dwelling* and *household*. The definitions (and, just as important, the instuctions given to Census enumerators on their interpretation) have varied somewhat from one Census to the next, generally in attempts to correct inadequacies shown up in usage. The basic definition of 'dwelling' has been a 'reasonable' degree of privacy, usually defined by structural separation. For the 1971 Census, though, a more pragmatic definition, based on 'reasonable separation' was introduced. The 'household' is defined on the basis of existing housekeeping arrangements, not on preferences; hence the comment that the Census is 'not an enquiry into emotions or intentions'. Of course, it is emotions and intentions that planners need to know something about in order to assess housing need in the future (based on present deficiencies and future changes in the pattern of households).

Early work on classification of households, carried out by Ruth Glass and associates, was used as a guide in various land use planning studies.[12] Such classifications may be elaborate—for example, the system used by a Rowntree Housing Trust Study (see page 269)—whilst still lacking precise social meaning; for example, 'small adult households' includes together childless couples, unmarried people of the same sex sharing, parents under 60 whose children have left home. Thus although broadly representing stages in the 'life cycle' of households, it is not much help in forecasting housing need.

268

Often, studies have focused on one 'core' individual in a household, traditionally the 'head of household'. (It has been suggested that it might perhaps be more useful to identify the housewife, that is the person supervising the general housekeeping arrangements.) By selecting the 'core' individual in a household in this way, it is possible to distinguish stable units—the 'continuing households', and to forecast new ones—'emerging households'.

	Under 16	*16 or over*
Individuals over 60	—	1 (under 60)
Small adult households	—	2 (under 60)
Small families	1 or 2	1 or 2
Large families	3 or more	any number
or	2	3 or more
Larger adult households	none or 1	3 or more
Older small households	none	1 (60 or over)
or		2 (at least 1, 60 or over)

There is, of course, a degree of circular cause and effect involved, as one of the influences on household formation is the availability of housing.

To illustrate a straightforward and typical 'robust' approach to the forecasting of housing need, I shall outline the procedure followed in the Tyne-Wear Study, when an initial estimate of housing demand was required, based on a single figure population forecast, for traffic testing purposes. The analysis was carried out in two parts—first calculation of increases needed to the existing housing stock, secondly replacement needs due to obsolescence.[13]

There were three major steps involved in the calculation of additional houses needed in the Study Area by 1981:

how many people;
how many households;
how many new dwellings?

Since a target population total was given, the first question was answered. In order to deal with the second question, however, it was necessary to assess a population structure—so a breakdown into five year age and sex cohorts was made. The conversion of this population into a number of households was based on 'headship' rate analysis. The headship rates in 1966 were worked out from the Household Composition Tables of the Census—that is, the percentage of each age group who were either 'married couples', 'lone parent', 'one person' or 'other' households. These 1966 rates were then applied to the target date population and subsequently modified to take account of work done by the Ministry of Housing and Local Government on headship rates in the Northern Region.

The number of new dwellings needed was taken to be the difference between 'need' as established in the way described above, and the number of existing dwellings. The 1966 Census figures of dwellings were updated to the base date for the Study—1969—by allowing for known new building and demolitions. Two assumptions made were that the 1966 Census figure could be accepted as sufficiently accurate, and that an appropriate allowance for vacancies was 3% of the housing stock.

Thus, the shortfall between the assessed 1969 figure of dwellings and the estimated need in 1981 gave the number of new dwellings that would be required.

The second part of the calculation—housing replacements—took the first five years to 1973 as covered by known local authority programmes. Regarding the geographical distribution of efforts after that time, it was assumed that it would be in the same pattern as the incidence of old houses. (Age of houses was accepted as the best indicator of sub-standard conditions, quoting several recent studies as evidence on this matter.) The indicator used was pre-1914 housing stock that would be left in 1973. To determine what the total replacement programme would be in the Study Area between 1973 and 1981, a likely maximum and likely minimum assessment was made—relating largely to past performance. A medium rate was then selected for the purpose of the calculation.

A final stage in this work was to translate the composite estimate of housing requirements to 1981 into land needs. This assessment was based on two assumptions—that 'on site' replacement of housing in renewal areas would occur at 70% between 1969 and 1973 and 60% from 1973 to 1981; and that the average

270

gross density of new housing could be taken to be ten dwellings per acre.

Headship rate model

The Tyne-Wear Study process described above makes clear the crucial part in housing need calculations played by 'headship rates'. There is a Ministry of Housing and Local Government computer program which provides a headship rate model.[14]

The theoretical basis of the model is that the number of potential households (that is, families and other groups likely to want separate dwellings) is a function of the age, sex and marital status structure of the population, in that members of the population who differ in these characteristics have different headship rates expressing the probability of their being the head of a household. The expression of the theory is a matrix, in which the structural characteristics of the population provide the dimension of the matrix, and each combination of characteristics has a rate associated with it. The model is calibrated by using base period study area data to estimate projected headship rates for each population category, and the model is operated by substituting in the equation forecasts of the population in each category.

Four separate headship rates are calculated for four different kinds of potential household, and twenty four age/sex/marital status categories of population are defined, to which the headship rates are applied.

Apparently, the results of the model are particularly sensitive to inaccuracies in the forecasts of male deaths affecting the size of the older male population categories in which headship rates are very high. The following comment was made about headship rate analyses—'The fact that, using a formula of an almost ludicrous crudity, it is possible to make a reasonable estimate of the number of households formed . . . suggests that here is a phenomenon which is essentially orderly.'

The same writer says that if more attention had been paid to headship rates in the past, and particularly to changes in the time spans of the stages of the family cycle, much more about the housing situation could have been satisfactorily forecast. She does, however, continue 'It must be admitted that Needleman, and Beckerman *et al*, using headship rates, have not been conspicuously successful in their projections', but she ascribes this to a lack of sufficient attention to the processes at work as opposed to pure statistical projection.[15]

Once future households have been calculated, the next step involves the making of whole series of assumptions regarding *appropriate types* of dwellings. These assumptions have partly become institutionalised, either through legislation or 'planning principles'. In general, the land use planner has quite limited influence over new housing provision. He cannot control central government's financial policies to local authorities and the private sector, the actions of banks, mortgage companies, private builders and developers or even other officials in his own authority. He can exert some influence through development plans and development control, but he is far from being able (even if he had the knowledge) to lay down complete guidelines on sizes of dwelling, densities, building types, tenure and allocation of households to housing available. Nor can he control the treatment given to the existing housing stock. Perhaps his greatest influence is on location and density of new housing. Thus to summarise, the estimation of housing needs in a particular area involves the following elements:

1 Survey of existing resident population (either direct, or from already available sources)
2 Forecast of future resident population, in terms of households
3 Assessment of present and future requirements in terms of numbers of dwellings of different sizes, types, prices, facilities, tenure, location
4 Allocation of land for residential use, accordingly.

The calculation of housing need is also, of course, carried out at a national level. For example, to arrive at an estimate for the end of this century, in the 'Prospect for Housing' the following procedure was used—First, an initial assumption had to be made about the rate of population growth; the Registrar-General's calculations, which indicate a total population of 64·6 million for the year 2000 (since modified) were accepted. Secondly, this population total was converted into 'household need'—that is, 'the number of households in a given population that may be said to want separate housing', and, based on established trends, a need for 22·2 million dwellings was estimated.

Thirdly, an allowance had to be made for a vacancy reserve (for changes of occupancy, repairs and conversions and second homes). This brought the total estimate up to, say, 24 million homes needed.

Table 13.1.

Population and household need: 1970 to 2000

	1970	1980	1990	2000
Population	54.4	57.3	60.5	64.6
Private household population	53.5	56.2	59.5	63.5
Household need	18.3	19.5	20.7	22.2
Average household size (persons)	2.92	2.88	2.87	2.86

Household types: 1970 to 200

	1970 No.	%	1980 No.	%	1990 No.	%	2000 No.	%
Families Marriedcouple	13.3	73	14.1	72	15.1	73	16.0	72
Lone-parent	1.3	7	1.3	7	1.4	7	1.6	7
One-person	2.7	15	3.1	16	3.2	15	3.5	16
Other	1.0	5	1.0	5	1.0	5	1.1	5
	18.3	100	19.5	100	20.7	100	22.2	100

Household need related to vacancy rates: 1970 to 2000

	1970	1980	1990	2000
Household need	18.3	19.5	20.7	22.2
Vacancy rate	Number of dwellings required			
3.5%	18.9	20.2	21.4	23.0
4.0%	19.0	20.3	21.5	23.1
5.5%	19.3	20.6	21.8	23.4
7.0%	19.6	20.9	22.1	23.8
10%	20.1	21.5	22.8	24.4

SOURCE Buchanan & Partners, *The Prospect for Housing*, 1971

Fourthly, the factor of demolitions had to be allowed for, both for housing reasons (a high, but likely estimate was 7·4 million) and to accommodate other land uses (for which 1 million demolitions appeared likely).[16] (See Table 13.1.)

273

Assessment of existing housing stock

The assessment of existing housing stock—important on the 'supply' side of the housing balance—also poses considerable problems (see Figure 13.2). First, to take the relatively simple question of numbers, problems arise over definition of a 'dwelling', as discussed above. Thus, a house which has been converted into two or more dwellings, or is shared, may be deemed one or

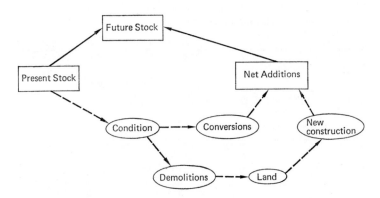

Fig. 13.2   Housing Stock—Present and Future

more dwellings according to the standards being applied. It is often difficult to obtain the facts needed without an elaborate survey. To illustrate, the extremely varied estimates of housholds which would be displaced and, therefore, need re-housing if the London motorway box were built, arose not only from differing assessments of tolerable noise and amenity levels, but also from lack of precise knowledge about the extent of sharing of the houses concerned.

Of course, the planner needs to assess the *quality* of the housing stock, as well as its quantity. For this, various standards of quality may be relevant. The lowest quality category, of course, is those dwellings declared unfit by the Public Health Inspector—the supposedly unambiguous slums. (Even with these, however, standards appear to vary from one place to another.) Above this level, standards may be based on the physical condition of the dwelling (structure and maintenance), existence of internal facilities and, more recently, the general standard of environment externally, including play space and parking. Another critical factor is the amount of space available to each individual and to each household which often hinges on the definition of a 'room'. These facts are not impossible to establish with time-consuming and expensive surveys, but a land use planner usually faces two problems:

1 defining appropriate standards, that is, *measures* of these various characteristics of housing
2 devising *short-cuts*, that will provide sufficient information about an area to provide a sound basis for policy, without total survey—for example, sample surveys, use of secondary sources of information or housing indices, or a combination of the three.[17]

The assessment of the structural condition and state of repair of a house is usually made by surveyors rather than planners. Ideas on internal facilities tended to stablise for a time, being those for personal hygiene and food storage and preparation. However, if the assessment of the housing stock is being undertaken as a basis for forward planning, it is necessary to consider future rather than present minimum acceptable facilities in a house. It is often said, for example, that present British standards for heating and storage are relatively low.

Studies have experimented with the use of several methods of appraising the number and quality of housing stock, to see how the results obtained with different indicators vary.[18] The Deeplish Study compared the separate use of age, condition, rateable value and value of house with a Composite Index.[19] Of course, a norm of a kind is provided by the recommended minimum standards for new building,[20] and by statutory building bye-laws and planning regulations. In general, if a single indicator of sub-standard housing is to be used, it is considered that the age of the property provides the best guide. More and more, it is emphasised that there are amenities external to the dwelling itself that are critical in providing satisfactory living standards—such as parking, play space and green areas—as well as convenient shops and schools. It is thus necessary to appraise *areas of housing* as well as individual dwellings.

Indeed, although a narrow interpretation of the functions of

275

land use planning might justify consideration of the physical characteristics of housing stock alone, a housing policy must be based on far wider considerations. This was emphasised in a report by SNAP (the Shelter Neighbourhood Action Project) in Liverpool, *A study in access.*[21] In 1971, Shelter workers in the Granby area of Liverpool could not understand the Corporation's decision to abandon the construction of 4100 houses because they had forecast a large surplus in housing stock, when many local families faced apparently intractable housing problems. On analysis they discovered that the so-called social indicators used in the survey (which are those used in many local authority housing surveys) tended to be heavily based in favour of physical characteristics. Such indicators do not in any way reflect the basic problem of the lack of access of various sectors of the population to any of the currently available housing.

I shall now describe three studies' approaches to the assessment of housing stock, using somewhat similar techniques of statistical analysis, but dealing with differing sizes of study area—one aimed to draw nationally valid conclusions, the second regional, and the third was concerned with part of central London.

The *Prospect for Housing* has already been referred to. A major element in the study was to develop a taxonomy for housing throughout the country that would make it possible to comprehend both the present characteristics of the national housing stock and likely future developments. The purpose of the study was defined in the report as 'to obtain an overall impression of the present housing situation, taking account of environmental conditions as well as dwelling characteristics. The conditions in question relate to such matters as parking facilities, the amount of private outdoor space, access to shared open space, proximity to industrial and commercial development, and the extent of traffic intrusion'[22]

The Northern and South East standard regions, which together embrace a wide range of housing conditions, were selected for analysis. The areas within those regions to be studied were selected as follows.

From a list of wards covered in the 1966 Census, a sample for all urban areas within the two regions was selected in two stages:

1 first all urban areas were stratified by population size, then the wards within each group were stratified by population size, and a sample of 450 wards was randomly selected, proportionate to the number of wards in each group

2 the sampled wards were then further stratified into five categories according to their distance from the centre of the local authority area and two wards were randomly selected from each group, making a total of 60 wards.

To these were added eight wards selected from the Tyneside conurbation and twelve from Greater London, giving 80 in all.

Each ED in the selected wards was studied, using 130 separate measures of population, households, dwelling and environment, gathered from the 1966 Census computer printouts, ordnance survey maps and local authority records (see Table 13.2). The analysis was carried out using 'factor analysis' and 'cluster analysis' to group the ED's into categories of similar types. (This technique is explained more fully in the Westminster example below.)

Table 13.2. *Measurement of Enumeration Districts* (after Buchanan)

Geographical:	Town size Distance to local centre Distance to regional centre
Population:	Institutional population Age distribution Mobility Birthplace of head of household Socio-economic group Economically active female population Car ownership Availability of amenities Household size Persons per room
Dwellings:	Age Condition Building type Tenure Occupancy
Environment:	Garage Parking facilities Persons per acre Dwellings per acre Private open space Land use Contiguous land use Road disturbance Railway disturbance

SOURCE 'Evaluation of housing stock and its environment', in *Journal of the Royal Town Planning Institute*, 1971

277

Table 13.3. *The Categories of Housing Areas* (after Buchanan)

Category	1	2	3	4	5
Category characteristics	Landscape	Semirural	Low-density urban	Private semi-detached	Public semi-detache
Population					
age		mainly under 45 / mainly over 45			
socio-economic group	managerial/ professional				semi/ unskille
birth place					
Household amenities					
size-number of persons	over 5 persons		2 persons		
persons per room			less than 0.5		1-15
car ownership	1–2 cars			1 car	no car
Housing					
type	detached			semi-detached	semi-detache
tenure	owner occupied			owner occupied	council rented
garden	spacious	large		medium	medium
persons per acre	−19	−39	−39	20–39	20–59
dwellings per acre	−9	−14	−14	10–14	10–19
Environment					
land use	open space/agricultural agricultural			residential	
road noise			some noise		
rail noise					
Type of Urban Area					
size	small-medium	small	large		
distance to regional centre		20–29 miles	over 30 miles		
Region				mainly in south	mainly north

(only those characteristics that tend to be determinants of the categories are indicated).

278

SOURCE 'Evaluation of housing stock and its environment', in *Journal of the Royal Town Planning Institute*, 1971

	7	8	9	10	11
)uter uburban erraced	Inner suburban terraced	Purpose-built flats	Central area terraced	Bedsitting room	Institutional
		mainly under 45			
	some common-wealth		some common-wealth	some common-wealth all amenities shared	
				1 person	
	1—over 15 (overcrowding)				
erraced	terraced	purpose-built flats rented unfurnished	terraced/ institutions		institutions
				rented furnished	
nall	small	none	some small, others none		
)—99	60 +	1100 +	60—99	60 +	
)—39	20 +	440 +	20—39	20 +	
			transport/ industrial /commercial		commercial
			very high very high		very high
conur-ation	in conur-bation				
	only in south		only in south	only in south	

An 11-cluster solution was finally accepted as nearest to reality and providing a satisfactory classification. Not every housing area will exhibit all the characteristics of its cluster, but the areas in one cluster will bear a closer resemblance to each other than to areas in the other categories (see Table 13.3).

To test the reliability of the method, detailed studies were made of one or two sample areas in each category. It was concluded from the study that this approach 'can provide basic information for future planning and policy decisions in much greater detail and on a much wider scale than was previously the case', and will enable the effect of imposing certain standards and the impact of various social changes on differing types of housing areas to be assessed'.[23]

The same firm of consultants took part in the Tyne-Wear Study, which incorporated a housing stock survey. Again, factor analysis was used for an overall survey with 97 variables considered. But in order to determine the local authorities' building programme requirements, older housing was specially assessed.

For pre-1914 housing, surveyors were required to make an assessment of the condition of a street block and were given detailed guide-lines to note either qualitative (e.g. good, fair, poor, bad), comparative (e.g. normal, above normal) or quantitative (e.g. percentage) measures of housing characteristics. The end product of this analysis was to be 'a penalty points' system—mentioned again in the final section of this chapter—which included both *environmental* and *dwelling* sections. The following measures were incorporated into the environmental section of the final scoring—landscape quality, traffic in street, external noise from traffic, non-conforming use and density, while the dwelling part was based on—external structure, external maintenance, front and rear space, off-street parking and house type, plus household hot water, fixed bath, inside WC. For the 'penalty points' calculations, each characteristic was given a quality grade from 0 to 6.

The other component of the housing stock considered as relevant to the local authorities' building programmes was inter-war housing, where the same basic approach was used, but with a different range of characteristics noted and then given a quality grading, namely:

280

maintenance of front garden/yard
size of front garden/yard
maintenance of back garden
size of back garden
long-term parking provision
short-term parking provision
house type
traffic flow
traffic parked in street
adjacent traffic noise
instrusive non-conforming uses
landscape quality
footpaths
derelict land
incidental open space
space between houses for garages
grass verges (and width)
old or disused buildings.

We will now discuss the Westminster Central Area housing study, and use this to explain more fully the mechanics of 'factor' and 'cluster' analysis.[24]

The spatial variations in the housing and related characteristics within the study area were examined, and described in the early part of the report, one by one. 'But many of the variables with which we are concerned are related to one another (e.g. we have seen that a high proportion of elderly household heads are at the lower end of the occupational status scale—that in the study area there is a significant association between age and occupational status)', the study explains, and therefore 'instead of characterising different parts of Westminster in terms of single variables (e.g. population density, or occupational status of residents), we can do so in terms of a composite measure which reflects a group of variables which are strongly associated with one another.'[25]

The statistical techniques used to do this in the study—factor analysis, and principal components analysis—permit the combination of a number of variables into a smaller number of groupings, called *components* which reveal the basic general patterns in the data. Each component reflects a group of variables which are strongly correlated (though it cannot be assumed that there is any causal relationship). The relative contribution of each variable to the overall component is shown by a *loading*, which is based on the statistical correlations between the variables. The loadings may be positive or negative, depending on the association —for example, a positive relationship between income and housing conditions, both increasing together, and a negative one between average income and the number of manual workers— and it is the variables with high loadings in either direction which are significant. Usually most of the total variance in the data will be accounted for by the first two or three components. The method becomes clearer with the following account of the results of the principal components analysis of 1966 Sample Census data for Westminster Wards.

The following table shows the 31 components used and their loadings on the first and second components which together account for 54% of the total variance in the data. The loadings between + and −0·4 are excluded as less significant:

Variables	Loading on Component I	Loading on Component II
1 % population under 15 years of age	0·72*	—
2 % women 20–24 currently married	0·45	—
3 % households with 5 or more members	0·45	—
4 % average number of persons per room	0·74*	0·53
5 % large households which are overcrowded	0·66*	—
6 % all private households of 2 or more members overcrowded	0·51	0·74*
7 % households sharing a dwelling	0·51	0·90*
8 % households sharing, without a stove or sink	0·51	—
9 % households sharing, lacking or sharing an inside WC	0·41	0·78*
10 % households with facilities for cooking, washing, etc.	—	—
11 % households sharing with no facilities	—	—

High loadings 0·6 and over, marked *

Variables	Loading on Component I	Loading on Component II
12 % households without a bath	0·59	—
13 % Local Authority tenant households	0·68*	—
14 % households renting private furnished	—	0·92*
15 % households renting private unfurnished	−0·54	—
16 % males in manual occupations	0·93*	—
17 % males in non-skilled manual occupations	0·76*	—
18 % females in manual occupations	0·78*	—
19 % females in non-skilled manual occupations	0·70*	−0·42
20 % total labour force in manual jobs	0·98*	—
21 % total labour force in non-skilled manual jobs	0·85*	—
22 % males with higher education qualifications	−0·86*	—
23 % females with higher education qualifications	−0·75*	—
24 % labour force in intermediate and junior non-manual jobs	−0·52	−0·41
25 % economically active persons who are women	−0·54	—
26 % labour force working full-time	−0·80*	—
27 % population born in India and other Asian Commonwealth countries	—	0·46
28 % population born in 'British' Africa	—	0·84*
29 % population born in 'British' Caribbean	0·60*	—
30 % population born in Ireland	0·59	—
31 % population not at same residence 1 year	−0·53	—
Percentage explained variance	37.0	17.0

High loadings 0·6 and over, marked *

The variables included in the analysis cover housing conditions and residential mobility as well as household composition and socio-economic characteristics of the population. 'The variables with a high and positive loading on Component 1 include those covering non-skilled and manual occupations, local authority tenure, large households, overcrowding and the proportions of the population born in Ireland or in the West Indies. In contrast the variables with a high but negative loading cover the proportions with higher educational qualifications, in privately rented unfurnished accommodation, those highly mobile (with less than one year in their current residence), and the proportions of the labour force in full-time employment, and of women in the labour force.' The study labels this component a social and economic index and it *explains* 37% of the total variance. The second component is partly an index of physical housing conditions, but the ward scores are difficult to interpret as quite different sets of relationships can be inferred from the data, largely because a ward is a rather coarse unit for this particular exercise.

Ward		*Score on* Component I	*Score on* Component II
1	Abbey	0·52	−1·04
2	Alderney	0·62	0·83
3	Aldwych	1·54	−1·12
4	Baker Street	−0·85	0·94
5	Berkeley	−0·94	−0·56
6	Cathedral	−1·00	0·02
7	Cavendish	−0·97	0·10
8	Churchill	0·74	−0·65
9	Church Street*	0·99	−0·84
10	Covent Garden	−0·34	−0·56
11	Dolphin	−0·99	1·59
12	Eaton	−0·91	−0·55
13	Ebury	1.13	−1·11
14	Grosvenor	−0·52	−0·96
15	Harrow Road †	2·61	1·68
16	Hyde Park*	−0·62	0·91
17	Knightsbridge*	−1·28	−0·71

Ward	Score on Component I	Score on Component II
18 Lancaster Gate †	−0·50	1·76
19 Lords †	−0·94	0·08
20 Maida Vale †	−0·93	0·66
21 Millbank	0·86	−0·85
22 Queen's Park †	1·69	−0·91
23 Regent's Park*	−0·77	−0·19
24 Regent Street	−0·66	−0·61
25 St. James	−0·45	−1·13
26 Soho	0·69	−0·01
27 Tachbrook	02·5	0·84
28 Victoria	0·43	−0·64
29 Warwick	−0·16	2·18
30 Westbourne †	1·70	1·39
31 Wilton	−1·00	−0·54

Twenty-one wards are wholly within the Central Area, four partly within (*), and six are wholly outside (†)

Despite its limitations, spatial contrasts indicating striking social polarity are revealed by the analysis, which provides a necessary framework for more detailed study of the extremely heterogeneous area.

Finally, in relation to analysis of housing stock, I would mention the questionnaire drawn up by Ines Newman for Community Action, for use by residents who wish to have their area declared a General Improvement Area. As well as the questionnaire itself, which has explanatory notes on why each piece of information is needed, she provides a check list for action in relation to GIA's and a clear guide to the writing of the report required by the 1969 Housing Act.

Production of housing policies and programmes

Having discussed separately above the analysis of housing needs and the assessment of housing stock, it is now important to consider how these are integrated to form a policy or programme for housing in an area. The Winchester Housing Needs Study provides a good illustration.[26]

The study was commissioned by the City Council in 1971 with two objectives—to provide a basis for policy formulation and to provide proposals for the monitoring of future needs. They were following the recommendation contained in 'Council Housing: Purposes, Procedures and Priorities', which stated 'Local authorities should take steps to ensure that they are better informed of the housing situation in their areas and the factors affecting it'.[27]

The study began with a general appraisal of Winchester and how it functions, and proceeded to more detailed analysis of what emerged as the key characteristics influencing the housing situation. The data inputs were provided by—a Household Survey, a study of Singly Occupied Dwellings, an analysis of the Private Property Market in Winchester to 1966–72, an Analysis of the Winchester Council Housing Waiting List, an Analysis of Winchester Council Tenants' Applications for Transfer, an Employment Survey, and a consideration of The Housing of Students.

It was agreed initially that the major relevant questions would include:

'a How many dwellings are required to meet current needs? Of what type should these be—in terms of tenure, cost, size and location?

'b How far does the current stock meet these needs? To the extent that there is a deficiency, how far can this be met by new building in the private and public sectors and by conversion and improvements in the existing stock?

'c What future changes in needs are ascertainable? What implications follow for housing policy?'

Regarding the first question, the conclusion reached was that it had two interpretations, either focusing on those already living in the City or else considering also those people who would some time move in. It was pointed out that housing requirements would largely depend on policy, but since the Council has only limited powers of control over housing, if a slow growth land use planning policy for Winchester is chosen, it could involve a continuing shortage of housing for local people. In this context, the role of Council housing—increasingly taking the place of the private rented sector—is crucial, for example, in catering for the elderly, the single and students, and also in providing low cost housing for owner occupation. But once a 'no-migration' assumption is relaxed, the question 'how many dwellings are required?' becomes incapable of mathematical answer. The estimate made of Winchester's housing need is shown in the following table:

Housing need 1971	Population	Dwellings
(a) 1971 Population	31 000	
(b) Subtract non-domestic population not requiring dwellings	2000	
(c) 1971 Population requiring dwellings	29 000	
(d) Dwellings required at 2·8 persons per dwelling		10 400
(e) Allow 3% for vacant dwellings		300
(f) Total dwellings required in 1971		10 700
(g) Number of dwellings: (a) 1966 Census: 9530 (b) Net increase 1966–71: 850 (c) Number of dwellings in 1971: (a) + (b)		10 380
(h) Shortage of dwellings 1971		320
Housing need by 1981 assuming no migration		
(i) Natural increase 1971–81	1000	
(j) Number of dwellings required for natural increase 1971–81 at 2·8 per persons per dwelling		360
(k) Number of additional dwellings need by 1981 to meet 1971 shortage and 1971–81 natural increase		680

Two recommendations of the study are highly pertinent to the above comments, the first was for a Housing Aid Service, a concept fully developed in the Seebohm Report,[28] and the second for a Monitoring System. It is suggested that the functions of the Housing Aid Service would include helping people (to register for a council house, to know what alternatives exist, how to get a mortgage, whether they are paying a reasonable rent, whether they can get an improvement grant or loan for conversion) and developing links with all agencies concerned with housing in the City.

This could also provide a valuable input to the Monitoring System, the elements of which are shown in the diagram opposite:

It is suggested that most of the information required is either already collected or easy to obtain, particularly if the Housing Aid Service existed but that the way information is presently collected and recorded would require adjustment so that it could be analysed. Stress is laid on the importance for policy development of a continuous flow of information and a method for its analysis so that special surveys are only occasionally necessary.

On the demand side, population is the key element, and changes need to be carefully documented. The Census and the Registrar General's Annual Estimates are the main sources, but additional information on incoming population can be gleaned from Electoral Registration records and from the Education and Health Departments. Information on employment can be obtained from the Employment Exchange and main employers.

On the supply side, information on housing is available in the rating list, from planning applications and from the Council's records of new building. The Monitoring System should aim to provide information 'which will show broadly what current trends are and where the major emphasis should be . . . unless all concerned are assured of the importance and relevance of the system, it is likely to fail'. The justification for the system is that 'Decisions of a political nature will still need to be made, but they will be better informed and, therefore, better designed to meet the problems of the City.'[29]

As the Winchester study points out, when housing is in short supply, it may be quite unrealistic to use a housing model that aims to assess demand for housing in isolation, with an implicit assumption that the demand can be met. In such a situation, it may even be more sensible to regard housing supply as the overall

288

limiting factor, and then forecast population and labour supply in relation to it.

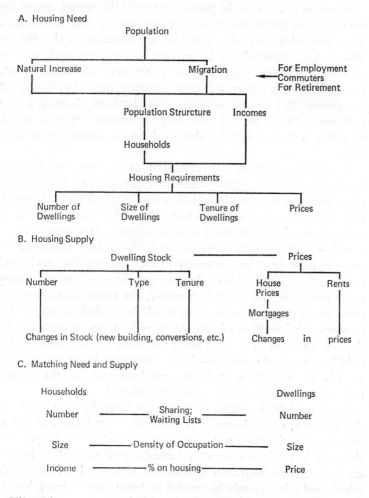

A. Housing Need

Population

Natural Increase — Migration ← For Employment / Commuters / For Retirement

Population Structure — Incomes

Households

Housing Requirements

Number of Dwellings | Size of Dwellings | Tenure of Dwellings | Prices

B. Housing Supply

Dwelling Stock ———— Prices

Number | Type | Tenure | House Prices | Rents

Mortgages

Changes in Stock (new building, conversions, etc.) | Changes in prices

C. Matching Need and Supply

Households | Dwellings

Number ———— Sharing; Waiting Lists ———— Number

Size ———— Density of Occupation ———— Size

Income ———— % on housing ———— Price

Figure. 11.3, page 204, shows in simplified form a model on such reasoning, developed at the GLC.[30] It can be used to establish, according to policy housing standards, hypothetical 'capacity' future populations, and hence work forces. By varying the policy assumptions, the consequences of them can be assessed—it is,

289

therefore, a type of sensitivity model. It may be used in conjunction with a demographic model, or they can be developed in relative separation and used to check each other's findings.

It will be noted that the particular model illustrated uses as the main unit of accommodation, a 'room' rather than a dwelling. Most critical among the variables are numbers and types of households, standards to be applied to housing stock and its existing condition, together with likely rates of improvement, conversion, demolition and new building, and the density of occupancy per room. Some of these are land use planning policy variables, others are independently determined factors, which planning policies must be designed to accommodate as they arise.

A similar approach was developed by land use planners working for the London Borough of Lewisham (see page 205). The relationships between housing, population and often also employment, form the basis of various models developed for land use planning, some of which are discussed in other chapters (see page 104).

A key question in housing policy is always how much investment to allocate to improvement of existing housing stock, and how much to new building. At one time this was viewed entirely as an economic question; fortunately, the much wider implications are now more often recognised. Nevertheless, the choice between rehabilitating or rebuilding older housing areas can be difficult to make. The need for guide-lines to decisions in this field has exercised model builders for some ten years, and various models incorporating different combinations of direct and indirect costs and returns have been produced.

Some models, for example those developed by Needleman in this country, or Rothenberg in the USA are primarily aimed at investigating the *investment* (that is resource allocation) aspects of this problem.[31] The costs of refurbishing or rebuilding houses are compared, taking into account the different levels of repair which will subsequently be needed and their respective values at the end of the time period considered. Although useful in showing the position in theoretical situations, it takes much modification to apply these models in practice. Early versions were not intended to be sensitive to the particular characteristics of any housing authority or area, and the variety of costs involved and the difficulty of obtaining realistic figures also complicate applications of the models.

The Department of the Environment some time ago issued guide-lines to local authorities, to indicate when rehabilitation should be considered. These relate the length of useful life to be expected from improved houses, and the standard that can be achieved to the costs which would be incurred. Considerable experience has now, of course, built up on rehabilitation of houses, improvements and environmental recovery areas, and the costs encountered.[32]

In the Leicester and Leicestershire Sub-regional Study, a model was developed to assess the feasibility of improvement to the housing stock throughout the study area.[33] It was a regression model based on the hypothesis that the average condition of housing stock is a function of the average age of that stock and of the average income level of the residential population.

Expressed as an equation, this was:

$$IMP = a + b\,AGE + c\,PCY$$

where IMP = zonal mean house improvement cost
AGE = zonal mean age of house
PCY = zonal mean per capita income
a, b, c = regression constants

and all the variables have forecast year $(t + n)$ values.

The model was calibrated with base year data for all one kilometre square zones in the sub-region, with more than 400 dwellings (separate calibration being carried out for the areas of Leicester City and Leicester County) to estimate the values of the constants, and for prediction values for the independent variables in the forecast year were inserted.

The output was the mean house improvement cost for each zone for each forecast year. It equalled the cost at constant prices of remedying a specified range of deficiences in structure, facilities and environment, and where it exceeded a predetermined amount dwellings were considered suitable for demolition.

A more satisfactory approach, which is not so dominantly financial, is the use of a form of cost-benefit analysis to compare new building with rehabilitation.[34] It is possible with such techniques to allow not only for relative standards of housing and costs in money terms, but also for intangibles such as disturbance to tenants, uprooting of communities, affection for existing architecture and so forth.

In the Tyne-Wear Study, already referred to above, a constrained cost-effectiveness method was developed 'to determine a "mix" of housing clearance, replacement and different degrees of rehabilitation which gives the best economic return for resources invested, which meets defined social needs, and is feasible in every future year in terms of constraints of available finance and physical limitations on the number of dwellings that can be cleared and replaced, or rehabilitated'.

The following assumptions were made:

1   That housing stock is divided into a number of 'clusters' of similar housing types; each ED is assigned to the most appropriate cluster.
2   To each cluster is assigned
    a an average standard of accommodation, defined in terms of 'deficiency points'
    b A cost of clearance and replacement at prevailing standards
    c A cost for varying standards of rehabilitation
    d An expected life (with or without rehabilitation) before clearance becomes essential to provide a minimum standard of accommodation.
3   Clearance is desirable when either clearance or rehabilitation is possible, but rehabilitation is more economic.

(Some aspects of this were discussed above in the section on assessment of housing stock, see page 269.)

The procedure consists of a series of steps, which are repeated until a satisfactory solution is reached. The preliminary is to establish for each year the number of buildings that must be cleared immediately and the number that need no attention at all. Once the budget is defined, that will establish the clearance/rebuilding capacity that remains in each year. Then, starting in the first year, the economically 'best' policy is defined for each cluster. If, in the first year, this 'best' solution exceeds the expenditure constraint, a switch to a cheaper policy is made first in the cluster where this will yield the largest reduction. Further reductions must be made in other clusters until the expenditure constraint is met. If the clearance constraint is exceeded, then reallocations must be made in favour of rehabilitation.

Next the housing stock is updated for all future years as a consequence of the policies selected for the first year, and the steps have to be repeated for each future year. It may be necessary to revise the early years of the programme if it is discovered in later years that it is impossible to avoid exceeding the constraints.

The process is continued until a programme is found that does not isolate the constraints for any year.

Of course, in operation, this procedure is expressed algebraically and the great number of calculations required are carried out mechanically.

Allocation of housing

I have, I hope, made clear throughout this chapter that housing must be seen for policy purposes as a much more complex matter than physical dwellings. A crucial element to the success or failure of housing policies is the 'fit' achieved between household and house.

For local authority housing, criteria are always used for the allocation of the housing stock although the land use planner is not normally involved in this.

A scheme for integrating housing allocation with the overall policies and duties of a housing authority is shown in Figure 13.3, based on work done for a group of Scottish 'new towns'.[35] It brings together the research and land use planning, the design and building and the allocation and letting aspects of a housing authority's work. There are three components illustrated here:

1 The overall model
2 The sub-model to determine the building programme
3 The sub-model to allocate dwellings.

It is quite crucial, if people are ever to be decently housed, that the *allocation* of dwellings to households is recognised for the decisive act it is. Many of the supposed failures of land use planning in relation to public housing stem rather from the narrow criteria used to select and then to match prospective

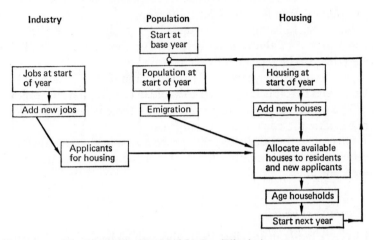

New Town Housing Model
(part of the overall housing / industry / population simulation)

Fig. 13.3   New Town Housing Model (after Pilgrim)

SOURCE   'Choice of House in a New Town', in *Regional Studies*, 1969

tenants and housing stock. Like many other problems of distribution, the allocation of housing lends itself well to handling by operations research methods, notably linear and dynamic programming.

References

1 Nevitt, A. A., *Fair Deal for Householders,* Fabian Society (1971).
2 See Nevitt, *op. cit.* (1) above.
3 Edwards, J. & Simpson D., *A Study in Access,* SNAP, Liverpool, Shelter (1972).
4 See Nevitt, *op. cit.* (1) above.
5 Buchanan, C. & Partners, *The Prospect for Housing,* A Study for the Nationwide Building Society (1971).
6 See Buchanan, *op. cit.* (5) above.
7 See Nevitt, *op. cit.* (1) above.
8 For example,
Greve, J. *et al., Homelessness in London,* Scottish Academic Press (1971).

9 See Nevitt, *op. cit.* (1) above.

10 Cullingworth, J. B., 'Housing Analysis', in *Regional and Urban Studies: A Social Science Approach,* edited by Orr and Cullingworth, Allen and Unwin (1969).

11 Angell, E., 'Housing Aspects', in *The Census of Population as a source of Information for Local Authority Planning Departments,* GLC Research and Intelligence Unit, Occasional Paper 2, page 12, November 1969.

12 Mainly at the Centre for Urban Studies, London; for example, Glass, R. & Davidson F. G., 'Household structure and housing need', in *Population Studies,* 4 (1950–1); also, Glass, R. & Westergaard J., *London's Housing Needs* (1965).

13 Working Paper 15, Housing Survey and Residential Needs, prepared for the *Tyne/Wear Plan (a land use/transportation survey),* by Voorhees and Buchanan (1970).

14 See Ministry of Housing and Local Government, *Population and Households, No. 1, Projecting Growth Patterns in Regions* HMSO (1970); also, Statistics for Town and County Planning, Series 3, *The Projection of Households;* Walkden, A. H., 'The estimation of future numbers of private households in England and Wales', in *Population Studies,* 15, November, 1961; Holmans, A. E., 'A forecast of effective demand for housing in Great Britain in the 1970's', in *Social Trends,* page 42, 1 (1970).

15 Hole, W. V. & Pountney M. T., *Trends in Population, Housing and Occupancy Rates, 1861–1961;* Building Research Station, HMSO (1971).

16 See Buchanan, *op. cit.* (5) above.

17 GLC Research and Intelligence Unit, *Ward Indices,* Occasional Paper 3 (1970); also PTRC, *Seminar on Housing Models,* London (1970).

18 Duncan, T. L. C., *Measuring Housing Quality: A Study of Methods,* Centre for Urban and Regional Studies, Occasional Paper 20, University of Birmingham (1971).

19 Ministry of Housing and Local Government, Joint Urban Planning Group, *Prospect of Renewal: Social Survey of Deeplish,* HMSO (1965).

20 For example, in the Parker Morris Report, *Homes for Today and Tomorrow,* HMSO (1961).

21 SNAP, *op. cit.* (3) above.

22 See Buchanan, *op. cit.* (5) above.

23 See Buchanan, *op. cit.* (5) above.
24 Williams, T., Anderson, J. & Goddard, J. *Central Area Housing Study*, City of Westminster Development Plan Research Report R1, July 1972.
25 *Op. cit.*, (24) above, page 33.
26 *Winchester Housing Needs Study 1971–2, Report,* Research Memorandum 13, Centre for Urban and Regional Studies, University of Birmingham, June 1972.
27 Central Housing Advisory Committee, *Council Housing: Purposes, Procedures and Priorities,* HMSO (1969).
28 *Report by the Committee on Local Authority and Allied Personal Social Services,* Cmnd. 3703 (1968).
29 See Winchester Study, *op. cit.* (26) above.
30 Described by Grigson, GLC Planning Department, at a Housing Seminar (1969).
31 Needleman, L., in, for example, *The Economics of Housing,* Staples Press (1965);
Rothenberg, J., in *Benefit–Cost Applications in Urban Renewal: A Feasibility Study,* by Rothenberg *et. al.,* Resource Management Corporation Report, prepared for US Department of Housing and Urban Development (1968).
32 See Ashworth, G., 'Environmental recovery at Skelmersdale', in *Town Planning Review,* page 263, **41,** July 1971.
Fleming, J., 'The central areas of our towns and cities— recondition or renew?' in *Housing,* page 8, **6,** January 1971;
Spencer, K. M., 'Older urban areas and housing improvement policies', in *Town Planning Review,* page 250, **41,** July 1970.
33 *Leicester and Leicestershire Sub-regional Planning Study,* **2,** Chapter 3, (1969).
34 For example, Lichfield, N., *Study on Skelmersdale.*
35 By the Local Government Operations Research Unit, see Pilgrim, B., 'Choice of house in a new town', in *Regional Studies,* page 325, **3** (1969).

14 Shopping

Introduction

Shops have a particular importance: as well as being the crucial link point in the sophisticated barter mechanism of our society by which labour is exchanged for goods, they also provide one of the main day to day reasons for people to meet each other.

Shops are thus a part of the social patterns of the community as well as the economic. This social function obtains whether one is discussing the all-purpose village shop, a large and complex city centre in which many other activities apart from shopping take place, or a hypermarket located on the edges of town.

In assessing existing shopping provision, and making estimates of future needs and ways of meeting them, land use planners are subject to several influences:

1 the *economic* hard facts about the profitability of shops in any location, which ultimately sets the limits of what is possible
2 the *social* function of shopping, either on its own, or as a complement to other 'town centre' activities, which may sometimes tempt planners to delude themselves about economic realities
3 the *value* of shopping and ancillary commercial uses as a rateable asset—this may suggest provision in one authority's area that is excessive when viewed in a wider context.

Land use planners' responsibilities toward shopping provision are discharged through the general mechanisms governing the use of land—the positive mechanism of making land available and the potentially negative mechanism of development control powers. In addition, land use planners may play a more active part by encouraging local authorities or private developers or a combination of public and private initiative to redevelop existing centres or build new shops.

More perhaps than with any other type of land use there is a temptation to boost the prosperity of one particular area by building shops, to the detriment of surrounding areas. An ambitious shopping development in one town or part of a city may succeed, but at the expense of run-down in older neighbourhood centres. It is vital, therefore, that some co-ordination of shopping provision is exercised over appropriate larger areas.

For the reasons suggested above, and also, no doubt, because of all the all-pervading philosophy of 'more is more', the tendency of planners, and notably of consultants, has been to recommend over-provision. Also, because the nature of shopping has been changing rapidly and somewhat unpredictably in recent years.

However, let it be said that it is easier with shopping than with many other forms of land use to gauge whether the planner has been right or not in his recommendations. Overprovision or poor location of shops leads to frequent changes of tenant, lower shop rentals, vacant shops. Underprovision is indicated if people are involved in long and difficult journeys and if shops are crowded.

This chapter can only refer to the very crucial matter of changing shopping habits—to self-service stores, to a polarisation of specialist shops and highly efficient but impersonal supermarkets, to cash and carry and other forms of discount shopping, to mail order business, to one-stop hypermarkets, to specialisation of shopping centres within a city, and so on—and the changes in consumer habits and demands that are generating these, including higher average disposable incomes, increasing car ownership and usage, and more teenage spending power. The excellent report of the NEDO Retailing Group—*The Future Pattern of Retailing*—has helped to give some factual substance to many of these previously rather vaguely defined factors, and at least points to the most likely futures for shopping.

The land use planner, therefore, has to seek the *dynamics* of the activity under study—in this case, retailing—and not be content with some grasp of the manifestation of the dynamics at one point in time. As Oliver Marriott demonstrated amply, by taking too superficial a view of the changes in shopping habits, and assuming that past trends are a perfect guide to future economic and social realities, mistakes may be made that are costly and with us for a long time.[1]

Purpose of studies

Before describing the methods planners have adopted to assist them in their work on shopping, let us list some of the questions about shopping to which the land use planner needs to seek answers.

The first group relate to *existing shopping provision* and include:

What is the existing pattern of shopping provision in the area— what is the total number of shop units and the square footage in different categories (for example, grocers, confectioners, furniture stores, and so on)?
How much of the area is sales space and how much storage or preparation area?
What different types of management are the shops under, such as independent, chain store, co-operative?
What are the prevailing rents and apparent profitability in different parts of the shopping centre?
What employment is generated by the shops, what transport needs and what requirements for waste collection? Are all these needs adequately met?

The second group of questions focus on *Existing usage of shops* :

What are the existing patterns of usage of shops in the area?
Are as many as possible of the types of shop a consumer needs available?
Are the shops themselves overcrowded?
Are the facilities for walking, parking and public transport adequate?

The third group of questions relate to *Scope for improvement* :

What is the scope for future improvement? Could the shopping area be improved by any degree of rebuilding or extension?

To what use is the surrounding land put at present?

Could the centre be improved by traffic management or alteration of transport facilities?

Are there any activities other than shopping which should be encouraged?

The final group are concerned with *Future provisions*:

What should the future provision be at macro-level—that is, throughout the city or sub-region?

What are the future household patterns and disposable incomes going to be in the area?

What is the expected car ownership and public transport provision?

If an overall increase in shopping floor-space is deemed appropriate, where should it be encouraged to take place?

Would any new development be better undertaken by the public authority, by private investors or some partnership of the two?

What physical form should the development take, and should it be combined with recreation and welfare facilities?

In essence, these questions concerning future provision are the familiar four—How much? Where? When? How?

Answering the questions

Information relating to *existing* shopping provision and usage can be obtained by the land use planner in part from published information (notably the Census of Distribution), and in part from specially conducted surveys incorporating observation of land use and questions to shoppers and shop-keepers about how satisfactory the shops and shopping areas are deemed to be. *Future* improvement or addition provision involves forecasting, and it is on this aspect of shopping that I will concentrate first; particularly on predictive models. Although they have acknowledged limitations, several types of shopping model have been developed to the extent that they are operational, and have been used to assist decisions by planners, retailers and developers. In fact, models have probably become an accepted tool of study for shopping to a degree that is exceeded in planning only by transport. For a critique of the application of models in shopping

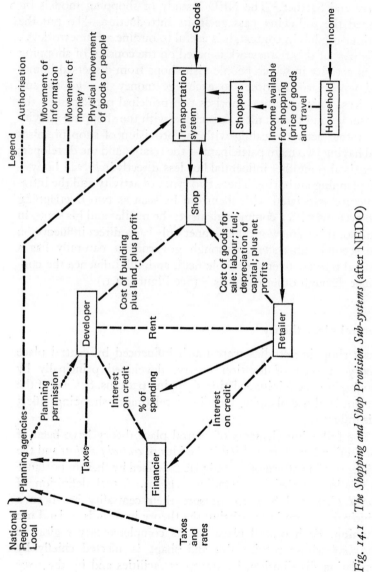

Fig. 14.1 The Shopping and Shop Provision Sub-systems (after NEDO)

SOURCE Urban models in shopping studies, 1970

Legend

•••••••• Authorisation

———— Movement of information

–––– Movement of money

━━━ Physical movement of goods or people

301

studies, which suggestes there is often quite fundamental lack of understanding of models, the reader is referred to an article by Batty and Saether.[2] The NEDO study of shopping models included the following passage in its introduction—'To put the various models in context, it is useful to outline a framework . . . One part of this framework is based on the concept of shopping as an activity in which people visit shops from dispersed homes and workplaces in order to exchange money for goods and services. This activity comprises two principal participants—the consumer and the retailer. Associated with the shopping activity is another activity dealing with the provision of shop premises and having two main participants—the retailer and the developer; there is also another influential but less directly involved body— the planning authority. These two types of activity and the infrastructure associated with them can be seen as two overlapping sub-systems with a common element: the retailer and his shop. In terms of this framework the planner only has a direct influence on the second sub-system, although government naturally has a general interest over the whole field, and will influence the consumer through other channels.'[3] (See Figure 14.1.)

Central place theory

Early shopping studies were much influenced by central place theory—a type of location theory, developed principally by geographers examining existing shopping patterns. Several of the current land use planning techniques relating to shopping reflect this influence.[4]

The following elements of central place theory have been of continuing importance. First is the idea of *central functions* and the existence of a pattern of central places defined by their importance in relation to their surrounding regions. Actual definition of *central places* and how to measure their centrality has been a principal concern in translating the theory into tools cf land use planning. Each central place has its complementary region or *hinterland* whose precise size and shape is affected chiefly by population distribution, by transport facilities and by the *range* of goods and services the centre provides.

302

Ideally, each consumer seeks maximum freedom of choice for his purchases together with minimum expenditure—of time, effort and money. The aggregate behaviour of many consumers, therefore, has a framework of maximum distances people are willing to travel for particular types of goods and services—thus defining the range—and minimum numbers of shoppers required to provide a sufficient market for any particular type of goods—which is the *threshold* population size. These bounding constraints have been incorporated into shopping models.

Finally, central place theory provided the concept of a *hierarchy* of central places, each with its own hinterland, in which the lower order centres provided only highly dispersed central services, and were themselves within the hinterlands of higher order centres.

In the theoretical development of these ideas von Thunen, Lösch and Christaller are outstanding[5]; and in early practical applications Smailes, Brush, Bracey, Carruthers, Thorpe and Rhodes, Berry and Garrison and many others.[6]

Some comments on the validity of central place theory in present conditions are given towards the end of this chapter (see page 319).

A model framework

The process of setting up a practical model from the elements of central place theory involves four important steps—
1 identification of a hierarchy of trade centres
2 delineation of the trade areas of each centre
3 description of retail sales within each trade area
4 prediction of sales or shopping floor space for a projected period (see Figure 14.2).

1 Identification of hierarchy

Classification of shopping centres in an area into a hierarchy must be based upon some index of size and/or function. Since 1961, the basic information source has been the Census of Distribution, which provides data on total sales, retail employment and numbers of establishments for all local authorities. Sales figures, broken down by a commodity classification, are given for towns and are available for rural districts. Based on the 1961 Census, classifications of shopping centres in England and Wales have been produced by Carruthers and by Thorpe.[7] Before 1961, the classification of centres by sales was not possible and, therefore, depended on functional characteristics only, such as shops of a certain type, banks, cinemas, bus services, rateable values and so on.[8]

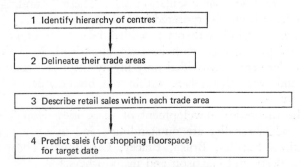

Fig. 14.2   A Model Based on Central Place Theory

2 Definition of trade areas

A variety of techniques has been used to delimit the hinterlands of centres, including surveys of consumers, study of bus routes and traffic patterns, and subjective judgement. Alternatively, a gravity model has often been used. More recently, probabilistic estimates of the proportions of total spending taking place in different centres have been made rather than an assumption of rigid catchment areas.

3 Description of sales

The next step is to attempt to find a formula which can describe the known pattern of sales in the area (as given in the 1961 Census, for example) by relating population and average per capita expenditure within the defined trade areas.

4 Prediction

Once a sufficiently satisfactory descriptive equation has been produced it may be used for prediction by substituting known or anticipated changes in population and income. Any planned alterations to transport facilities or to the pattern of shopping centres must, of course, be taken into account. The disadvantages of this approach are that it is based on *retrospective* relationships and is a *static* model. Thus it is now usual to find it used in a considerably modified form, or elements of it incorporated into other models. Examples of two specific recently developed shopping models will now be given.

Gravity model

The gravity principle has been applied to several aspects of planners' work, including studies of shopping. The example of the application of a gravity model to the prediction of shopping requirements which is outlined here was an early method developed by a Study Group of the West Midlands Branch of the Town Planning Institute.[9] Several aspects of the approach might now be handled differently, but the process is clearly explained and easy to follow. Like other planning gravity models, it builds on the 'law' of retail gravitation as formulated by Reilly, which states that—'Two cities attract retail trade from any intermediate city or town in direct proportion to the populations of the two cities and in inverse proportion to the square of the distances from these two cities to the intermediate town.'[10] Reilly based this 'law' on empirical study of American urban areas in the 1920's and early 1930's.

The West Midlands study area included 111 competing shopping centres and was divided for the purposes of the model into almost 300 population zones comprising sub-divisions of local authority areas. The shopping centres on the immediate edge of the study area were included and allowance was made for some trade to West Midland centres originating outside the area.

Information on distances shoppers travel and frequency of visits to different centres was obtained from a field survey.

An important distinction was made between accessibility trade and attraction trade. The *accessibility* trade of a centre consists largely of those goods purchased regularly by a household (often called convenience goods) and was taken to be a function of the centre's accessibility to resident population subject to limitations imposed by the centre's own 'competitive level'. This competitive level was defined by the variety of shop types present in a centre. The *attraction* trade of a centre (consisting principally of durable goods and such relatively infrequent and important purchases of a household) was considered to be dependent on the centre's accessibility and on its attraction, which thus had to be measured in some way for the model. Generalised travel times from population zones to shopping centres were based on the proportion of car owners, the public transport services and estimated travel times on the road network to produce generalised *mean travel times*. The zonal accessibility trade expenditure and attraction trade expenditure were estimated by multiplying the forecast zonal population by a forecast mean per capita retail expenditure, split between the two types of trade, after any necessary deduction for expenditure in centres outside the model area.

The model was calibrated (that is, mathematically adjusted, until deemed sufficiently accurate) with data for 1964, and was then used to produce results for 1961 (*sic*) as a test of its accuracy. The output of the model was the total retail turnover in each shopping centre for the forecast year (see Figure 14.3).

The use of the model thus involved the following component decisions and calculations:

1 Definition of study area.
2 Division of study area into population zones.
3 Forecasting population totals for the target year and combining these with estimates of spending to obtain the total spending generated by each population zone.
4 Differentiation of two types of shopping spending—accessibility and attraction—and assessment of the proportion of total shopping spending going to each.
5 Application of these proportions to zonal spending totals to obtain zonal accessibility spending and zonal attraction spending.
6 Identification of all shopping centres within the study area and immediately adjacent.
7 Calculation of travel times from each population zone to each shopping centre.

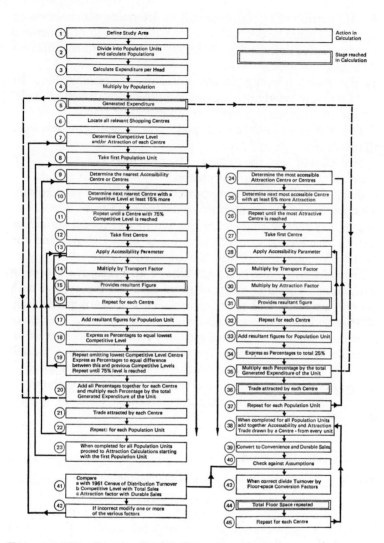

Fig. 14.3 Flow Diagram for Calculating Shopping Turnover and Floor Space

SOURCE   West Midlands Branch TPI, Predicting shopping requirements, 1967

8 Application of a gravity formula to determine which shopping centres could be deemed to serve which population zones and the relative accessibility of the various centres to the different zones.

9 For each shopping centre, decisions concerning both its 'attraction' relative to all other centres for 'attraction trade' and its 'competitive level' for 'accessibility' trade.

Thus the *key elements* of older predictive shopping models were all involved:

—definition of relevant trading areas of centres
—estimation of attraction of centres
—calculation of the spending power of the relevant population
—estimation of the significance of distance and travel times.

The way these elements are handled in this model should be compared with the central place theory model above, and the gravity potential model, which is outlined below.

I should point out here that almost all predictive shopping models incorporate elements of more than one theory, but with varying emphasis and modifications. This makes it particularly difficult to label any practical model unambiguously. The reader may thus find the same study cited by different writers as an example of more than one type of forecasting shopping model. I should also mention the use of the term 'step by step approach' for practical procedures for forecasting shopping requirements, which may well include elements of central place or gravity theory.[11]

Gravity potential model

An example of a retail potential model incorporating a modified gravity formula is Part 2 of the Haydock Park Study.[12] The model does not begin by dividing the area of study into shopping hinterlands (as in central place theory) but assumes that money is drawn from all parts of the region to each and every centre. The model concentrates on durable goods sales which represent the greater part of the turnover of all but local shopping centres.

It is postulated in the model that four factors are critical to the durable sales potential of a centre—its size, the number of people to whom it is accessible, how prosperous they are, and what competing shopping facilities exist. The area of north-west England covered by the study included 47 shopping centres and was divided into some 240 zones based on local authority areas. The object of the study was to investigate the impact of the introduction into the area of a new centre at Haydock Park. The model was calibrated by finding the values for the constants in the equation that gave the best results, using data for the base year 1961, for which Census of Distribution information was available. The formula used was:

$$SAL_j = \sum_{i=1}^{m} RSP_i \frac{\dfrac{APO_j^b}{TT_{ij}^a}}{\displaystyle\sum_{k=1}^{n} \dfrac{APO\,K^b}{TT_{ik}^a}}$$

where SAL_j = durable sales in centre j

RSP_i = retail spending in zone i

APO_j = size or attractive power of centre j

TT_{ij} = interzonal travel time between zone i and centre j

TT_{ik} = interzonal travel time between zone i and zone k

m = total number of zones of spending power

n = total number of centres

a, b = exponential constants

and all variables have forecast year $(t + n)$ values

The shopping centre attractive power was measured indirectly by an index:

$$F = 2V + 3D + C + M$$

in which V = total variety shops

D = total department stores

C = total chain stores

M = total markets

which proved to give the best results of various possible measures assessed. For the projection year, 1971, adjustments were made to the attractive power of different centres in the light of known

309

planned changes. Similarly, allowances were made for improvements in the travel times from zone centroids to shopping centres.

The sales for each shopping centre in 1971 were then derived by distributing the forecast retail expenditure for that year between the centres. The model thus assumes that the relationships expressed in the model can be regarded as persisting over a ten-year period.

The Haydock model is, in fact, a version of the retail potential model first developed in Baltimore by Lakshmanan and Hansen,[13] which has been widely used in a number of forms, with variations particularly in the measures of shopping centre attraction and the distance factor.[14]

Other approaches to shopping models

Comprehensive models, incorporating retail components

In 1964 a form of retail interaction was used as part of the comprehensive model developed for the city region of Pittsburgh by Lowry.[15] The total population and distribution of basic industry were assumed to be given exogenously, and the model generated estimated of residential population, retail employment and land use for one-mile grid squares using gravity interactions in successive iterations, proceeding towards an equilibrium solution. As discussed elsewhere, this model has now been adapted for use in various planning studies, including several in this country.[16]

Intervening opportunity

A concept which is used a great deal in journey-to-work studies has also been employed in shopping models—that is Stouffer's theory of *intervening opportunity*.[17] Harris adapted this theory into a retail location model for the Penn-Jersey Study in 1964.[18] The model postulated that the number of shopping trips (or sales) from an origin to a destination (shopping centre) is proportional to the number of intervening opportunities. Unlike gravity formulations, interzonal distance does not appear. Instead the number of possible destinations are ranked in order of increasing impedance from an origin to provide an 'absorption' model. Harris also incorporated in the model specific provision for variation in the demand exerted by different socio-economic classes of the population. The intervening opportunities model has since been developed and used in other shopping studies.

Entropy

Wilson has suggested that a shopping model could appropriately be based on the principle of *maximum entropy*, in which the probability of a particular shopping trip occurring depends on the number and distribution of points of origin, that is—shoppers, and points of destination, that is—shopping centres.[19]

Individual consumer behaviour models

All the models described above look at population behaviour in the aggregate.

Bacon has suggested the use of a model of individual consumer behaviour, which can incorporate the real world influences on the individual and show what the likely shopping pattern would be.[20] He describes his, at present very simplified, approach thus:

'The model deals with a situation where the consumer may have a large number of different goods to purchase and a large number of shopping centres where these goods can be bought. Not every centre sells all goods and the consumer, in a rational world where the only relevant factor is the distance to any shopping centre, will minimise the total costs of shopping'. Bacon's analysis begins with 'the basic feasible solution', which allocates the purchase of each of the goods to the nearest centre to home which sells that good. He then makes two essential adjustments—for 'external economies', where trips to nearer centres are eliminated if they can be phased with essential trips to further centres, and for 'joint economies' where trips are preferred to centres offering more than one of the required goods. Even from this simple model, a few interesting observations can be made. First, even in a model which assumes no price differentials between shopping centres, goods need not be bought at the nearest shop which sells them, since *external* economies or *joint* economies are achievable.

Secondly, the 'local' shop—defined as that which sells goods frequently purchased—may lose trade to centres which are more distant but which sell both the same goods and others giving rise to external economies.

Thirdly, if shoppers change their frequency of shopping over time then the places that they use may also change, since foodstuff shopping—the staple of local shops—will be bought on trips to the larger centres where external economies are available.

Fourthly, it can be seen that those shops which are most numerous will not all be equally successful, since those locating on their own will merely attract local trade, whereas those locating in centres with other types of shops will attract local trade and trade generated by external economies. 'Thus even in a plain with purchasing power spread evenly over the plain and all shoppers having identical shopping patterns it would seem that shops selling identical goods will have different turnover. This is a function of the existence of several goods and sharply distinguishes this model from those of the one good case where shops would sell the same amounts when they had located optimally.'[21]

There are thus interesting aspects to shopping behaviour suggested by this model, which Bacon indicated he hoped to explore further.

Any micro approach to shopping models would benefit a great deal from more information on the details of shoppers' habits. In recognition of this need, the Building Research Station recently conducted a detailed survey of women shoppers in Watford.[22]

Rent models

Another approach to shopping models has been developed by urban economists who have produced models representing the relationship between land use, location and rent.[23] Although such models based on classical price and rent theory have as yet only limited usefulness in dealing with broader land use planning issues, the analytical framework they provide is helpful in exploring the inter relationships of such variables as quantities of land available for shopping use and its location, turnover and profit margins, and operating costs and rents.

The comment on rent models in a recent assessment was as follows—'In practice, these methods are primarily concerned with the assessment of shop rents and the valuation of land. The approach is informal and relies very much on a personal judgement of the situation. Official statistics are relatively unimportant and much of the information used is quantitative, and a great variety of sources may be tapped. A survey of the existing property in the shopping centre is usually the major basis for judgement, but this is supported by data on recent activity in the property market together with the expressed intentions of retailers interested in new shops. A knowledge of the cost structure of different types of trader is also very useful.'[24] Although such pragmatic methods may be denigrated by believers in more systematic analysis, they are the stock in trade of the majority of firms providing commercial advice on shopping developments.

Floorspace needs

In general, the final output of shopping studies is needed by a land use planner in terms of floor space, not sales. Thus it is necessary, as a last stage in shopping prediction calculations, to convert sales figures into the amounts of floor space required.[25]

This is usually done in two stages.

The first stage is to *disaggregate total retail sales* into sales of different types of goods and services (already done in some types of predictive model). This has to be based on observations of expenditure patterns, as, for example, in the Family Expenditure Survey, or as derived from specially collected data (such as the Building Research Station's Survey, mentioned above), which may give more reliable detail of geographical and income variations peculiar to the study in question. Such patterns of expenditure must, of course, be adjusted to allow for anticipated changes in the future.

The second stage is to apply factors of *turnover* per square foot of shopping space to the anticipated spending in each shopping category to convert the sales figures to square footage of retail floorspace (see Figure 14.4). Normally, this conversion gives actual *selling* space, and an additional proportion of space is allowed for storage and preparation area. A further assessment must then be made of the servicing and access needs of the shopping area to provide an overall acreage allocation required for the additional shops (obviously some preliminary assumptions on layout and design are required at this point).

Sales per gross sq ft per annum at 1961 prices

Trade category	1' 1962	2 1968	3 1970 (1980)	4 1971 (1981)	5 1971 (1981)	6 1971	7 1981	8 1981
Food			35 (39)			33 (40)		
Grocers	32	40						
Other food	30	35						
Confectionery & tobacco	26	22	30 (34)					
Convenience goods				34 (41)	31 (34)			35
Non-food					20 (27)	33		
Durable goods				25 (29)	26 (28)			35
Clothing & Footwear	25	20	25 (31)					
Household	20		20 (24)					
Other non-food	20							
General stores	30							
Pharmaceutical			30					
Hardware			15					
Furniture			12					

1   D Diamond and J P Gibb, "Development of new shopping centres: area estimation", *Scottish Journal of Political Economy*, June 1962: the 1959 survey of retailers updated and used for Skelmersdale New Town

2   R K Cox *Retail Site Assessment*, Business Books Ltd, 1968

3   D Diamond and J P Gibb (1966), Livingston New Town – based on experience in East Kilbride

4   Drivers Jonas and Company for Runcorn New Town

5   Consultant's forecast for Craigavon New Town, Northern Ireland

6   Development Analysts Ltd., *Economic Survey of South Devon – Report on Shopping Needs*, 1965

7   Consultant's forecast for development in Greater London

8   General estimate suggested by a consultant in an unpublished paper

Fig. 14.4 Conversion Factors (after NEDO)

The floorspace conversion factors, like the expenditure patterns, have to be based on observation of current practices, for example by using the Census of Distribution, land use surveys,

314

or data on shopping already available from studies, and these again must be adjusted to allow for future changes in retailing methods and efficiency in the use of space. Whatever method is used to obtain sales figures, whether it be sums on the fingers or a complex shopping model, the significance of sound assessment of the floorspace implications is just as great.

Figures of sales per square foot in existing centres vary a great deal depending on the age and layout of the shops, the type and style of trading, the income levels of the shoppers and hence the marketing policies of the retailers and so on. Some discussion of the existing situation and the likely future is to be found in an article by Rhodes and Whitaker,[26] and the relationship between retail turnover and number of shops is mentioned in a recent article by Price, which is discussed below.[27] However, the most comprehensive coverage of this aspect of shopping studies is to be found in the two NEDO publications, which also contain a most valuable section on sources of data on past and present conditions for use in shopping models.[28]

The matter of growth in incomes and changes in budget patterns has received some attention; for example, Colbourne produced a model for use in a shopping study of Greater London which attempted to predict the effects of income growth on spending.[29] Expenditure was seen as consisting of two parts—a 'committed' part and a 'supernumary' part, which were expressed in the model thus:

$$p_i \, q_i = C_i \, p_i + b_i \left(m - \sum_{j=1}^{n} C_j p_j \right)$$

where n = the number of commodities
p_i = the unit price of commodity i
q_i = the quantity of commodity i purchased
C_i = the 'committed' quantity of commodity i
m = total expenditure
b_i = the proportion of all 'supernumary' expenditure devoted to commodity i

The parameters b and c were assumed to have a constant rate of change over time. This model has also been developed for use in other studies.

Service floorspace

I have concentrated so far on methods used to forecast the amount of retail floorspace required in a centre. There are several aspects of shopping studies that are of great interest and significance to land use planners not yet mentioned—notably employment generated by retailing, accommodation of traffic, including pedestrian movement, of parking needs and of servicing. Some of these receive attention in other chapters. Mention must be made here, however, of the service trades and ancillary uses to be found in shopping centres. Data on expenditure in these establishments have been very poor, and in order to estimate service floorspace requirements it has invariably been necessary to assume some ratio between retail and service floor space.

In 1961 the Census of Distribution covered only two service trades on a local basis—shoe repairers and hairdressers. This was claimed to be largely because of the practical difficulties involved: for example, for dry cleaners it is impossible to obtain meaningful local figures for the establishment since it is often only a receiving office. The shopping centre contains a number of service businesses, of which some are services in the distributive sense and others professional services—for example solicitors and accountants. Land use planners are interested particularly in the first group, which compete for shopping space. The need is thus for 'local figures of those services which compete most effectively for ground-floor space in shopping centres: for example, banks, building society offices, travel agents, launderettes and motor car showrooms'.[30]

1971 Census of distribution

The 1971 Census incorporates some improvements in definition of shopping centres and trades included. For the 1961 Census, the centres all over Britain were defined by enumerators trained by the Business Statistics Office, using as their guide-line that the limits of shopping areas should be taken as that point where the ratio of shops to all premises fell below one in three. For the 1971 Census, centres outside Greater London were identified from shopping centre maps (produced by Charles E. Goad Ltd.) and

316

in Greater London, delimitation was undertaken by the Boroughs with GLC co-ordination. The kinds of businesses covered in 1971 were the retail trade, the motor trades, the repair, maintenance and installation of consumer goods, the hiring out of consumer goods, hairdressing, laundering (including launderettes), dry cleaning, pawnbroking, the relaying of sound or television broadcasts. The intention was to process the information for grid squares, from which information relating to a particular centre could then be compiled.

The Census of Distribution has, in recent years, undoubtedly been the main source of information for building up theories and methods relating to shopping behaviour, and testing them against reality. (Of course, there is a great deal of *unpublished* information on shopping, which is collected both by those firms of planners/surveyors who act as consultants to many of those involved in retailing, and by market research firms.)

I shall now mention two studies based on Census of Distribution data.

Studies relating to central place theory

The first of these is by Price, who emphasises the need to recognise *migrant custom* as an element helping to explain the pattern and relative importance of shopping centres.[31] He examined the relationship between the total number of shops in individual towns throughout England and Wales and the total turnover achieved in those towns as shown in the Census of Distribution. Regression analysis showed a significant relationship between the two variables, but with an important and interesting pattern of residuals. Price considered that the influence of over-provision of shops and spatial variation in income both failed to give a satisfactory explanation for regional differences in the distribution of residuals. He concluded that the important factor influencing the pattern of anomalies was the role of migrant custom between a town and its dependent area.

Price's results suggest a significant difference between central towns with surrounding rural areas, to which the classical notions of central place theory apply, and those in heavily urbanised areas.

317

In his article, Price surveyed other work relating to the significance of geographical variations in incomes. He mentions Cox, who described a method of estimating income and expenditure in British towns based on a technique familiar in marketing and advertising surveys, employing proxy variables.[32] Perry recently extended the ideas to a study of census tracts in South Hampshire.[33] Coates and Rawstron attempted to show the distribution of incomes throughout the country using Inland Revenue data.[34]

The second study, by Dawson, was based on the hypothesis that the traditional hierarchial classification of settlements has been too narrow and that it is the particular pattern of functions of any town that is of interest, not just one pre-selected aspect.[35] As he put it:

'In recent years a considerable amount of work has been carried out on the methods of functional classification of towns, while the ways that types of town function have been ignored.'

He used a series of variables to measure retail intensity in towns in the East Midlands and, by multivariate analysis of the variables, identified five groups of towns. He further analysed four of these groups and established significant differences, which certainly did not relate only to the size of places.

As he says:

'The implications of the approach and findings of this study for classical urban hierarchy concepts are of interest. The basis of the urban hierarchy is a comprehensive functional size grouping of places ... The urban hierarchy provides one method of viewing inter-town relationships, the study presented here allows for a second way of approach. No doubt others exist.'[36]

A third study, which is interesting in relation to Dawson's, focused on the need for more definition of central place concepts when applying them to intra-urban behaviour. Clark and Rushton studied the shopping behaviour of a sample of households in Christchurch, New Zealand.[37]

'Each of the households was asked to identify their major supply centre for six commodities ... Their spatial behaviour patterns could then be compared with patterns of behaviour that would occur if behaviour conformed to the classical postulate of

318

central place theory, wherein consumers used the nearest centre offering the good.'

They reached the conclusion that the central place behaviour premises require modification and that a probabilistic model of spatial behaviour would be more accurate. They suggested, too, that it might be useful to adapt the 'indifference zone' idea for use with the attractiveness index in analyses of intra-urban consumer behaviour. The indifference zone would be defined in terms of a range of sites which the consumer regards as equally competitive.

Another paper suggesting the need to modify conventional central place theory is that by Schiller on location trends in specialist services.[38] He points out that 'Central place theory is basically concerned with centres, with why shops tend to cluster and hence with the concept of the inter-dependence of the centre and its hinterland. Despite much empirical evidence that this concept is breaking down, and despite its rejection by many of the leading theorists . . . the centre-hinterland idea is still widely used in the UK. This is because in aggregate terms it still applies . . . It is only when groupings such as 'durables' are broken down to finer categories that the inadequacy of the hierarchy idea at this level can be seen.'

The arrival of the car is surely the one overwhelming fact which has destroyed not the theory but the traditional application of it . . . since the centre has lost its *raison d'être*—accessibility. Road congestion and parking difficulties make it positively less accessible than other places at similar distances. The effect of this change depends upon the type of shop or service:

1 convenience shops selling standardised and branded goods can be expected to find the advantage of being in the centre obsolete
2 shops with a 'fashion' and 'comparison' function need to cluster, and may be expected to stay central
3 the high order specialist functions—the subject of Schiller's paper are freed to move from the centre.

Schiller developed a theoretical distribution of specialised services using a Rank Size rule, and then compared it with reality.

The conclusions he drew (reinforced by other studies, especially that of Leigh on Vancouver) include the following:

1 'There is the possibility that polarisation is occurring between

the large CBD with a substantial office and tourist population, and non-nuclear locations either beside a main road or in a pleasant possibly rural environment. Activities would choose between these two according to their market.

2 The second idea concerns the geographical segregation of the community by class or income level. It seems likely that segregation is increasing ... The result is that the main towns in the OMA lose their high-income population to the surrounding countryside in the same way as London itself.

The polarisation idea and the importance of the income level of an area both lead to a common conclusion. They suggest that a major factor in determining the location of specialist activities is the intrinsic attractiveness of the area itself ... Perhaps the development of an Index of Attractiveness would be of more help to a specialist service seeking a location than a refinement of the gravity model.'[39]

Forecast for the Greater London Development Plan

As a useful summary of many of the points made in this chapter on shopping, I shall now outline the sequence undertaken to produce shopping floorspace forecasts for the GLDP.[40]

It has been pointed out that:

'On account both of the statutory requirements and the scale of the problem, the forecasts made by the GLC were much broader than is usually the case. Retail turnover in London in 1981 was forecast in six large segments and an estimate made of the floorspace that would be appropriate for this order of trade. By analysing the present trade of the centres a London-wide definition of 'large centre' was obtained, and, within the six segments of London, a forecast was made of turnover and floorspace in large centres as well as for the segment as a whole.'

To produce a forecasting model:

the first step was to establish base data for 1961 on square footage of retail floorspace—the supply, and on expenditure—the demand, based on 1961 population, average household income and spending. These base data were built up using the 1966 GLC Land Use Survey, information on floorspace changes supplied by each Borough, the 1961 Census of Population, the Family

320

Expenditure Survey, plus information on spending and income from the London Traffic Survey, the 1965 British National Travel Survey (for spending by non-Londoners) and the Census of Distribution 1961.

Eventually it was judged that a satisfactory picture had been built up of retailing supply and demand in 1961, and the validity of the model was tested by simulating the retail system in 1950. The forecast for 1981 could then be made.

The following assumptions were necessary for the forecast:

1   the population of London would accord with the estimates given in the GLDP
2   relative price levels would remain unchanged
3   that there would be a standard and constant rate of growth in income, at 2·6 per cent per annum per household in Greater London, and 2·5 outside
4   that the changing distribution of households between income groups would be reflected in the average expenditure patterns for each socio-economic group
5   that trade in large centres would increase at a rate faster than in the rest of the segment (from 26% of total retail turnover in 1961 to 33% by 1981).

There were then three steps to carry out:

1   Assessing total retail expenditure in 1981—
    this involved judgements about socio-economic groups, average income changes and spending patterns.
2   Allocating this total expenditure to the different segments of London—
    this was based in general on trends evidenced between 1950 and 1961.
3   Estimating the appropriate amount of floorspace for the forecast trade—
    this was related to known intensification of use of floorspace, but 'the increase in efficiency was not applied uniformly . . . the average was applied directly to central London, but elsewhere the change was related to the turnover per square foot in 1961, so that those segments above the average in 1961 would increase their turnover per square foot at a slower

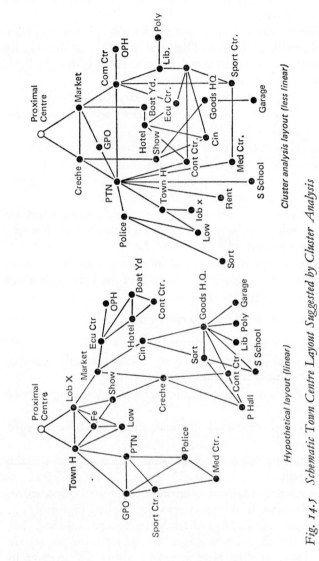

Hypothetical layout (linear)

Cluster analysis layout (less linear)

Fig. 14.5 Schematic Town Centre Layout Suggested by Cluster Analysis

SOURCE 'Computer aided analysis' by J. Roberts, in Official Architecture and Planning, 1969

rate . . . and those below the average would increase at a faster rate.'[41]

From these forecasts of turnover per square foot in 1981 the gross square footage was calculated.

Layout of shopping centres

To conclude this chapter, I would refer at least briefly to the question of shopping centre layout. Since fairly large areas of land may well be involved, with a mixture of activities and complicated access and servicing problems, land use planners may be needed to consider the design of their layout, together with architects and valuers.

One of the techniques which has been applied to this type of problem is cluster analysis (a form of factor analysis), which can illuminate the functional linkages between different town centre activities and hence suggest appropriate physical relationships.[42]

Figure 14.5 illustrates one use of cluster analysis—applied as a test to a possible layout for a new town's centre. The pattern on the left is an analysis of the hypothetical layout, which was essentially linear; on the right is that suggested by the cluster analysis, which is much less linear. Such schematic layouts can be brought into use by the architect as an aid to his design.

The process involves listing all the activities to be accommodated in the centre and assigning a weight to every functional interrelationship between each pair of activities. On the basis of these weights, a matrix is drawn up from which the overall pattern of relationships can be assessed and, if wished, presented graphically.

Perhaps it is a good note to finish the chapter with a reiteration that the whole question of making sure that centres are adaptable to changes in social and economic factors over time is crucial. An approach to do this—with obvious advantages for both traders and shoppers—has been suggested by the Institute for Centre Planning, in Denmark.[43]

References

1 Marriott, O., *The Property Boom* (1969).

2 Batty, M. & Saether, A. 'A note on the design of shopping models', in *Journal of the Royal Town Planning Institute*, page 303, **58**, 7, July/August 1972.

3 NEDO, *Urban Models in Shopping Studies*, Distributive Trades EDC, page 15 (1970).

4 For a convenient summary of central place theory, see Robinson, K., *Central Place Theory—1. A Review*, Working Paper 2 (1968); *Central Place Theory—2. Its Role in Planning with Particular Reference to Retailing*, Working Paper 9 (1968); both published by the Centre for Environmental Studies.

5 Losch, A., *Economics of Location*, New Haven (1954); Christaller, W., *The Central Places of Southern Germany*, Prentice Hall (1966).

6 For example,
Smailes, A. E. & G. Hartley, 'Shopping centres in the Greater London Area', in *Transactions of the Institute of British Geographers* (1961);
Bracey, H. E. 'Towns as rural service centres', in *Transactions of the Institute of British Geographers*, 19 (1953);
Carruthers, W. I., 'Service centres in Greater London' in *Town Planning Review*, page 5, 33 (1962).
Thorpe, D. C. & Rhodes, T. C. 'The shopping centre pattern of Tyneside urban region and large scale grocery retailing', in *Economic Geography*, January 1966;
Green, F. H. W., 'Motor bus services in S.W. England considered in relation to population and shopping facilities', in *Transactions of the Institute of British Geographers* (1948);
Berry, B. J. L. & Pred, A. *Central Place Studies: A Bibliography of Theory and Applications*, Regional Science Research Institute, Philadelphia (1965).

7 Carruthers, W. I., 'Major shopping centres in England and Wales, 1961', in *Regional Studies*, page 65, 1 (1967);
Thorpe, D., 'The main shopping centres of Great Britain in 1961: their locational and structural characteristics', in *Urban Studies*, June 1968.

8 For example, see Bracey and Carruthers, *op. cit.* (6) above.

9 West Midlands Branch of the Town Planning Institute, *Predicting Shopping Requirenents*, August 1967.

10 Reilly, W. J., *The Law of Retail Gravitation*, New York (1931).

11 See, for example, NEDO study, *op. cit.* (3) above.

324

12 Manchester University Department of Town and Country Planning, *Regional Shopping Centres—A Planning Report on N.W. England, Part 2—A Retail Shopping Model* (1966).

13 Lakshmanan, J. R. & Hansen, G. W. 'A retail market potential model', in *Journal of the American Institute of Planners*, page 134, 31 (1965).

14 For example,
Rhodes, T. & Whitaker, R. 'Forecasting shopping demand', *Journal of the Royal Town Planning Institute*, May 1967;
Tees-side Survey and Plan, **2**, Chapter 14 (1969);
Leicester and Leicestershire Sub-regional Planning Study, **2**, Chapter 5 (1969).

15 Lowry, I. S., *Model of Metropolis*, Rand Corporation (1964).

16 For example,
Cripps, E. & Foot, D. 'A land use model for sub-regional planning', in *Regional Studies*, page 243 (1969);
Batty, M., 'An activity allocation model for the Notts-Derby Sub-region', in *Regional Studies*, page 307, October 1970.

17 Stouffer, S. A., 'Intervening opportunities: a theory relating mobility and distance', in *American Sociological Review*, page 845, 5 (1940).

18 Harris, B., *Regional Growth Model—Activity Distribution Sub-Model* Penn-Jersey Study Paper 7.

19 Wilson, A. G., *Notes on some concepts in social physics*, Centre for Environmental Studies, Working Paper 4, June 1968.

20 Bacon, R. W., 'An approach to the theory of consumer shopping behaviour', in *Urban Studies*, page 55, **8**, February 1971.

21 See Bacon, *op. cit.* (20) above.

22 Building Research Station, *Shopping in Watford Survey*, June 1971.

23 Such as,
Alonso, W., *Location and Land Use*, Harvard University Press, Cambridge (1964);
Wingo, L., *Transportation and Urban Land Use*, Resources for the Future, Washington, DC (1961).

24 See NEDO study, *op. cit.* (3) above.

25 For a thorough discussion, see NEDO study, *op. cit.* (3) above, pages 97–104.

26 see, Rhodes & Whitaker, *op. cit.* (14) above;
also, 'A further note on forecasting shopping demand', in *Journal of the Town Planning Institute*, page 53, 53 (1967).

27 Price, D. G., 'Analysis of retail turnover in England and Wales', in *Regional Studies*, page 459, 4 (1970).

28 See NEDO study, *op. cit.* (3) above, pages 97–104.
29 See NEDO study, *op. cit.* (3) above.
30 See NEDO study, *op. cit.* (3) above.
31 See Price, *op. cit.* (27) above.
32 Cox, W. E., 'The estimation of incomes and expenditures in British towns', in *Applied Statistics,* page 252, **17** (1968).
33 Perry, A., 'Spatial variations of income in Southern Hampshire', in *Area,* page 12, **1** (1970).
34 Coates, B. E. & Rawstron, E. M., 'Regional variations in income', in *Westminster Bank Review,* page 28, February 1966.
35 Dawson, J. A., 'Some structural relationships in the retail economy of East Midlands towns', in *Journal of the Town Planning Institute,* page 348, **56,** 8, September/October 1970.
36 See Dawson, *op. cit.* (35) above.
37 Clark, W. A. V. & Rushton, G., 'Models of intra-urban consumer behaviour and their implications for central place theory', in *Economic Geography,* page 486, **46,** July 1970.
38 Schiller, R. K., 'Location trends in specialist services', in *Regional Studies,* page 1, **5,** (1971).
39 See Schiller, *op. cit.* (38) above.
40 Greater London Council, *Greater London Development Plan—Written Statement,* and *Report of Studies* (1969).
41 Petterssen, G. & Willson, J. M., 'Forecasting retail expenditure and floorspace', in *Greater London Research,* GLC Intelligence Unit, page 21, **11,** June 1970.
42 Roberts, J. A., 'Computer aided analysis', in *Official Architecture and Planning,* page 1186, October 1969.
43 Institute for Centre Planning, *Seven Shopping Centres: Planning for Change and Flexibility* (1968).

15 Leisure

Introduction

This chapter is about techniques used in planning for people's leisure activities. Unlike the previous few chapters—where at least the central activity was clear—if nothing else—it is inescapable that I begin by trying to define what is meant by 'leisure'. I have deliberately used the term leisure, since this covers a wider range of activities than recreation; although it will be found that many of the studies mentioned in this chapter are of recreation.

There are many definitions of the word leisure, and of related terms, such as recreation, which have been carefully formulated by research groups. For example, the International Study Group on Leisure and Social Science defined leisure as consisting of 'a number of occupations in which the individual may indulge of his own free will—either to rest, to amuse himself, to add to his knowledge and improve his skills disinterestedly and to increase his voluntary participation in the life of the community after discharging his professional, family and social duties.' Maw comments that factors entering into individuals' choices about their free time are:

1 commitment
2 cost
3 social exclusiveness
4 energy expenditure (see Figure 15.1).

The Countryside Recreation Glossary said 'Leisure is the time available to the individual when the disciplines of work, sleep and other basic needs have been met', and recreation is 'Any pursuit engaged upon during leisure time, other than pursuits to which people are normally 'highly committed'.[1]

	Fully Committed Essential	Partly Committed Optional	
		Highly Committed	Leisure
A Sleeping	Essential sleep		Relaxing
B Personal Care and Exercise	Health and hygiene		Sport Active play
C Eating	Eating		Dining out Drinking
D Shopping	*Essential shopping	Optional shopping	
E Work	*Primary work	Overtime Secondary work	
F Housework	*Essential house-work Cooking	House repairs Car maintenance	Do-it-yourself Gardening
G Education	*Schooling	Further education Homework	
H Culture and Communication (non-travel)			Television/radio Reading Cinema/theatre Hobbies Passive play
J Social and Institutional Activities		Child-raising Religion Politics	Talking Parties Dancing
K Travel	Travel to work/ school		Walking Driving for pleasure

*not essential during a holiday period

Fig. 15.1 Use of Time (after Maw)

Further definitions continue to appear—some less formal, as —'Recreation is not an easily defined, homogeneous entity. Indeed, it is much easier to define what it is *not* than to say what it *is*. It does not include work. Nor does it include certain personal and social obligations that all people have, such as sleeping and washing. Beyond this, however, it is impossible to speak with any great certainty. It is easier, and perhaps more useful, to consider the *functions* of recreation in a modern society and, then, to outline the more important ways in which these functions are carried out . . .

'One point is clear. The notion that life today consists of 'eight hours of work, eight hours of sleep and eight hours of recreation in each day' simply cannot be sustained in the light of the empirical evidence that is increasingly becoming available to us. Instead, the concept of recreation and of the role which it occupies in contemporary society needs to be considered in positive terms. It can no longer be conceived solely as a residual— as something which happens to be left over to each person after work and other necessary chores have been completed.'

This discussion of recreation, by Burton, goes on to mention the three main positive functions which recreation performs: it provides relaxation; it provides entertainment; and it provides a means for personal and social development. Thus, far from being an alternative to work, it presupposes the existence of it—to provide a contrast or complement to it.[2]

I have taken the field of interest of this chapter, therefore, to be techniques that help with land use planning for all those activities not undertaken to earn money or as routine 'personal maintenance'; unfortunately, though, work done by planners has concentrated heavily on certain facets of leisure and this is reflected in the material that follows. The greatest imbalance is the attention paid to countryside as opposed to urban leisure.

Perhaps more than any other single aspect of planning, it is certain that we will see considerable development of techniques related to planning for leisure in the next few years—for the now, tediously often, repeated reasons: that many people in the community have more time free, higher real incomes, the use of motor cars and an educational background and general conditioning that stress the delights of various forms of leisure activity. (Compare with 'consciousness 3' in *The Greening of America*).[3]

The Chapter is in three broad sections—first, techniques that relate to *demand* for leisure facilities, second, those concerned with *supply*, and finally, a discussion of techniques considering *demand–supply interaction*.

Demand

Provision and management of leisure facilities are the province of many different groups and agencies, both public and private. But, whether their dominant motive is commercial or altruistic, they must concern themselves with *demand* for their services. The concept of 'demand' in relation to leisure was clarified at a recent seminar, in an attempt to make sure that everyone was using certain terms to mean the same things.

'Demand as used by the recreation planner is a slightly different concept from that used by the economist, although it has the same roots. It is defined as the number of persons (or units of participation) requiring to take part in a particular recreation activity and hence is manifested as a demand for facilities. There are several components in "existing demand" (see Figure 15.2) either for

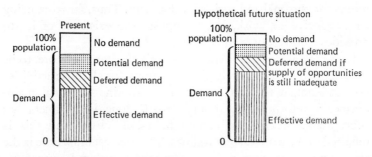

Fig. 15.2   Components of Demand

recreation as a whole or for any particular activity. These consist of effective demand, which is present participation, and what is sometimes termed *latent demand* which comprises *deferred demand* (those who would like to participate and have the means and time to do so but are unable to because of the lack of recreation facilities or the lack of knowledge of the existence of such facilities) and *potential demand* (those without the means or time to participate, but who could be converted into *effective demand* at a later date if their social/economic state changed). Finally

330

there is of course the element of *no demand*—the old, the sick, the uninterested and so on. In predicting demand at a future date, the planner is only concerned with the level of potential effective demand—that is all those people with the purchasing power (time and money) to be able to consume (i.e. participate) at that point in time. If all those who are predicted as requiring recreation facilities could be supplied with them there would be no deferred demand; resource limitations, however, constrain the situation and the planner is therefore concerned with deciding the best way in which to deploy resources so as to minimise the shortfall of supply in relation to predicted effective demand.'[4]

I personally find this definition of types of demand confusing, but it was produced as a consensus view after careful consideration, so had presumably better be accepted to put an end to the semantic confusion.

Efforts to assess demand in the future generally begin with information on usage in the present and recent past, and Burton has suggested that there are six principal ways of collecting such data—interview surveys; self-administered and particularly postal surveys; observation; documents compiled for other purposes; physical evidence; and mechanical and electronic devices.[5] What follows is based on his summary. He is generally critical of the studies done to date—'Most recent recreation studies in Britain have been limited in objectives and severely restricted in scope. Generally, the objective has been to provide improved background data about current trends in recreation habits, for the use of planners and others concerned with the provision of facilities.... Too often the objectives of recreation studies have been expressed in very broad and general terms—such as 'to provide detailed information on the use of (demand for) recreation facilities which will serve as a basis for planning'.'

Interview surveys

Interview surveys' major advantage is their flexibility. The two groups of interview survey are categorised by:
1 type—standardised, semi-standardised or non-standardised
2 location—whether household, or on site.

When the same information is to be collected from each respondent, a standardised interview is used, with the wording and sequence of questions decided in advance, and the manner of asking. A semi-standardised interview may be set up with only a list of data the interviewer is expected to obtain or a list of questions whose order may be varied. A non-standardised interview makes no attempt to obtain the same categories of information from each respondent, and the questioning stems from the interviewer's understanding of the overall objectives of the inquiry.

Household surveys may involve all members of the household, selected members or one individual only, and be on any scale from a neighbourhood to national.

Site surveys may be of the users or the suppliers of the facility.

Burton says 'The interview survey has become the most popular method of obtaining data about recreation demands in recent years. All major national and regional demand studies during the past decade have employed it (with a few exceptions) . . . Most have been by household interview: although Burton, the Greater London Council and the British Travel Association have all conducted large-scale site interviews.'[6]

In general the problems encountered have not been with the conduct of surveys, but in the planning and analysing of them. The first problem has been to identify and obtain an adequate sample of respondents, the second to ensure comparability of data between surveys. Sampling is the selection of part of an aggregate of material to represent the whole. The major problem is to avoid bias. With recreation studies, there are two particular problems—determining the size of the sample that is required and ensuring it is 'representative'; both problems arise from the wide range of diverse pursuits embraced in the term 'recreation'.

An example of this problem arose with the Pilot National Recreation Survey.[7] The survey—probably the most comprehensive study in this country of general recreation habits—was intended to provide information on how patterns of recreation are changing, and what influences them. The emphasis was on informal pursuits requiring large areas of land. A random sample was attempted to represent the total population of the country, urban and rural, and in all regions. 3167 respondents were interviewed in standardised household interviews. The

Survey	1	2	3	4	5	6
Occupation						
Employed or unemployed	x	x	x	x	x	x
What firm (name)						
Type of firm				x		
Job actually done	x	x	x	x	x	x
Any qualifications						
Length of working week	x		x			
Any overtime	x					
Paid weekly or monthly	x					
Income						
Actual income						
Income groups	x				x	
Social Class						
Self-rating	x					
Rating by interviewer	x	x	x			
Education						
Type of school attended	x				x	
Operator of school						
Co-educational or single sex						
Age left school	x	x		x	x	
Any further education					x	
Any qualifications						
Car						
Ownership	x	x	x	x	x	x
Use made of it	x					
Household Goods						
Television	x		x	x	x	
Washing machine	x					
Refrigerator	x					
Telephone						x
Housing						
Type of dwelling	x			x	x	
Garden yes/no				x	x	
Owned or rented	x			x	x	
Length of residence					x	
Previous place of resid.				x		
Age of dwelling	x					x
Sex						
sex	x			x	x	x
Age						
Date of birth	x					
Actual age		x		x	x	x
Age group			x			
Marital Status						
Two groups				x		
Three groups	x				x	
Five groups						x
Household Composition	x	x	x	x	x	x
Holidays						
Length of paid holidays	x					

Surveys

1 Pilot National Recreation Survey (BTA)
2 The People's Activities (BBC)
3 Survey of Major County Cricket (NOP)
4 Surveys of Use of Open Space (GLC)
5 Leisure and Planning Inquiry (GSS)
6 Village Life in Hampshire

Fig. 15.3 Profile Data Obtained for Six Recent Recreation Studies

SOURCE *Experiments in Recreation Research*, by T. L. Burton & A. J. Veal, Allen & Unwin (1971) sample was moderately successful in avoiding bias, but proved inadequate in size for anything other than simple descriptive analysis and statement of broad conclusions.

The same problem of securing adequate data about minority activities was encountered in the two other recent national recreation surveys—the BBC's study, 'The People's Activities', and the Government Social Survey's 'Leisure and Planning Inquiry'.[8]

One way to obtain data about minority activities is interviewing at the site of the activity, although it is often difficult to produce an unbiased sample. Several studies of this kind have been undertaken in recent years, including 'The Non-residential Use of the Crystal Palace National Recreation Centre' by the Central Council of Physical Recreation. Burton's study of the use of Windsor Great Park on summer weekends and the GLC's survey of the use of parks and open spaces in London.[9]

The other major problem with recreation studies—that of ensuring comparability of data—has two aspects; the type and quantity of data sought about recreation activities, and the information about the characteristics of those involved, termed 'profile' data. Since 'recreation' is a collective term embracing many activities, it is often difficult to define and classify activities unambiguously. The difficulties about profile data are not, of course, unique to recreation studies and a working party recently set up by the British Sociological Association has already produced some suggestions.[10] Figure 15.3 shows the items of profile data collected in six recent major recreation surveys, which can be compared on only four items.

Self-administered surveys

These are surveys in which the questionnaires are completed by the respondents without any interviewer. The major difficulties are in obtaining a sufficiently high response rate to avoid bias. In general such surveys are postal, with normal response rates between 30 and 50 per cent. Efforts at increasing response rates centre around improvements to the form of the questionnaire and explanatory material, and better methods of contacting respondents. Thus a recent study of school-children, and another of theatre-goers secured high rates of response. Another means is to offer rewards, for example a draw based on the questionnaires completed.[11] Such surveys also have the danger of a bias to the literate (and extrovert?).

Self-administered surveys have been particularly important in securing data about recreation supply, for example, the 'Initial Appraisals' of facilities for sport and recreation made by ten of the Regional Sports Councils in 1967–8. A questionnaire was sent to every local authority and the survey covered swimming pools and baths, indoor sports halls, sports and athletic stadia, golf courses, water recreation areas and places for general leisure although the coverage varied somewhat between surveys. They show very well the significance of definitions—the Southern Region shows only two sports halls, while the county of Lancashire has 247.[12]

Observation

Observation is potentially a useful method of social research, particularly for small-community and small-group studies. It can be defined as 'purposeful and selective watching and counting of phenomena as they take place'. To be systematic, it should be:

1 suitable for investigating the problems of interest
2 appropriate to the populations and samples under study
3 reliable and objective.

Moser has suggested the method has significant weaknesses on all these counts.[13] Perhaps its usefulness is most often as a complementary technique to interview surveys. Two examples of observation studies are Hole's work on children's play on housing estates, and Wagner's study of the public use of the National Trust property at Ashridge, undertaken as part of 'Outdoor Recreation on Common Land'.[14]

Documents

There are two main kinds of documentary source—continuous and discontinuous records. Continuous records, ranging from Census data to club membership lists and sales and ticket records, can be obtained fairly cheaply and are easy to sample, but have drawbacks associated with 'selective deposit and selective survival'. They have not been much used in recreation research, an exception being a study of the 'Norfolk Holiday Industry', in 1961, using records of bread sales as a method of measuring the flow of holiday-makers.[15] Some small studies have used club memberships as an indication of demand. The main use of documents has been to provide supplementary information, especially profile data.

The most important discontinuous source, half-way between a self-administered questionnaire and a diary, is proving of increasing use in recreation studies—that is, the *time-budget diary*. The object is to secure a complete record of the way in which a period of time has been used. There are some difficulties with bias, but the main problem arises in grouping and coding activities. This problem was not apparently given much importance in the largest time-budget study recently undertaken—the 'Cross-national Time-Budget Study', which included research teams in ten countries, co-ordinated from Vienna.[16]

It was, however, in another important time-budget study—the 'Household Activity Systems Study' by Chapin and Hightower.[17] The study was exploratory, concerned with developing a typology of household activities and experimenting with different techniques for identifying activities that could be used in later studies. Eventually, it was decided that an act qualified for separate identification if sufficient respondents recognised it as such. This led to nine major categories of activities:

1 Income-producing and related activities
2 Child-raising and family activities
3 Education and intellectual development
4 Religious and human welfare activities
5 Social activities
6 Recreation and relaxation
7 Participation in club activities
8 Participation in community service and political activities
9 Activities associated with food, shelter, medical and similar needs

These were divided into 62 sub-groupings, some of which were further divided.

There have been recent time-budget studies in Britain, including that by Maw, as part of his leisure model study, which is discussed further below, and the BBC's Audience Research Department's study, reported in 1965.[18]

Physical evidence

Physical evidence constitutes traces surviving from past events and behaviour, mainly *erosion* or *accretion* (notably litter of various kinds). Coppock hopes to use aerial photographs' evidence of erosion in a Pilot Survey of Tourism in Part of the Borders.[19]

Mechanical and electronic devices

Such devices may be used as a means of recording data on their own, or as a supplement to other methods. They are most useful in providing information on attendance, incidence and so on, for example traffic on a road, or feet passing over a stile.[20] Hidden cameras and microphones have also been used in studies, where they would seem to be most suited to psychological investigations.

The above description of sources for recreation information has largely been based on Burton's survey, but reference should also be made to Cherry[21] and to Burton and Cherry[22].

Influences on demand

Having discussed methods of collecting information relating to demand and its determinants, it is perhaps appropriate, before considering actual studies, to consider briefly what such determinants are. This will provide a persepctive against which to assess the studies carried out.

Clawson and Knetsch considered the factors in demand for a particular recreation area to be:
1 Factors relating to the potential recreation users as individuals:
a their total number in the surrounding tributary area
b their geographic distribution within this tributary area
c their socio-economic characteristics (age, sex, occupation, family size and composition, educational status and race)

337

d their average incomes and the distribution of incomes among individuals

e their average leisure, and the time distribution of that leisure

f their specific education, their past experiences and present knowledge relating to outdoor recreation

g their taste for outdoor recreation

2 Factors relating to the recreation area itself:

a its innate attractiveness, as judged by the average user

b the intensity and character of its management as a recreation area

c the availability of alternative recreation sites, and the degree to which they are substitutes for the area under study

d the capacity of the area to accommodate recreationists

e climatic and weather characteristics of the area

3 Relationships between potential users and the recreation area:

a the time required to travel from home to the area, and return

b the comfort or discomfort of the travel

c the monetary costs involved in a recreation visit to the area

d the extent to which demand has been stimulated by advertising[23]

In studies carried out to assess or forecast recreation demand, some of these factors have conventionally received much more attention than others, and there have been few attempts to evaluate systematically the relative significance of the different factors in varying circumstances. Some attempts to fill these gaps will be described below. Clawson and Knetsch's list should be compared with those elements expressed in Figure 15.4—Factors influencing the Consumption of Outdoor Recreation, as set out by Law.[24]

Studies of demand

Studies of demand may focus on one activity, one area or one recreation location. An example of a recent demand study concerned with one particular type of activity is the *National Survey of Angling*, which, so the report says, 'confirmed angling's claim to be Britain's number one participant sport'.[25] The objects of the survey were to find out:

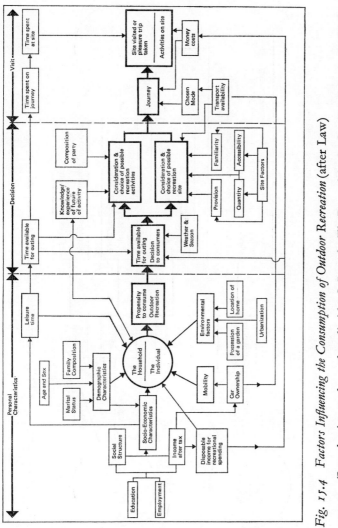

Fig. 15.4 Factors Influencing the Consumption of Outdoor Recreation (after Law)

SOURCE 'Introduction to demand studies' by S. Law, in *The Demand for Outdoor Recreation in the Countryside*, Countryside Commission (1970)

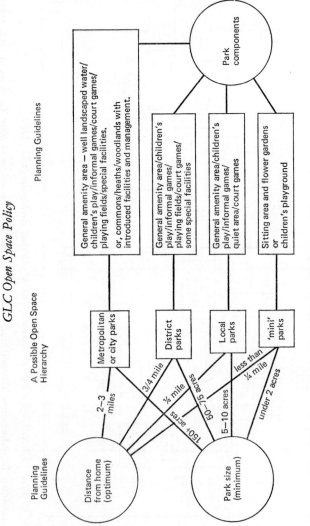

Fig. 15.5(a) Open Space Policy Formulation—Elements of Demand

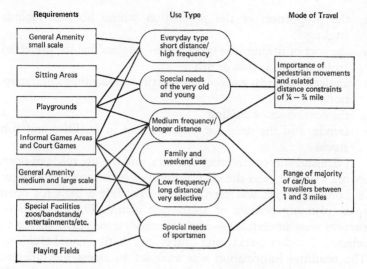

Requirements	Use Type	Mode of Travel
General Amenity small scale	Everyday type short distance/ high frequency	Importance of pedestrian movements and related distance constraints of ¼ – ¾ mile
Sitting Areas	Special needs of the very old and young	
Playgrounds		
Informal Games Areas and Court Games	Medium frequency/ longer distance	
General Amenity medium and large scale	Family and weekend use	Range of majority of car/bus travellers between 1 and 3 miles
Special Facilities zoos/bandstands/ entertainments/etc.	Low frequency/ long distance/ very selective	
Playing Fields	Special needs of sportsmen	

Fig. 15.5(b)   Open Space Policy Formulation—Planning Guidlines and Possible Hierarchy

Park Type	Function	Minimum Size (acres)	Maximum Distance From Home (miles)	Components
Metropolitan	Weekend type (bus and car travellers)	150	2 – 5	General recreation areas/ playing fields/ special facilities
District	Weekend type (mainly pedestrian travel)	50	¾	
Local	Everyday type (short visits / workers)	5	¼	General recreation areas/court games/ children's play areas
Small local	Old people/ young children/ workers	Under 5		Gardens/ sitting area/ children's play areas

Fig. 15.5(c)   Criteria for Determining Nature and Distribution of Parks and Open Space

341

1 the proportion of the population whose hobbies include angling
2 the sort of fishing that takes place—anglers' habits, preferred areas, sites and types of fish
3 anglers' problems and opinions on present facilities and restrictions
4 the economics of angling
5 trends, and the need for improvement in facilities and fish stocks.

A demand survey covering one area, and the use made of open spaces within it, was the GLC's study of parks and open spaces in London, which was carried out to provide a basis for open space planning policies of a strategic nature. Three groups of surveys were undertaken—a home interview survey, a survey in selected London parks, and interviews with school-children. The resulting information was analysed to assess the different demand groups within the population as a whole, to classify types of recreation demand, and finally to suggest a hierarchy of provision which would satisfy the demands identified. The hierarchy comprised open spaces of different types and sizes, within certain maximum distances of a person's home. Figure 15.5 shows the elements of demand, and the planning guidelines and possible hierarchy, produced in formulating the open space policy.[26] The GLC's subsequent work on facilities outside their own administrative area is discussed below.

Demand models

Based either on survey material or on judgement alone, models may be developed to explore, explain or predict demands for leisure facilities. Many take into account the interaction between demand and supply, and these are considered below.

Travel pattern models

In a recent survey article, Houghton-Evans and Miles said, 'To provide adequately for future recreational travel, highway and planning authorities require a simple accurate method for predicting attendance at a recreation site ... yet the application of traffic models to recreational travel has received relatively little attention.'[27]

The gravity model has been used to describe present-day recreation travel patterns to isolated parks. It has also been the basis of some forecasting studies, and is being developed further. Since travel patterns to facilities are affected by the availability of local alternative leisure opportunities, the intervening and competing opportunities models would seem to be appropriate, and have been used, particularly in the USA. These, however, require the use of a trip generation model to forecast the total number of recreation trips; such trip generation models are usually of a regression type, based on socio-economic and locational factors. With such model analyses allowance can be made for improved travel times to individual sites, or for new recreational sites not previously available.[28]

Houghton-Evans and Miles concluded that work done so far generally comprises isolated studies of weekend activity in various popular areas of countryside, and such studies are difficult to compare and correlate. One investigation, based on household interviews in Northfield, Birmingham, 'showed "driving for pleasure and to walk" to be the most popular recreational activities, with an average of 13 car trips per household per annum. The greatest number of trips were to localities adjacent to the survey area, followed in descending order by trips to "water oriented" sites and "countryside" sites up to approximately one hour away. Social groups 1 and 2 (professional occupations) favoured countryside sites, whilst 3 and 4 (skilled and partly skilled occupations) preferred the 'man-made' sites, such as stately homes and their grounds, or country parks.'[29]

Some of the other findings from studies have been—

Travel mode—on-site surveys have found a heavy dependence on the car as travel mode—Wager, in a study of outdoor recreation on common lands, which included 20 commons in various parts of England, found 76% of parties of visitors had arrived by car; of visitors in the New Forest interviewed, 92.5% had travelled there by car; in Windsor Great Park, 93%.[30]

Trip distance—The Pilot National Recreation Survey found trip distances are usually short—38% of recreation motorists made a round trip of under 50 miles and only 27% travelled over

343

100 miles. The catchment for commons was basically local—less than 20 miles; for Windsor Great Park, a sub-regional attraction, it was about 30 miles, but for the New Forest, 38% of visitors had travelled quite far—thus qualifying it as a 'regional' attraction. These findings may be compared with a suggested classification of recreational facilities:

Local   —to draw visitors from 5–10 miles away
Sub-regional —to draw visitors from 20–30 miles away
Regional   —to draw visitors from up to 50 miles away.[31]

Occupancy rates—the pattern of recreational travel is highly concentrated around the weekend, and high occupancy rates of motor cars obtain—the Peak District survey found 3·5 persons per vehicle, Box Hill survey found 3·2 persons per vehicle, Windsor Great Park survey found 3·8 persons per party, Lake District survey found 3·0–3·5 persons per party.[32]

Activities at destination—another factor investigated in recreational travel studies is commonly activity at destination. The following descriptions of findings are typical—'Once at a country site, the majority of visitors are able to satisfy their recreation needs within a few yards of a parked car, or by remaining inside. It seems many people want only visual contact with the countryside.'[33] 'It would seem that for many, 'wanting to be on one's own' does not mean solitude, but rather being left quietly to pursue one's own activities'.[34]

'Two factors which emerged from the New Forest study are fundamental: the natural gregariousness of a high percentage of visitors and their almost universal reluctance to move far from their cars.'[35]

Lake District model

Mansfield developed a model to explain the demand pattern generating trips to the Lake District.[36] The factors influencing trips made from a town to a particular beauty spot were taken to be:
the relative attractiveness of the beauty spot;
the money cost of travel to the beauty spot and alternative resorts;
journey time expended in reaching each resort;
population of the town.

344

It was assumed in the model that the first two items would remain constant in the short-term.

The formula was

$$\frac{Y}{P} = a + [c + t]f(X) + tM + gw$$

where Y = number of person trips from zone i to the Lake District

P = population of zone i

X = distance of zone i to the Lake District

M = a dummy variable, measuring motorway access

a, c, t, g = constants.

The model, when fitted to survey data for day and half-day trips, explained up to 99% of the variation in trip numbers, although the motorway and car ownership variables contributed very little to the predictive power of the equation.

Mansfield used the model to investigate the value of time, and the elasticity of demand for recreation trips. Some of his findings were subsequently incorporated into the Morecambe Bay Barrage studies, in which he was concerned with the evaluation of recreation benefits from the alternative possibilities under consideration. The evaluation of benefit involved predicting usage.[37]

Economic methods of assessing demand

Also incorporated into the Morecambe Bay studies was the 'Clawson' method—an approach to demand measurement and prediction derived from economics. As the name suggests, Clawson was among the first to explore how far the theories of economics could be helpful in recreation studies, and he and others in the USA developed such methods especially in relation to water resource projects.[38] They have now also received a good deal of attention in this country.

In a paper by Kavanagh, the approach is introduced thus— 'What is important when it comes to decision making about the quantity of resources to be devoted to recreation is an objective view. . . . The commodity 'outdoor recreation', conceptually at least, can be treated like any other economic commodity. According to economic theory, normally the quantity demanded of a commodity per period of time is inversely related to the price per unit . . . '[39]

Or, put more simply by Clawson and Knetsch. 'In choosing to use parks and other recreation facilities and to spend time, money and trouble in so doing, people behave in a way that is not fundamentally different from the way they purchase other items. In a good many ways we can think of society, or the economy, producing good parks, playgrounds and other recreational facilities in much the same way it produces and enjoys automobiles, dishwashers, roads and nearly everything else. Economic analysis is as applicable to outdoor recreation as it is to any other of man's wealth-getting or income-spending activities. It is a particularly useful vehicle for focusing on two important aspects of outdoor recreation; the question of worth or values, and the determination of patterns or regularities.'[40]

Clawson's early attempts to evolve a practical method from economic theory centred around the construction of a demand schedule for a recreation facility, the schedule reflecting how much people would be prepared to pay for their enjoyment. The notional price is taken to be a measure of the benefit they derive. Clawson's demand schedules related to the population distribution round the recreation facility, and to the transportation, food and lodging costs people incurred in using it. Knetsch later suggested the inclusion of other factors, notably the income of the recreationist, the availability of substitute recreation areas and some measure of congestion.[41]

Each subsequent use of the method has produced some further refinement.[42]

The Water Resources Board sponsored a study in which the Clawson method was applied to activities at Grafham Reservoir.[43] One of those involved in this work has described quite simply the process involved. Gibson begins by quoting from Clawson, 'the whole outdoor recreation (visit) is, to a large extent, a package deal; it must be viewed as a whole, in terms of cost, satisfaction and time, for all members of the family as a group (and) the demand curves must be derived first for the whole experience.' There are, it is suggested, five identifiable phases in the recreation

346

experience, each of which is important in decision making by recreationists—planning or anticipation, travel to the recreation site, on-site experiences, travel back and recollection.

There are two main stages in measuring demand, as explained by Gibson. The problem used as an example is to estimate a demand curve for an outdoor recreation activity, such as trout fishing, on a reservoir, close to an area of urban population—

1 Recreational experience 'as a whole'—demand curve

It is assumed that the population of the area is located in, say, four concentric zones around the reservoir—each zone being homogeneous in relation to population and socio-economic characteristics. The basic data are represented in the following table—

Zone	Mean distance from reservoir (miles)	Price of trip (new pence)	Number of trips from zone in time period
A	20	25	300
B	40	50	200
C	60	75	100
D	80	100	0

The table can be interpreted thus—there is no user charge to be paid by anglers, but they incur costs in travelling, as shown. An inverse relationship obtains between costs from a zone and number of fishing trips at the reservoir originating in it. When the data in the table is plotted on a graph, it gives the demand curve for the recreation experience as a whole.

2 Fishing—demand curve

To obtain the demand curve for the specific recreation—trout fishing—the following calculations must be made. With no user charge paid to fish at the reservoir, total fishing trips from all zones are 600, and this gives the first point on the demand curve.

To obtain other points, the effects of increasing user charges at the reservoir are traced. If there is a charge of 25p, each angler now confronts two-part costs, the user charge and travelling costs, giving data as in the table below, which is based on the assumption that anglers in all zones will respond in the same way to different levels of costs.

Zone	Mean distance (miles)	Total price of trip (new pence)	Number of trips
A	20	50	200
B	40	75	100
C	60	100	0
D	80	125	0

By repeating this procedure for higher user charges a complete demand curve can be obtained, as shown in Figure 15.6.

Empirical studies, also at Grafham Reservoir, and as reported by Clawson for several parks in the USA, are regarded by supporters of the method as confirmation that it is an effective simulation of actuality. There is, though, an extensive critical literature making minor criticisms in most cases, but doubting whether the method has any fundamental validity in others.[44] As mentioned above, this (Clawson) method was incorporated into the studies made recently in connection with a possible barrage at Morecambe Bay.[45]

Supply

Studies of the supply side of planning for leisure concentrate on present and future resources available to meet demands. Most published studies concerning supply policies for leisure facilities relate to the countryside and to public enterprise. It is tantalising that we do not know more of the methods of commercial operators in this field.[46] One commercial operator prepared to disclose something of his own supply policies is Lord Montagu, owner of

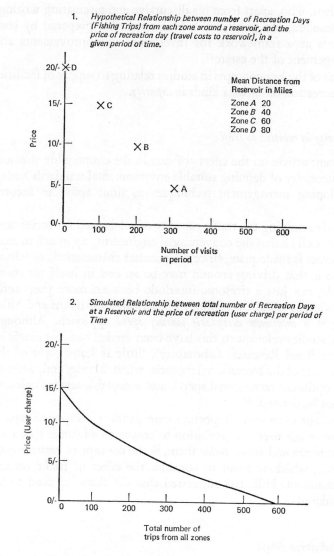

1. Hypothetical Relationship between **number** of Recreation Days (Fishing Trips) from each zone around a reservoir, and the price of recreation day (travel costs to reservoir), in a given period of time.

Mean Distance from Reservoir in Miles

Zone A 20
Zone B 40
Zone C 60
Zone D 80

Price

Number of visits in period

2. Simulated Relationship between total number of Recreation Days at a Reservoir and the price of recreation (user charge) per period of Time

Price (User charge)

Total number of trips from all zones

Fig. 15.6   Derivation of a Demand Curve

SOURCE 'An economist's approach to the measurement of recreation demand' by N. Kavanagh, in *The Demand for Outdoor Recreation in the Countryside*, Countryside Commission (1970)

349

Beaulieu, who, apart from his discursive and fascinating writings on Beaulieu, has published a long-term plan prepared by consultants as a framework for investment in improvements and management of the estate[47].

One of the key concepts in studies relating to supply of facilities for recreation of various kinds is *capacity*.

Capacity in relation to traffic

A recent article on the effects of cars in the countryside stressed, 'the necessity of defining suitable environmental standards and of developing management techniques to limit activities accordingly.'[48]

In determining the traffic capacity of roads used for recreation, it may well be that the conventional engineering approach to road capacities is inadequate, since the peculiar characteristic of leisure traffic is that driving around may be an end in itself for many people, not just a tiresome interlude between more purposeful activities, as is most travelling. Thus Houghton-Evans and Miles suggest a *minimum acceptable journey speed* approach. Although some studies relevant to this have been carried out (for example, by the Road Research Laboratory), 'little is known yet of the behaviour of the recreational motorist when driving, and, without this, optimum recreational speeds and acceptable service volumes cannot be defined.'[49]

Perhaps even more important than defining acceptable capacities on roads used for recreation to ensure an adequate speed for the vehicles and those *inside* them, is the concept of *environmental capacity*, which sets out to consider the effect of traffic on the environment. Hills has suggested that six elements need to be considered—

1 Pedestrian delays

In some areas the comfort and safety of the pedestrian may be considered to take priority over the needs of moving traffic, such as a village street, and in such cases maximum acceptable traffic flows could be determined.

2 Noise

In studies of the New Forest, an attempt was made to define environmental standards on the basis of noise, smell and visual intrusion. The noise investigation was in two parts:

a measurement of traffic noise on selected roads;

b noise from vehicles and various other sources in the open forest.

Measured noise levels were checked against people's subjective judgement of their nuisance value.[50] The Building Research Station has developed a Traffic Noise Index, which allows for the range of noise climate as well as general levels, and which would seem suitable for environmental studies.

Hills has suggested the use of an Environmental Passenger Car Unit—EPCU—variant of the familiar PCU, which would weight different vehicle types according to their effect on the environment. The ratings of different vehicles would be changed according to the character of the environment.[51]

3 Fumes

Although a minor irritant, the New Forest Study found fumes could be ignored, except where many vehicles were halted by traffic congestion.

4 Vibration

Vibration is closely linked with noise, and could be accommodated in the EPCU rating.

5 Visual intrusion

The problem of parked cars was considered by Furmidge, who asserted that a visual study is an essential component of rural capacity studies; and, when identified, cases of visual intrusion require the consideration of a landscape architect.[52]

6 Encroachment of vehicles on footpaths

The problem of encroachment of vehicles on areas not intended for them is quite a serious one, although it does not receive much emphasis. This, like the other aspects mentioned, requires positive management policies to preserve environmental standards.

Management of traffic through physical and psychological controls has received some attention, and is clearly increasingly important. Measures include control of traffic volumes by constrictions, gateways, cattle grids and prohibitions plus car parks; the composition of traffic can be managed by the type and condition of roads provided, by direct controls such as loading gauges and by prohibitions. The distribution of traffic at different time periods also merits consideration. Speed is commonly controlled, for example by road bumps.

An attempt at control of traffic in a recreation area, which the organisers regard as very successful, is the Goyt Experiment in the Peak District National Park. A valley was under extreme visitor pressure at peak summer periods and two of the three approach roads are very narrow. The aim—to retain accessibility for visitors, whilst preserving the beauty of the valley—was achieved by providing car parks at the three approach points, together with a mini-bus service to points of interest. At the same time, walks, a nature trail, picnic facilities and various other amenities were introduced.[53]

Capacity and management

The Dartington Amenity Research Trust (DART) has been concerned with the integration of recreation demands on the countryside and the wider rural economy, and two themes which have emerged are:

1 Planning for recreation with due regard to conservation of natural resources (thus a concern with their capacity for human use)
2 The management of recreation enterprises in rural areas.

The present Director of DART, in his previous appointment, carried out a capacity study in Donegal, as a basis for planning for tourism and recreation, while safeguarding the natural environment.[54] The purpose of the study was to develop a method that could be used by rural authorities to achieve a balance between conservation and development. Capacities are needed as a guide to the number of people who can be accommodated without crowding, without causing physical or ecological damage and without straining facilities such as roads and car parks. The assessment of demand and of capacities in the Donegal Study was somewhat arbitrary; three types of capacity were defined:

a existing capacity;

b potential capacity, which takes into account possible improvements;

c necessary capacity (which is really demand made on resources).

A simple formula was used—

$$P = \frac{1}{3}\left(\frac{A}{2} + 2B + \frac{C}{3}\right)$$

in which P = leisure purpose trips
A = over-night visitors
B = day visitors
C = local residents;

this had no basis other than pragmatism and when used in Wharfedale in 1968 to check the theoretical capacities against actual usage, the latter were found to be far heavier.[55]

The Wharfedale Study conclusions were that local adjustments to a capacity formula would always be needed (as the Donegal Study had suggested); also, that the overall concept is probably more applicable to large areas of outstanding natural beauty than to the countryside around large cities. It was decided that for Wharfedale a more direct approach relating environmental standards to volumes of traffic would be more meaningful.

It would seem that to assess capacity in an area, or at a particular recreation facility, the following five steps are involved:

1 compilation of an inventory of recreation resources and facilities
2 estimation of present levels of use of each site and facility
3 assignment of capacities to each site and facility
4 comparisons of the levels of use and the assigned capacities to reveal over and under-usage
5 estimation of alternative methods, costs and management techniques for bringing use and capacity into better balance.

353

In a paper on this subject of capacities and management, Butterfield considered the factors which limit the capacity of an area of land or water for sustaining public recreational use:

'1 first of all physical characteristics—available space, topography, soil condition, vegetation, etc.

2 the attitudes of the public—what activities are demanded and what standards are felt to be tolerable

3 the attitudes of the owners or managers are also critical and may obviously differ from those of the public

4 finally, the investment in facilities—roads, car parks, accommodation slipways, moorings and so on.'[56]

He points out that 'our four classes of limiting factors can be shown to inter-act in such a way as to make capacity difficult to quantify, even if consideration for capacity is a good guiding rule.

'Quantification might mean the acceptance of some equilibrium but unless there are particular environmental qualities to conserve, the equilibrium may be difficult to place.' He illustrates with the example of three historic house country parks (which could in fact represent different stages in the development of the same park)

Park	Investment made	Effective capacity
A	Limited capital additions for recreation	15 per acre
B	Modest capital invested in attracting public	85 per acre
C	Heavy capital investment in public attractions and facilities	125 per acre[57]

He suggests that 'Although no hard conclusions can be drawn from our (DART's) work to date, the analysis of finances of recreation enterprises does suggest that, at present levels of admission and other charges, resource-based day recreation is not a profit-making business unless:

1 much of the capital resources are inherited (as with historic houses) or paid for under other heads (as with gravel pits) and thus do not appear in the recreation enterprise accounts, or

2 a strongly commercial attitude is taken with elements introduced which maximise expenditure per visitor, which naturally
   has an effect on the resource and on the recreation experience.
   Even where one of these factors applies, real profits may be
   low and, indeed, subsidies may be needed from public or private
   funds.'[58]

Classification of facilities

It was stated above that an element in capacity studies is the
compilation of an inventory of resources. At a grand scale, the
Outdoor Recreation Resources Review Commission, in the USA,
recommends classification of facilities and resources thus—

   1 High density recreation areas, these are intensively developed
and managed for mass use, and especially suited for day and
weekend visits. Development can include provision of a road
network, sanitary and eating facilities and playing fields, thus
allowing for a wide range of activities by a large number of
people.

   2 General outdoor recreation areas, such areas could sustain
varied activities and be developed for many specific recreation
uses, such as camping, picnicking, fishing, water sports, nature
walks and outdoor games.

   3 Natural environmental areas, in these, recreation is combined
with other uses, leaving the natural characteristics largely unchanged. Activities might include hiking, hunting, fishing, camping, picknicking, canoeing and sight-seeing, but special measures
will be needed for fire control, visitor safety and to prevent
vandalism.

   4 Unique natural areas, these are individual areas of high scenic
splendour or scientific importance. Adequate access for the
enjoyment and education of the public should be provided
wherever consistent with the main management objective of
preservation, and improvements should thus be the minimum
consistent with public safety and protection of the resource.
Access by vehicle should be restricted to the perimeter.

   5 Primitive areas are defined as undisturbed roadless areas,
characterised by natural wild conditions, including 'wilderness'

areas, which should be managed to preserve their primitive condition and isolation.

6 Historic and cultural sites, sites of major historical or cultural significance closely associated with vacation and recreation travel.[59]

Urban recreational provision

Another study concerned with supply of opportunities for leisure pursuits was that carried out by the London Borough of Southwark.[60] A Leisure Survey in the Borough showed that almost three-quarters of weekday recreation activities took place in the home, and even at the weekend it was well over half. As Betty Haran said, in describing the study, 'We concentrate on outdoor activities and facilities with a tendency towards active pursuits . . . for the vast majority recreation is time spent at home and the biggest single item is watching television.'

However, the land requirements generated by those recreation activities which are not home based cause particular difficulties in an inner city area where competition for land is acute and land acquisition costs enormous. Thus, 'what has to be done is an estimate of the capital and annual costs of desirable standards of recreational provision'; and in this there are two separate elements:

1 To ensure that there is a 'reasonable' allocation of resources for recreation
2 To allocate this money between different needs for facilities, all of which are in short supply.

Betty Haran emphasises—'To sum up this issue: land use forecasting and planning is one element in resource planning and for this to be done adequately a restructuring of local authority committees and finance is required.'[61]

Demand and supply studies

The one facility which Southwark particularly examined was swimming pools, and it was a swimming pool that Maw used to test his leisure model's accuracy.[62] Maw's study began with an analysis of people's use of time, based on their recorded time budgets, from which he concluded, 'Leisure time is significantly constrained within a relatively fixed framework of essential

356

activities and their associated time and place ties, particularly on weekdays. Choice of leisure activities is also restricted by income, social class, age and other characteristics of the population.'

His model incorporated a large number of variables, which are shown in Figure 15.7. All the variables must be measured

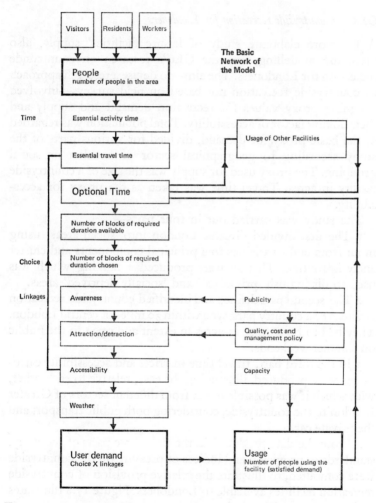

Fig. 15.7   Leisure Model: the basic network of the model (after Maw)

before the model can be used in any particular situation—some can be measured from sources already available, some require special surveys and some are impossible to determine by normal survey methods. The effectiveness of the model in simulating reality was tested in a comparison of its predictions with actual usage of a north London swimming bath.

GLC—Countryside recreation for Londoners

A far more elaborate study of leisure facilities' supply, also involving modelling, was the GLC's research on countryside recreation for Londoners. The aim—to devise a research approach to countryside recreation not based on field surveys—involved assigning proxy values for recreation demand and supply and their linking factor of accessibility. Total population was regarded as the basic proxy for demand, divided for various parts of the study according to geographical sector of London or social grouping. The proxy used for supply was the size of a countryside facility in acres. Travel time was taken as the proxy for accessibility.

The study was carried out in four parts—

1 The first divided Greater London into 'social areas' using input from eight variables to a principal components and cluster analysis routine. This analysis produced a ranking which was used to distinguish 'privileged' and 'socially deprived' areas.

2 The second part defined and identified countryside recreation facilities of a country park type within 30 miles of central London. They had to be at least 25 acres in extent and open to the public on summer weekends.

3 In the third part, travel time matrices and accessibility cartograms were produced, illustrating the ease, relative to each other, with which it was possible to get from different sectors of Greater London to the countryside, considering both public transport and the private car.

4 From the data produced in the first three parts of the study, standards of provision and indices of pressure on the countryside were computed, to illustrate the relative provision of countryside recreation facilities available to Londoners. Figure 15.8 illustrates various aspects of the study.

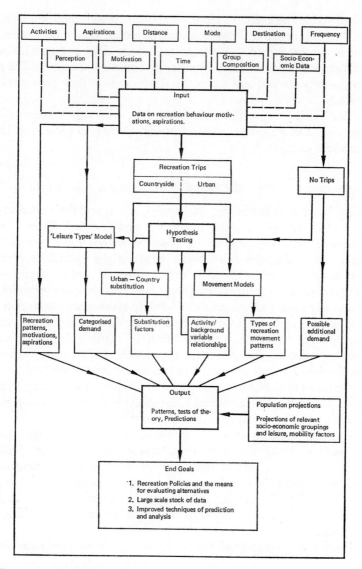

Boxes top row:
Activities | Aspirations | Distance | Mode | Destination | Frequency

Perception | Motivation | Time | Group Composition | Socio-Economic Data

Input

Data on recreation behaviour motivations, aspirations.

Recreation Trips

Countryside | Urban

No Trips

'Leisure Types' Model

Hypothesis Testing

Urban — Country substitution

Movement Models

Recreation patterns, motivations, aspirations

Categorised demand

Substitution factors

Activity/ background variable relationships

Types of recreation movement patterns

Possible additional demand

Output

Patterns, tests of theory, Predictions

Population projections

Projections of relevant socio-economic groupings and leisure, mobility factors

End Goals

1. Recreation Policies and the means for evaluating alternatives
2. Large scale stock of data
3. Improved techniques of prediction and analysis

Fig. 15.8   GLC Weekend Recreation Survey—Structure of Analysis

The conclusions expressed by Law and Perry in one of their discussions of the study are, 'The various indices and standards calculated in the exercises reported above cast an interesting light on the relative provision of countryside recreation for Londoners but it can be shown that the methodology does not provide a feasible alternative to formal studies of demand and supply.' They do go into some detail as to the shortcomings they see in the work.[63]

The GLC is now, in fact, preparing, with other interested agencies, a more formal research study relating to recreation in the south-east.

Some comments on the demand and supply relationships

Some interesting comments on demand, supply and their relationship were made in a paper by Burton and Cherry.[64] They first discussed demand, stressing its origin as an economic technical term, describing the relationship between the quantities of a product that people will purchase and prices. It is often confused in work on leisure facilities with consumption—the quantity which is actually purchased or consumed at any given price. Consumption derives from both demand and supply factors, and figures of use or attendance are thus the effect of existing demand and existing supply. For products for which the normal market mechanism does not work, which includes many leisure facilities, we confront, therefore, the problem of how to measure the demand for them. Most recreation studies are not really telling us anything about demand, only consumption.

The measurement of supply involves an accurate inventory of available facilities for recreation. Studies have compared the relative value for this of maps and photographs, documentary sources, self-administered postal surveys and observation; also, the possibility of using demand surveys as a means of determining available supply, by asking respondents to record all the facilities they use.

Finally they discussed the socio-economic determinants of recreation behaviour, which have been shown to affect the volume of participation in many recreation pursuits. However, 'what very few studies have shown, is the extent to which these factors affect demand and, more important, which aspects of these factors are most important.'

360

Chi-square tests of the significance of these factors produced some interesting results.

Those characteristics which were significant at the 1% level of probability included all of the four demographic characteristics; of the employment and status characteristics, the following—job status, personal income, socio-economic group, length of actual working week, length of usual working week, and method of pay; of the education characteristics, the following—type of school last attended, age left school, and amount of further education received; and all of the five home and equipment characteristics.

2 There were no characteristics which were found to be significant at the 5% probability level, but not at the 1% level.

3 There were six characteristics which were found to be not significant even at the 1% level of probability—these were all associated with either employment and status or education.

Burton and Cherry continue—'We should hasten to add that these results were based upon the significance of these characteristics in determining the *number* of recreation activities undertaken during one calendar year, 1968. Further tests are still being made of the significance of these factors in determining the types of activities undertaken and the frequency with which they are undertaken, rather than simply the volume of activities.'[65]

Simple theoretical model

Much of the work alluded to by Burton and Cherry was undertaken at the Centre for Urban and Regional Studies, University of Birmingham, and one of the Centre's most recent ventures was the development of a 'theory' and its extension into a 'model' for recreational facilities, described by Veal.[66]

The context of the method was taken to be a public or private body which is involved in administering facilities of one type for recreation and considering expansion (the eventual test situation taken was public libraries). The first requirement is to understand the existing situation thoroughly:
the number and locations of the facility in question
the relative accessibility of these facilities to the user population
the attractiveness of each individual facility.

361

These are the characteristics of supply that affect directly the use of, or demand for, facilities. Another factor is the socio-economic characteristics of the population.

'These various concepts can now be defined in a form suitable for use in a model:

X_{ij} is a measure of the use made of facility j by residents of zone i, in a given period of time. The unit used might be person-visits per annum, or person-hours per annum, or total expenditure. In the subsequent discussion, this quantity will generally be referred to as 'number of users'.

A_j is the attractiveness or attraction factor of facility j. There may be, in fact, several of these factors for each facility . . .

'These factors could reflect such things as the newness or size of the facility, prices charged (if any) and the availability of car parking.

D_{ij} is the distance of zone i from facility j. Distance might be measured in miles, as 'the crow flies' or by road, or in terms of time taken to travel from the zone to the facility, or in some combination of time and distance.

E_i represents one or more socio-economic characteristics of the population of zone i: it could be, for example, the number of females under 65 years of age.

P_i is the resident population of zone i.

'There are assumed to be N facilities and n zones in the planning area.'

Veal explains further—'X_{ij} is the dependent variable; that is, it is postulated that its value depends on the value of the other variables specified—the independent variables. Thus, the more attractive (A_j) a facility is, the more people will use it, or the more intensively they will use it. The further away (D_{ij}) a facility is, or the less accessible it is, the fewer people will use it, or the less intensively they will use it. This is because of the deterrent effect of distance—the costs and inconvenience of overcoming it —and because at greater distances people are often less aware of the existence of a facility. The socio-economic structure of the population (E_i) will also affect participation rates, so that, for example, an area with a lot of old people will, other things being equal, tend to have fewer active sportsmen than an area containing a high proportion of young people. For some recreation activities,

362

the income levels of the population may also be important, as will the overall total population (*Pi*) of the area.'

It is suggested that a model developed along these lines could be used to forecast the level of use of facilities which could be valuable in formulating policy, which would, of course, take into account factors considered important other than optimum level of usage of facilities.

Potential surface approach to rural planning

An approach to the analysis and policy resolution of conflicting demands on land, first used for economic and urban problems, has begun to be applied to rural planning. The East Hampshire area of outstanding natural beauty was chosen for a case study, by the various agencies concerned, to develop a rural planning method.[67]

Four distinct stages were involved:

1 Resources and activities

The first stage was to identify the resources available in the area, and the nature and extent of the activities going on. The categories for recording information were wildlife, landscape, agriculture, forestry and 'other uses' (settlement and services, communications, mineral workings, defence establishments, recreational activities). The results of an appraisal of these different factors, and their relative significance to different parts of the study area was expressed on 1-inch-to-the-mile maps; trends in land use practices and changing levels of demand, were, of course, taken into account.

2 Zonation

The second stage was to sub-divide the study area into units for which planning policies to resolve land use problems could be formulated. The result was a map dividing the area into 136 zones, which were subsequently reduced in number by combining adjacent zones where two different interests were not, in fact, in conflict (such as landscape and wildlife) or where the differences were largely of degree.

3 Interactions

The next stage was to examine the effects of different uses of the land upon the resources of the study area and upon each other, considering multiple use of land and the effects of neighbouring activities. The interactions were summarised in a table (see Figure 15.9) which allowed rapid identification of conflict situations and possible areas for new activities.

4 Policy formulation

After the analysis described, a basis was available for deciding policies for rural land use. Five factors were considered in relation to any demands for changes:

1   Whether proposals are in accord with established objectives—national, regional or local; public and private.
2   To what extent they would affect other land uses or resources.
3   What sort of location they prefer.
4   What conditions to ameliorate their effect on other interests should be imposed (or vice versa).
5   What method for implementing the proposed policy can best be used.

The policies evolved for the study area were of two types, described thus—

'1 Precise location and control policies, needed in the zones of greatest potential conflict or for activities which were extremely unacceptable to other interests. Examples were most recreation sites; certain agricultural practices in areas of high wildlife value; and the location of horticultural buildings in areas of high landscape value. Methods of implementation suggested were controls along the lines of Town and Country Planning legislation or management agreements.

'2 Policies covering practices not tied to specific location, such as many agricultural practices or pleasure motoring. In many cases these activities seemed suited to policies of publicity, exhortation, or promotion of codes of practice, and possibly

364

Fig. 15.9 *Extract from Accessibility Chart*

Activities	Points of View	Zone 1					Zone 2					Zone 3				
		Agriculture	Forestry	Landscape	Conservation	Recreation	Agriculture	Forestry	Landscape	Conservation	Recreation	Agriculture	Forestry	Landscape	Conservation	Recreation
26 Road improvement — Large scale	2	2	4	5	2	2	3/2	4	5	2	2	2	4	5	2	2
26 Road improvement — Small scale	2	2	4	5	2	2	2/2	4	5	2	2	2	4	5	2	2
27 Telephone wires — Large scale	1	2	2	5	3	1	4/2	2	5	3	1	2	2	5	3	3
27 Telephone wires — Small scale	1	2	2	5	2	1	2/2	2	5	2	1	2	2	5	2	2
28 Walking, picnicking — Large scale	2	2	2	2	1	3	2	2	2	1	3	2	2	2	1	1
28 Walking, picnicking — Small scale	2	2	2	2	1	3	2	2	2	1	3	2	2	2	1	1
29 Fishing — Large scale	4	–	2	2	1	4	–	2	2	1	4	–	2	2	1	1
29 Fishing — Small scale	2	–	2	2	1	2	–	2	2	1	2	–	2	2	1	1

management agreements. It is interesting to note that the technique developed has produced a rather similar result to the existing development plan 'white land' pattern of policies, but it has revealed that in rural areas now covered by general 'white land' policies there are certain areas analogous to urban areas which need far greater detail of planning because they are areas of greater potential conflict between different interests.'[68]

The conclusions of the study were that much more can be done in such situations with existing powers than is generally realised, and that it is quite possible to develop techniques of analysis to produce policies for planning rural areas which are just as acceptable as their equivalents for urban areas.

Conclusion

It is very difficult to draw any neat conclusions about techniques for planning for leisure. In essence, as with all planning, *choices* are involved about the allocation of the community's resources, notably land and investment. To make these choices, all those concerned in planning for leisure have to make an analysis (which is often implicit) about the relative costs and benefits of different courses of action, and which developments would be in conflict with each other and which would be mutually compatible or even reinforcing. Behind these cost and benefit assessments lie the values of the community as a whole. Thus many of the techniques described have been concerned with identification and measurement of factors on the 'supply' side and the 'demand' side, and how they influence each other, which are necessary pieces of knowledge in trying to operate—whether in an explicit technique or by 'common sense' equivalents—an approach to the planning of facilities for leisure pursuits which will represent an appropriate allocation of the community's land and other resources to this group of needs, as compared with all its other needs.

Those areas of technical expertise commonly suggested for urgent further work reflect the inadequate understanding at present of the real value of leisure, an inability to express such valuation in investment decision situations, and a wish to improve the use made of resources allocated for leisure pursuits—

366

for example the four fields for development suggested by Cherry were: attitude and motivation research, capacity studies, management techniques and cost-benefit analysis.[69]

References

1 Countryside Commission, *Countryside Recreation Glossary* (for CRRAG) (1970).
2 Burton T. L., *Experiments in Recreation Research,* Allen & Unwin, London (1971).
3 Reich, C. A., *The Greening of America,* Penguin (1971).
4 Law, S., 'Introduction to demand studies', in *The Demand for Outdoor Recreation in the Countryside,* Countryside Commission, page 5 (1970).
5 Cherry, G. E., 'Research techniques in recreation planning', in *Recreation Land Use Planning and Forecasting,* PATRAC, page 31 (1969).
6 Burton, T. L., *Windsor Great Park: A Recreation Study,* Wye College Studies in Rural Land Use, No. 8 (1967); Greater London Council, *Surveys of the Use of Open Spaces—1,* Research Paper 2 (1968); British Travel Association/Peak Park Planning Board, *Peak District National Peak Survey* (1963), Summary Report, and Study Reports.
7 British Travel Association/University of Keele, *Pilot National Recreation Survey,* Report 1 (1967).
8 British Broadcasting Corporation, *The Peoples' Activities,* Audience Research Department (1965); Sillitoe, K., *Planning for Leisure,* Government Social Survey, HMSO, London (1969).
9 Central Council of Physical Recreation, *A Preliminary Analysis of the Non-Residential Use of the Crystal Palace National Recreation Centre* (1965); Burton and the Greater London Council, *op. cit.* (6) above.
10 British Sociological Association, series of appraisals, some now published in *Comparability in Social Research,* Heinemann Educational Books (1969).
11 Newcastle-upon-Tyne City Planning Department, *Evening Leisure Survey,* see Sutherland, A., *Methods of Data Collection.*
12 Regional Sports Councils, *Initial Appraisals* (1967–8).
13 Moser, C. A., *Survey Methods in Social Investigation,* Heinemann (1958).

14 Hole, V., *Children's Play on Housing Estates*, National Building Studies Research Paper 39, HMSO (1966);
Wager, J. F., 'Outdoor recreation on common land', in *Journal of the Town Planning Institute*, page 398, **53,** 9, November 1967.

15 Norfolk County Council, *Report on the Norfolk Holiday Industry* (1964).

16 Cross National Time Budget Study, see Robinson, J. P. & Converse, P. E. *Sixty-six Basic Tables of Time Budget Data for the U.S.*, Draft Report, University of Michigan Survey Research Centre (1966).

17 Chapin, F. S. & Hightower, H. C. *Household Activity Systems— A Pilot Investigation*, University of North Carolina, Urban Studies Research Monograph (1966).

18 see BBC, *op. cit.* (8) above.

19 Coppock, J. T., *Pilot Survey of Tourism in Part of the Borders: Methods of Data Collection*, University of Edinburgh, Department of Geography.

20 As used, for example, in a survey of visitors to the Wye and Crundale Nature Reserve, as reported in Cullingworth, J. B., 'Planning for leisure', in *Urban Studies,* page 1, **1,** 1, May 1964.

21 See Cherry, *op. cit.* (5) above.

22 Burton, T. L. & Cherry, G. E. 'The nature and measurement of recreation demand', in *The Demand for Outdoor Recreation in the Countryside,* Countryside Commission (1970).

23 Clawson, M. & J. L. Knetsch, *Economics of Outdoor Recreation,* Johns Hopkins Press, for Resources for the Future, page 60 (1966)

24 See Law, *op. cit.* (4) above.

25 Steering Committee for the National Survey of Angling, with the Natural Environment Research Council, *National Survey of Angling,* (1969–70).

26 Law, S., 'Open Space provision and policy in Greater London', in *Recreation Land Use Planning and Forecasting,* PATRAC, page 11, (1969);
also, 'Planning for outdoor recreation in the countryside', in *Journal of the Town Planning Institute,* page 383, **53,** 9 (1967).

27 Houghton-Evans, W. & Miles, J. C. 'Weekend recreational motoring in the countryside', in *Journal of the Town Planning Institute,* page 394, November 1970.

28 Duffell, J. R. & Goodall, G. R. 'Leisure in town and country', in *The Surveyor and Municipal Engineer,* page 32 131 (3945) (1968).

29 Buchanan, C. & Partners, *The South Hampshire Study,*
Supplementary Volume 2, HMSO (1966);
see Burton, *op. cit.* (6) above;
see Wager, *op. cit.* (14) above.

30 As (29) above.

31 As (29) above.

32 See Houghton-Evans & Miles, *op. cit.* (27) above.

33 See Wager, *op. cit.* (14) above.

34 See Buchanan, *op. cit.* (29) above.

35 Mansfield, N. W., 'Traffic policy in the Lake District National
Park', in *Journal of the Town Planning Institute,* page 263, **54,**
6 (1968).

36 Mansfield, N. W., 'The estimation of benefits from recreational
sites and provision of a new recreational facility', in *Regional
Studies,* **5,** 2, (1971).

37 Clawson, M., *Methods of Measuring the Demand for and Value of
Outdoor Recreation,* Resources for the Future, Reprint No. 10,
Washington DC (1959).

38 Kavanagh, N. J., 'Economics of water recreation', Chapter 4
in *Recreation Research and Planning,* edited by T. L. Burton,
page 78 (see page 88), Allen & Unwin, London, (1970).

39 See Clawson & Knetsch, *op. cit.* (23) above.

40 for example, Knetsch, J. L., *Economics of including recreation as
a purpose of water resource projects,* Resources for the Future,
Reprint No. 50, Washington DC (1965).

41 Including Smith, R. J. & Kavanagh, N. J. 'The measurement
of benefits of trout fishing: preliminary results of a study at
Grafham Water', in *Journal of Leisure Research,* Autumn 1969;
Stevens, J. B., 'Recreation benefits from water pollution control',
in *Water Resources Research,* **2,** 2 (1966).

42 See (41) above.

43 See, for example, Seckler, D. W., 'On the uses and abuses of
economic science in evaluating public outdoor recreation', in
Land Economics, **42,** page 485 (1966).

44 See Mansfield, *op. cit.* (35) above.

45 A small amount of useful material has been collected, but
not published.

46 'Planning for the tourist: Beaulieu', in *Architect's Journal,*
March 1967.

47 Houghton-Evans, W. & Miles, J. C. 'Environmental capacity
in rural recreation', in *Journal of the Town Planning Institute,*
page 423 December 1970.

48 See (47) above.

49 See Buchanan, *op. cit.* (29) above.

50 Hills, P. J., 'Case studies of environmental management', in *The Surveyor and Municipal Engineer,* **127,** 3848 (1966).

51 Furmidge, J., 'Planning for recreation in the countryside', in *Journal of the Town Planning Institute,* page 62, **55,** 2 (1969).

52 Countryside Commission & Peak Park Planning Board, *Goyt Valley Traffic Experiment—Interim Report,* March 1971; also, Burrell, T. S., 'National Parks—managing the scene', in *Official Architecture and Planning,* page 855, October 1970.

53 An Foras Forbartha, *Planning for Amenity and Tourism,* Dublin (1966).

54 Miles, J. C., *Weekend Recreational Travel—A Review and Pilot Study,* University of Leeds, unpublished thesis (1969).

55 Butterfield, J. H., 'The capacity and management of recreation resources in the countryside', in *Recreation Land Use Planning and Forecasting,* PATRAC, page 35 (1969).

56 See Butterfield, *op. cit.* (55) above; See also Report in *Recreation News,* 31, July 1971, of British Tourist Authority's Historic Houses Committee Course on Management of Country Parks, Historic Houses and Castles.

57 See Butterfield, *op. cit.* (55) above.

58 Bureau of Outdoor Recreation, Department of the Interior, *Outdoor Recreation Space Standards* (1967).

59 Haran, B., 'Review of the problems of recreational provision in an inner area', in *Recreation Land Use Planning and Forecasting,* PATRAC, page 7 (1969).

60 See Haran, *op. cit.* (59) above.

61 Maw, R., 'Construction of a leisure model', in *Official Architecture and Planning,* page 924, **32,** 8 (1969).

62 Law, S., & Perry, N. 'Countryside recreation for Londoners—a preliminary research approach', in *GLC Intelligence Unit Quarterly Bulletin,* page 11, 14, March 1971. also, *GLC Department of Planning and Transportation Strategy Branch Research Memo RM* 267, November 1970; see also, Cracknell, B., 'Accessibility to the countryside as a factor in planning for leisure', in *Regional Studies,* page 147, **2** (1968).

63 Law & Perry, *op. cit.* (62) above.

64 See Burton & Cherry, *op. cit.* (22) above.

65 See Burton & Cherry, *op. cit.* (22) above.

66 Veal, A. J., in *Experiments in Recreation Research and Planning*,
by T. L. Burton, Allen & Unwin, London (1971).
67 Countryside Commission, *Rural Planning Methods* (1968);
a full report is given in *East Hampshire AONB—a Study in
Countryside Conservation*, Hampshire County Council (1968).
68 In Rural Planning Methods, *op. cit.* (67) above.
69 See Cherry, *op. cit.* (5) above.

16 Transport

Introduction

In talking about transport we are concerned with the movement of people and goods. People need to move from place to place to get from homes to work, schools, shops, friends and other destinations; goods must often be moved many times during production and before reaching the place of eventual use or consumption. The means for achieving these movements of people and goods are varied, but the notable ones in our society are cars, buses and lorries, trains and planes, as well as feet.

The techniques used by those concerned with planning for transport needs are often complex, but what is at the root of them is the familiar approach of planning—trying to assess present and future patterns of need, what facilities exist to satisfy such needs now, and what further provision should be made.

Although such assessments are made at the national level, as in motorways or ports policies, the most frequent scale of study is for the individual town or city, or the sub-region. It is studies of this type which are most amenable to the methods described below. In general, although rail transport makes some contribution to the overall needs for movement in a town or city, the facility most under pressure and most suitable for expansion is the road system. In fact, rail will be of use for certain types of movement—commuter trips, freight moving long distances, for example, but generally not for the complicated mesh of shorter distance and multi-purpose trips, for which the private car is often most convenient for the individual user, but most inconvenient in aggregate for the planner.

Most of this chapter is devoted to an outline of the transportation planning process (see Figure 16.1). There is also a brief section on environmental considerations.

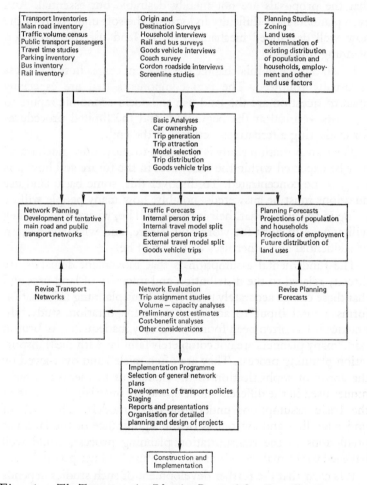

Fig. 16.1   The Transportation Planning Process (after Proudlove)

SOURCE 'Some Comments on the West Midlands Transport Study' in *Traffic Engineering and Control*, 1968

The transportation planning process

The London motorway box is only one of many instances of transport proposals provoking violent hostility. In such cases, the emotional outrage of objectors runs smack into an impenetrable wall of seemingly incontrovertible hard fact, demonstrating that the proposals are not merely desirable but essential. And even planners have difficulty in locating the soft underbelly of the now well developed mechanism of the land use/transportation planning process.

I shall outline in this chapter the different stages in this process as usually followed. The two components that are especially open to question are the land use and socio-economic inputs to forecasts—critical at the beginning, and the limited procedures for evaluating alternatives—critical at the end.

The transportation study is designed to show how much travel may be expected within the study area in the future and how it is likely to be concentrated. To discover this, some basic land use questions must be answered—notably, how many people will be living in the area, what their incomes will be, what activities they will engage in both for work and leisure, and what the pattern of residential and other uses of land will be.

The fundamental assumption is that movement demands are directly related to the distribution and intensity of land uses and that these can be accurately predicted. Thus planning information forms a vital input to any land use/transportation study. In practice it has often been found to be very inadequate. As Bruton said, 'many planners are not completely familiar with the transportation planning process. They are often misled and over-awed by the apparent sophistication of the numerous mathematical techniques used in the different models, and are invariably unaware of the basic assumptions underlying these models. This lack of understanding and awareness of the significance of the land use predictions in the transportation planning process, could well have led to the making of unrealistic future land use predictions.'[1]

It is clear that the further development of such studies depends in part on improved land use forecasting techniques and in part on a greater understanding of the interrelationships between land development and transport systems.

374

The land use/transportation planning process culminates in the financing and implementation of the projects chosen to maintain (or improve) the efficiency of the transport system. The projects should be chosen on the basis of evaluation of alternative possibilities in both economic and social terms—such alternatives must derive from an estimation of future demands for movement and awareness of shortcomings in the existing provision.

In essence, this is a three part framework—

The present—a survey and analysis stage, which assesses present demand for movement, how it is met and what relationships exist between the characteristics of the study area and the demand for movement.

Forecasting futures—the extrapolation of such relationships to produce estimates of future travel demands, together with the possible ways of meeting them.

Choice of action—an evaluation procedure to assess which of the transportation proposals would provide the maximum benefits to the community at minimum costs.

In terms of work organisation a sequence of eight steps may be identified:

1 the collection of land use, population, economic and travel pattern data for the present day situation;
2 the establishment of quantifiable relationships between present day movements and the land use, population and economic factors;
3 the prediction of land use, population and economic factors to the target date for the study;
4 the prediction of the origins, destinations and distribution of the future movement demands, using the relationships established for the present day situation and the predicted land use, population and economic factors;
5 the prediction of the person movements likely to be carried by the different modes of travel at the target date;
6 the assignment of predicted trips to alternative co-ordinated transport systems;
7 the evaluation of the efficiency and economic viability of the alternative transport systems proposed;
8 the selection of a balanced transport system which best serves the needs of the future.

The work stages 1 to 6 above are normally handled by a series of models, which, although interdependent in the process as a whole, are best explained individually. A considerable amount of information is required for the operation of these models; since some of the data is used in more than one model, it is simpler to mention data collection before discussing the models.[2]

Collection of basic data

There are four categories of information required, concerning
1 the people who live in the study area
2 travel patterns
3 existing travel facilities
4 land use

The first, concerning people, is collected largely by home interview; the second, travel patterns, by home interview and traffic survey; the third, existing travel facilities, by various surveys and observations, and the fourth, land use, is generally obtained from land use planners.

Home interview survey

In general, a sample of residents in the area is selected from electoral registers or rating lists. The size of the sample tends to vary with the size of the area under study. In a small town, perhaps 1 in 5 households will be interviewed; a much lower proportion (1 in 25 to 1 in 100) in a large city. From every household in the sample, information is obtained about the members of the household—age, sex, occupation, place of work or school, car ownership—and about all their travel on, say, the previous day. The origin and destination of each trip, together with its purpose, the travel mode used and the time taken will all be noted.

Travel pattern surveys

The area of study is delimited by an external cordon and divided into internal traffic zones. These zones are selected in terms of natural boundaries and dominant land use, taking into account

376

the areas used by other agencies recording information which might be useful, e.g. ED's. There is a standard system for assigning coding numbers to these zones, and another one for the external zones—those outside the cordon—which cover the whole country, increasing in size away from the study area.

Interviews with the drivers of a sample of vehicles crossing the external cordon (sometimes by supplying a prepaid post-card questionnaire) establishes three types of movement affecting the area:

through movements, that is, external to external, sometimes divided into stopping and non-stopping journeys; external to internal; and internal to external. The latter, and a fourth type, purely internal movements, are established from the home interview survey—also, sometimes, by using an internal cordon or screen line for a traffic check. An internal check has the further advantage that it can be compared with the grossed-up estimates of travel derived from the home interview survey.

Of course, commercial vehicles, as well as private vehicles, are studied.

Existing transport facilities

An important element of the collection of basic data is the survey of existing transport facilities. The data is obtained from surveys of the road network, public transport facilities and parking provision, and the use made of them, and is, in effect, a stock-taking of the major highway and public transport networks, the existing demand for and supply of parking accommodation, and the present day traffic volumes and travel times.

Thus the typical patterns of travel in the study area at the present day are established, and any over or under utilisation of the transport and parking facilities.

Planning data

Information is needed on present and future patterns and intensity of land uses, which is normally obtained from the planning authorities.

Information on retail sales (to gauge shopping trips), places of employment and educational establishments must be pieced together from published Censuses (including Distribution, for shopping, and Population, for journey to work), the planning authorities, the home interview and other special surveys.

The Census of Population provides a check to the household survey information on the socio-economic characteristics of the inhabitants of the study area.

Once all the data has been assembled, it must be grossed up where derived from samples, and coded and processed for computer input.

Trip generation

In order to assess future travel demand, the present day determinants of trip production must be understood. Once those characteristics of land-use, population and transport facilities that influence travel demand have been identified, they are projected to the target date to provide estimates of the total amount and kind of travel demand. It is thus assumed that the present day relationships will hold over time.

Various techniques have been developed to produce figures of trip generation, generally identifying the traffic zones of origin and destination of trips. *Multiple linear regression analysis* is the technique most often used. It measures the separate influence of each factor in association with other factors, and the aim of the analysis is to produce an equation which embodies traffic, land use and socio-economic data.[3]

A development aimed to overcome some of the problems associated with the selection and formulation of variables is *category analysis*, as used, for example, in the second phase of the London Traffic Survey. This assumes that trip generation rates for different categories of household will remain constant in the future. Thus, by knowing the generation rate for each category of household, and how many such households there will be, the overall trip generation can be assessed. In general, reliable estimates of future trip generation for the short-term can be produced, but the longer-term predictions are more difficult.

Trip distribution

Trip distribution techniques are concerned to establish the links between zones, not the specific routes, nor the travel modes used.

There are two main groups of trip distribution techniques which are used. *Growth factor methods* which are based on the assumption that present travel patterns can be projected into the future, using expected differential zonal rates of growth. These methods are adequate for short-term predictions or for updating recent surveys. Their advantages are that they are easily understood and applied and require only an inventory of present day trip origins and destinations and an estimation of simple growth factors.

However, more widely used are *synthetic methods*, which attempt to utilise the causal relationships behind patterns of movement, by assuming them to be similar to laws of physical behaviour. Examples of synthetic methods are the gravity model, the 'electrostatic field' method and 'intervening' and 'competing' opportunities formulae, as well as multiple regression methods. (A comparison has been made of the effectiveness of four of these techniques, using work journey distribution as a test.)[4]

Traffic assignment

This is the process of allocating the travel pattern derived from the trip generation and distribution calculations to a specific transportation system. A complete description of either the proposed or existing transportation system and a matrix of interzonal trip movements are required.

The general procedure is for the computer to select the minimum path between zones, assign estimated trips to this path and accumulate traffic volumes for each section of the route (see Figure 16.2).

The output is an estimate of traffic volumes on each link of the transportation system (more sophisticated assignment techniques also include directional turning movements at intersections).

There are three basic types of technique used for traffic assignment. The choice of procedure to be adopted in any particular transportation study depends largely on the purpose of that study and the degree of sophistication required of the output.

379

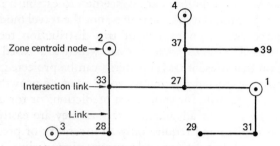

(a) *Highway network description — links and nodes*

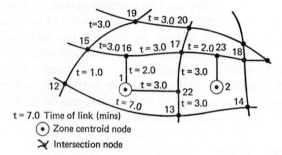

t = 7.0 Time of link (mins)
⊙ Zone centroid node
✗ Intersection node

(b) *Network for calculation of minimum path*

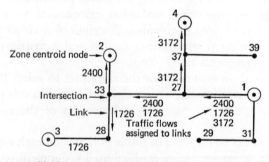

(c) *Minimum path tree calculated from Node 1 in sample network*

Fig. 16.2 Traffic assignment (after Bruton)

SOURCE *Introduction to Transportation Planning*, Hutchinson (1970)

Division curves

For any trip, there are usually several alternative routes, each with its own 'travel resistance' derived from its characteristics of speed, distance, travel time and level of service. The driver evaluates these to choose his route.

A quantified measure of the travel resistance of different routes can be used to produce diversion curves, which indicate what proportion of drivers are likely to switch to a new route if constructed. Three different types of diversion curve are in current use—their names imply the factors they consider:

a the travel time ratio curve
b the distance and speed ratio curve
c the travel time and distance saved curve (see Figure 16.3).

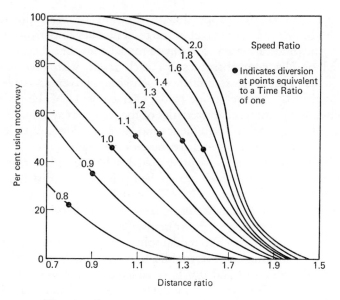

Fig. 16.3   Diversion Curves

'All or nothing' assignments

This technique for traffic assignment is also based on the assumption that vehicles will take the travel path with the least resistance

—the measure normally used is that of time. The disadvantage of this simple technique is that no account is taken of increasing congestion associated with increased traffic volumes, which, in practice, would influence drivers to transfer to other routes.

Capacity restraint assignment

As an improvement on the 'all or nothing' technique, capacity restraint assignments allow for the automatic lowering of assumed speeds on links of the travel network as the assigned traffic volumes on them approach the practical capacity. Therefore, their attraction to traffic decreases.

Modal split

Modal split is the proportionate division between different methods, or modes, of travel of the total number of person trips. Many methods are used to estimate modal split, but they are all based on the competitiveness of each mode with the others available. Three factors influence such competitiveness—characteristics of the journey to be made, characteristics of the person making the journey, characteristics of the transport system. Many of the factors known to influence modal choice are incapable of being quantified reliably and are therefore omitted.

The techniques used to give modal split are either *trip end* modal split models, which are applied prior to trip distribution stage, or *trip interchange* modal split models, which allocate parts of given trip movements resulting from the trip distribution forecasts to the competing modes of transport.

The trip end approach to modal split, unlike trip interchange, is capable of making separate public transport and private motor vehicle distributions and this is considered an important advantage. However, both types of model have been criticised as having a built-in bias in favour of the private car.

The process of a transportation study, as sketched above, has inherent weaknesses, quite apart from the use to which the results may be put. 'Significant advances in the development of the transport stages of the process have been achieved in recent years, yet the weakest part of the whole procedure is the land use and economic forecasting stage which is really fundamental to the whole process. Although many of the different models which go to make up the overall model appear to be complex and sophisticated, the assumptions on which they are based are at present weak. The transportation process is not the precise tool which some people like to think it. Rather it is a rational process, which isolates all those factors which apparently influence movement demands, and attempts to present a logically argued case for estimating future movement demands.'[5]

Perhaps land use/transport forecasts should more often be treated as exploratory devices, to assess what would happen if various patterns of land use or personal behaviour occurred in the future, or what would be the effects of various levels of investment in transport facilities and different planning policies.

They also have a monitoring role to play; the process should be a continuous one, 'rather than a "once and for all time" study, whereby regular comparisons should be made between actual and predicted land use and traffic developments. Any significant divergence between the actual and the forecasted developments should be analysed carefully to establish the reasons for the divergence and if necessary the original assumptions modified or amended to bring about a balance between the two values.'[6]

Nearly five years ago now, Peter Hall was stressing the necessity of transportation studies functioning in an *evaluative* sense.[7] 'The provision of future transportation facilities should itself help to condition the future pattern of land uses, in order to provide patterns of living, of working and of travel which will prove efficient at the lowest cost in resources to the community. At this point the process of model building must cease to be merely mechanically predictive, and must become evaluative. It must specify certain planning goals and seek to discover how these goals may be most rationally and economically achieved.'

However, Hall continues, 'evaluative models cannot proceed without a common measure of value which may be used to judge alternative courses of action', and from this it follows that, 'one of the largest question marks in urban model building at present concerns the development of evaluative techniques.'

Implicit assumption of values

There is no doubt that too little attention has been given to the implicit assumption of values within transportation studies (fundamental to Stages 7 and 8 above).

A recent article discussed the measurement of the utilities associated with the outcomes of alternative transport strategies, suggesting that, at the least, any evaluation framework should be based on the community's demands for accessibility and for environmental quality, taking into account income distribution goals (i.e. *who* benefits).[8]

The author suggested that, 'Before speculating on the appropriate form of an evaluation framework it is instructive to review the state of affairs which has existed throughout the past decade. During this period most transportation policy decisions in North America were made by the elected representatives on the advice of transportation planners with only cursory attention being paid to the other interest groups in the community.'

Thus, 'Transportation investment evaluations during this period were based on an aggregated view of the impacts of these investments and a concentration on those impacts associated with the movement of private motor vehicles on the transportation system. Investment costs were measured generally in terms of the capital costs of construction and the market prices of the land required for the rights-of-way. Few attempts were made to incorporate the costs arising from the displacement of people and businesses, the opportunity costs of the land consumed, or the environmental impacts of these investments.'

A recognition of the existence of community interests was the mechanism of the public hearing. 'The principal characteristic of most of these public hearings was the focusing of the negative reactions of the groups affected by transportation proposals. A major deficiency of this type of forum was the lack of any real communication between the planner, the elected representatives and the electorate. Transportation planners were generally incapable of conveying the real impact of proposals on the mobility and environment of the urban residents.'

His general conclusion was—'Perhaps this unwillingness to view transportation investment in broader terms and in terms of their differential impacts on the various community interest groups, is a direct reflection of the welfare economists' reluctance to address themselves to the distributional effects of investments.'

Environmental effects

One most important aspect of any transport proposals involving either building new roads or railways, or intensification of use of existing facilities, is the detrimental effect on environment—whether through visual intrusiveness, noise and vibration nuisance, or delay, danger and inconvenience to pedestrians. Thus, in any cost-benefit evaluation of transport possibilities it is usual to find some environmental implications taken into account (although there is always much to question in the methods chosen to measure the relevant factors, and often of those factors selected as relevant). Noise levels are forecast, both averages and peaks, visual intrusiveness may be assessed by indices of various types, the effects on pedestrians are gauged through likely delays at pedestrian crossing points and numbers of accidents.

An attempt at a more comprehensive assessment of the detrimental effects of alternative road network proposals was made recently by the London Borough of Camden. Their environmental scoring method evolved from a study of alternative road networks which the Borough undertook, to find ways of coping with its share of London traffic with the least harm to residential areas.

The starting point was therefore the network of all roads that might be used for through traffic—both main and back streets. Those streets obviously unsuited to through traffic were eliminated from consideration, leaving about 40 miles of road for analysis. Three possible solutions were then postulated—coarse, medium and fine networks of district and local distributor roads. At the same time, eleven 'environmental areas' were defined.

Once the three alternative networks were fixed, the next step was to quantify the environmental impacts of each, or of combinations of parts of them. To assess the two main aspects of traffic nuisance—conflict with pedestrians, and disturbance by noise, vibration and so on, reasonably objective and quantifiable factors were selected for measurement. They comprised—residential density, proximity of roads to shops, proximity of roads to schools, distance of frontages from the roadside and road gradient. Other factors known to be important but difficult to quantify—such as listed buildings and views—were left out. Most of the information was already held in the planning department.

The roads to be investigated were divided into 50-metre lengths, and the scores for each factor summed to produce an 'index of vulnerability' which, with all its crudeness, was most useful in comparative assessment. (The scoring of factors is shown in Figure 16.4(*a*). The figures were then converted to a

The factors were scored as follows :—

Pedestrian Activity Connected with Shopping

More than 300m from shops	0
200 – 300m	1
100 – 200m	2
under 100m	3
at shopping frontage	4

Pedestrian Flow at Schools

More than 300m from school	0
200 – 300m	1
100 – 200m	2
under 100m	3

Frontage Separation

Frontages over 25m apart	1
20 – 25m	2
15 – 20m	3
under 15m	4

Gradient

Under 1 in 50	1
Between 1 in 50 and 1 in 35	2
Between 1 in 35 and 1 in 25	3
Steeper than 1 in 25	4

Residential Density

Non-residential	0
Under 30 p.p.a.	1
30 – 50	2
50 – 70	3
70 – 100	4
100 – 136	5
136 – 170	6
over 170	7

Fig. 16.4(a)   Camden—Quantifying Environment (after Mason)

SOURCE 'Camden Discovers a Method of Quantifying Environment' in *Municipal Engineering*, 1970

A	B	C	D	E	F	G	H	J	K	L	M	N	P	Q
Link Number	No. of 50m sections	Frontage Separation	Road Gradient	Proximity to School	Proximity to Shops	Resid-ensity	Principal Traffic Route	Total Environmental Index	Traffic flow factor 'coarse'	Traffic Flow Factor 'Medium'	Traffic Flow Factor 'Fine'	Index of Detriment 'Coarse'	Index of Detriment 'Medium'	Index of Detriment 'Fine'
69	5	9	15	6	11	24		53	10	10	10	530	530	530
70	9	13	9	0	16	61		69	36	25	10	2484	1725	220
72	4	4	4	0	1	26		22	10	10	10	220	220	220
106	6	7	6	0	15	42	X	49	157	118	118	7693	5782	5782
107	9	11		0	24	32		80	51	10	10	4080	800	800
												Coarse	Medium	Fine
Total of above links. Excluding principal traffic routes:												142677	190779	200246
Total as % of medium network score:												75	100	105
Total over all links in Camden on the three networks:												853419		967143
Total as % of medium network score:												89	100	101

Fig, 16.4(b) An example of the total network evaluation in Camden. Scores in C, D, E, F and G are allocated to each 50m section using the values decided and then totalled for each link. Column G shows the residential density scales for both sides of each link except where marked with an asterisk. The two-sided score is divided by two when calculating the environmental index: J = C + D + E + F + ½G. Principal traffic routes are shown with an X in column H.

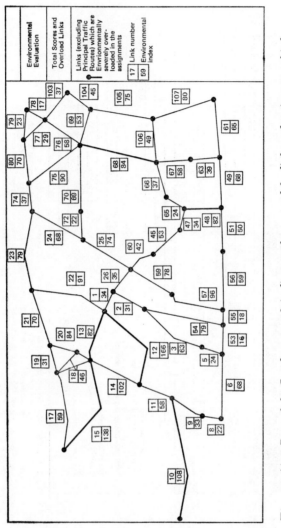

Fig. 16.4(c)   Part of the Camden network in diagram form scored for links and environmental index

logarithmic scale for different flows of vehicles. The last step was the multiplication of the traffic flow factors and environmental index for each length to give an 'index of detriment'. A summation of the detriment indices throughout the length of each network gave a comparative figure for each of the three (see Figure 16.4(c)).

Efforts to refine the method, which is clearly of great potential usefulness, centre on more accurate scoring of the different elements involved to relate more closely to the detrimental effects of traffic as actually perceived by people, and differential scoring of various types of vehicle.[9]

Environmental capacity

There have been several significant changes in attitudes to transport planning in the last decade, which can in large part be traced to the influence of the Buchanan Report on Traffic in Towns.[10] Buchanan stressed the inter-connection of land use and traffic, and also that 'accessibility' and 'environmental considerations' often pulled in opposite directions. Thus to secure a satisfactory environment, even when more resources were devoted than might be strictly necessary in engineering terms alone, some sacrifice of accessibility might be involved.

From such ideas has evolved the concept of 'environmental capacity'—that level of traffic which is acceptable in environmental terms—as a supplement to the well-established notion of engineering 'traffic capacity'. The definition of environmental areas, which are protected from through traffic by traffic management measures, is one important way of ensuring that environmental capacities are respected.

Hills, in an aritcle discussing case studies of environmental management, amplified different aspects of determining environmental capacity.[11] He suggested the use of an EPCU—Environmental Passenger Car Unit—variant of the PCU, which would weight different vehicle types according to their effect on the environment. Six different aspects of the environmental influences of traffic can be distinguished: noise, fumes, vibration, pedestrian delays, encroachment and visual intrusion.

Noise has perhaps received most attention. The Building Research Station has developed a Traffic Noise Index, which allows for the range of the noise climate as well as general levels. Vibration is closely linked with noise and can be accommodated in noise measures. Fumes are an irritant and coming increasingly under attack from environmental action groups. Pedestrian delays have traditionally been considered in any evaluation of transport improvements, along with drivers' time, and accidents.

Encroachment of traffic physically on to areas intended for pedestrians occurs in both city and country—mostly on to roadside pavements and verges—and although penalties may be imposed, it may often be difficult to provide enough supervision to ensure that the encroachment does not occur.

Visual intrusion is a very significant element in preserving environmental standards, and relates to both moving and parked cars. Work has been done to attempt to quantify in some way people's perception of, and sensitivity to, different kinds and degree of intrusion, often in association with the other elements mentioned above. For example, in studies carried out by Buchanan and associates in Edinburgh, and in several of their other recent studies, a complex machine which records several aspects of traffic nuisance levels has been used.

A recent article by Hopkinson, although not actually dealing with traffic, has some interesting points to make about our current attitudes to visual intrusion, suggesting that it is 'another form of environmental pollution, along with noise, dirt and chemical pollution, and means are being sought for its evaluation.'[12]

Traffic management

I do not think it appropriate to discuss traffic management in any detail, but it has been mentioned already and the principle is important. Essentially it is applying legal constraints (such as one-way systems) and relatively small-scale physical adaptations to existing streets. The object may be to increase usage, decrease it or alter its pattern, as necessitated by the traffic and environmental objectives.

390

The London Transportation Study

The London Traffic Survey was initiated in 1960 by the LCC and the Ministry of Transport (with help from London Transport and British Rail). In 1962, a number of surveys were carried out to ascertain the existing travel pattern in London and to establish the basic relationships between person and household characteristics and travel characteristics. Although large in scale, the survey was originally conceived quite narrowly, but has steadily developed into a more comprehensive approach, and particularly a much greater emphasis on public transport. It is now called the London Transportation Study.

In the second phase of the study the first comprehensive forecasts were made of future travel demands in London. 'The procedures used were conventional and demonstrated the amount and mode of travel which could be expected in future if car ownership continued to increase rapidly and if cars were used with the same relative freedom which existed in 1962.'[13] These results were taken to represent 'potential demand'. This provided a main framework for exploration of policy, but it became clear that extension of the study to a third stage was necessary to provide:

1 a forecast of the pattern of public transport demand
2 testing of alternative combinations of road and public transport networks
3 a realistic estimate of actual volumes of travel by car in which the demand was in balance with the capacity of the network tested
4 an economic evaluation of the network tested.[14]

Thus, in phase three, various different road plans, public transport improvements and combinations of the two were examined. To test and evaluate these alternatives various new techniques were worked out. 'A transportation model was developed to deal with a large congested system of roads operating in conjunction with an extensive public transport system. The model made use of speed reductions in relevant areas to reflect congested road conditions and the consequent reduction in traffic demand on the roads and transfer where appropriate to public transport.'

The estimates of traffic depend on overall assumptions of future population and employment levels and distribution.

Sensitivity tests on these factors and the effects on transport demands were carried out, but the availability of further information, particularly Census of Population results, necessitated further testing. The effects of a smaller Greater London population, it has been suggested, might cause some difficulties in the effective operation of public transport; in relation to roads, it would help to bring demands and capacities into better balance.

The attempts to estimate costs and benefits of alternative overall transport plans for Greater London have been hedged around with qualifications, for example,

'It seems highly unlikely that traffic conditions will be left to find their own level in future. On the other hand it is not clear to what extent control measures will be either technically feasible or politically and socially acceptable. It may be safe to conclude that the true rate of return on urban road investment in future will lie somewhere within a range, the precise position representing a

Table 16.1   *Example of Cost and Benefits*

Plan

		Plan 1	Plan 3
Route length (miles)		150	345
Construction cost (£m)		59	513
Property cost (£m)		313	1145
	Total cost of roads	372	1658
Parking (£m)		79	183
Total capital cost (including parking) (£m)		451	1841

		Plan 3 minus Plan 1
Benefit due to change in journey costs (£m)		29.9
Benefit due to extra capacity (£m)		53.8
Benefit measured by tax paid by generated traffic (£m)		41.7
Increased maintenance (£m)		− 3.6
	Total Benefit	121.8

SOURCE   'The London Transportation Study and Beyond' by T. M. Ridley & J. O. Tresidder, in *Regional Studies*, 1970 political and social choice between greater expenditure and greater submission to control of individual freedom.'[15]

An attempt at cost-benefit analysis of two alternatives is shown in Table 16.1, not because of the significance of the figures, but to show the form of the analysis.[16]

The information needs of the transport planner

Perhaps an appropriate final point to emphasise in this chapter on techniques of transportation planning is the prodigious requirement of these techniques for information of different kinds. Bayliss has suggested that transportation—already a complex field—will involve increasingly sophisticated research and shows signs of an outstanding high documentation growth rate.[17]

Relevant to this problem are the increasingly diverse backgrounds of those involved in transportation studies (since people bring with them the approaches and techniques of their first disciplines) and the importance of awareness of comparable studies abroad. The increasing realisation of the relationships between different forms of transport and between transport and other aspects of the environment also implies a wider range for the information a transportation planner must have at his command. It becomes important, therefore, for any reports of research or of studies to be made available rapidly and in an easily digested form.

Needless to say, these problems are not unique to the transport aspects of planning.

References

1 Bruton, M. J., *Introduction to Transportation Planning*, Hutchinson, London (1970).
2 See Bayliss, D., 'Information needs of the transportation planner', in *GLC Intelligence Unit Quarterly Bulletin*, page 3, 15, June 1971.
3 Used, for example, in Buchanan, C. & Partners & Atkins, W. S. *Cardiff Development and Transportation Study*, Main Study Report, Supplementary Technical 5.
4 Lanson, H. & J. Dearinger, in *Proceedings of the American Society of Civil Engineers, Highway Division*, 93, HW2 (1967).
5 Bruton, *op. cit.* (1) above.
6 Bruton, *op. cit.* (1) above.

7 Hall, P., 'New techniques in regional planning: experience of transportation studies', in *Regional Studies,* page 17, 1 (1967).

8 Hutchinson, B. G., 'Structuring urban transportation planning decisions', in *Environment and Planning,* page 251, 2 (1971).

9 Mason, D., 'Camden discovers a method of quantifying environment', in *Municipal Engineering,* page 2427. 147, 47, 20 November 1970,

10 Buchanan, C., *Traffic in Towns,* HMSO, London (1963).

11 Hills, P. J., 'Case studies of environmental management', in *The Surveyor and Municipal Engineer,* 127, 3848 (1966).

12 Hopkinson, R. G., 'The quantitative assessment of visual intrusion', in *Journal of the Royal Town Planning Institute,* page 445, 57, 10 December 1971.

13 Ridley, T. M. & Tresidder, J. O. 'The London Transportation Study and Beyond', in *Regional Studies,* page 63, 4 (1970); see also, London County Council, *The London Traffic Survey,* 1 (1964);
Martin, B. V., *Transportation Studies: London,* Proceedings of Transportation Engineering Conference, Institution of Civil Engineers, London (1968);
Greater London Council, *The London Traffic Survey,* 2 (1966);
Tresidder, J. O., Meyers, D., Burrell, J. & Powell, T. 'The London Transportation Study: Methods and Techniques', in *Proceedings of the Institution of Civil Engineers,* 39 (1968);
Crawford, K. A. J., 'The 1971 Greater London Transportation Survey', in *GLC Research and Intelligence Unit Quarterly Bulletin,* page 15, 16, September 1971.

14 Ridley & Tresidder, *op. cit.* (13) above, page 65.

15 Ridley & Tresidder, *op. cit.* (13) above, page 70.

16 See also, Barrell, D., *Cost-benefit analysis in transportation planning,* Oxford Working Papers 10 (1972).

17 Bayliss, *op. cit.* (2) above;
on information needs see also, White, B., *Source Book of Planning Information,* Clive Bingley, London (1971).

17 Perception

Introduction

Part 3 of this book, and, indeed, to a large extent the book as a whole, has tended to imply that any person's life is devoted to the pursuit of classifiable planning activities, undertaken neatly one at a time—now I shop, now I travel, now I work and so on. Such a schema totally leaves out consideration of the way an individual continuously responds to everything around him, receiving complex impressions though all five senses that produce disturbance of either pleasurable or another kind. Whilst a land use planner must certainly be concerned with provision of adequate amounts and types of land and buildings for the activities of people's daily lives, it is essential that he is also aware of, and concerned about, people's perception of what is around them.

There has been a lamentable gulf between the psychologists and sociologists working on aspects of people's responses to the world, and adequate recognition by land use planners of its relevance to their tasks. Lately, however, the whole subject of perception has been receiving increasing attention by land use planners. Indeed, there now seems to be some danger of wide-spread aversion as a result of the facile over-publicity to which 'amenity', the 'quality of life', 'ecology', and related matters have been subjected.

In this chapter I shall provide an introduction to perception, mentioning first the visual awareness of the stationary and the moving observer, then perception of space and of other people, followed by perception through senses other than sight, and, finally, the difficulty of evaluating aspects of perception.

Analysis and classification of visual elements

One of the roots of present day land use planning was civic design—hence an early emphasis on the city beautiful, timeless and unvarying aesthetic codes and concentration on what things look like. Various techniques distilled this approach, analysing and classifying elements in townscape and landscape as visually good and visually bad, and such methods are still very much with us.

Gordon Cullen's ideas are familiar to many, and particularly the notation he developed as 'the observant layman's code for his environment', which was described as 'an attempt to optimise humanism in the face of expediency'.[1] The notation comprised 'scales', which indicated the function and intensity of use of a piece of land or a building, as well as its appearance, and 'indicators', which were more concerned with the significance of objects as elements in the landscape. By a combination of scales and indicators, the essential characteristics of any area could be analysed, classified and communicated.

It was explained that 'a system of notation is a way of passing on precise opinions about a particular situation. The advice may not be taken, but this is a way of giving it.' The implications of the notation are that it will assist in developing a more refined eye for visual effects, but also that people's reaction to landscape is both uniform and predictable.

This assumption of *ascertainable group values* necessarily underlies all landscape classification studies which do not confine themselves only to identification of elements in the landscape, but set out to assess 'quality'. One such attempt to establish a comprehensive and qualitative classification for use in planning work was that by Fines, who used East Sussex to test the methodology. First, a small group of people were shown photographs of test views. From their comparative rankings of the views, a scale of values (as shown in Figure 17.1) from 0 to 32, arranged in six descriptive categories was derived, applicable to townscape, as

396

well as landscape. This scale was then used in the field by Fines
to evaluate the views and sequences of views, which were subsequently converted to land-surface values, 'the criterion being
the value of a particular tract of land to the totality of views in
which it features'.[2]

This technique has been criticised for several reasons, for
example, by Brancher, who singled out the inadequacy of the

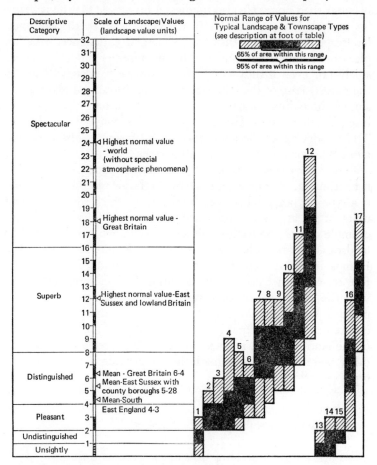

Fig. 17.1   Scale of Landscape Values (after Fines)

SOURCE 'Landscape Evaluation: a research project in East Sussex' in
Regional Studies, 1968

'representative' group of people Fines first assembled to show his test views, his subsequent use of the evaluations of only one part of that group, the notion that 20 photographs could represent the range of scenes in the world, the conversion of rankings of photographs to a cardinal scale of measurement and so forth.[3]

In fairness to Fines, he presents the inevitable defence in planning that since evaluative decisions must be taken, some method is better than none. He also implies in his article that he is aware his analysis is only partial—'In its relationship to the observer, landscape is multi-dimensional. The total experience, whether pleasant or unpleasant, obtained by the observer is not dependent solely—or even mainly—upon the response to visual beauty in the purest sense of the harmony of form, colour and texture in a single three-dimensional pictorial composition, but upon an interplay of sensory, psychological and sequential experiences The sensory experiences are not derived from visual satisfaction alone but from an amalgam of all five senses.'[4]

Research into methods of landscape classification and evaluation is continuing, of course, and one method now receiving attention is a type of 'potential surface' analysis, in which the constituent units of an area are scored according to various criteria. An example of the application of such a technique, which included landscape among other facets of rural planning, was the East Hampshire Study. As well as landscape, wildlife, agriculture, forestry and other uses of the countryside, including recreation, were the 'claimants' on rural resources. The aim was to produce policies which would resolve conflicts in these claims, and ensure maximum compatibility. Thus the effects of different uses of the land upon the resources of the study area and upon each other were assessed systematically to provide a basis for two types of policy:

1 'precise location and control policies, needed in the zones of greatest potential conflict or for activities which were extremely unacceptable to other interests'
2 'policies covering practices not tied to specific locations, such as many agricultural practices or pleasure motoring.'

The means suggested to implement the policies range from use of town planning legislation, management agreements with land owners, promotion of codes of practice to publicity. In general,

398

the conclusions of the study were that 'much more can be done with existing powers than has been generally assumed' and that 'there seems every reason to believe that plans can be made for the countryside which will be as acceptable and as valuable as those for our towns'.

The method was refined in a subsequent study on Sherwood Forest, and continues to be developed at present. Such classifications are basic to certain types of rural planning, for example, the work by planners of the Canadian National Parks to assess the different perceptible landscapes in their country.

The moving observer

Still concentrating on visual perception, a third group of techniques is those methods developed in relation to roads. The moving, rather than static, observer introduces a new scale of perception. Thus, Lynch (whose approach is discussed later) investigated with colleagues the 'view from the road'.[5] In this country, one of the earliest planning studies of this type was that relating to views observed by users of the Durham motorway.[6]

The study first assessed the range of visual perception relevant to motorway users, then examined all land that would be seen from the projected motorway and analysed how the landscape could be improved by planting, earth moulding, removal of eye-sores and so on.

A promising pilot project concerned with roads and amenity, though with a wider coverage than simply visual effects, has been carried out by the London Borough of Camden. Essentially, a method was devised to score streets, in order to provide a comparison between different traffic patterns and their detrimental effects on the streets' environment. The factors selected for consideration, and how they were scored, are shown in Figure 16.4(a), on page 386. The 'environmental index' thus produced was multiplied against traffic flow factors to give an 'index of detriment', for each link on the traffic network.

The discussion of the pilot project stated that the work would be further refined, hopefully to 'enable more accurate scoring of the different elements of the equation so that they relate more closely to the perceived detrimental effects of traffic'.[7]

Space perception

Lynch, mentioned above, has been very influential in drawing the attention of planners to the inadequacies of conventional visual classifications. What such methods tend to ignore is that people interpret their surroundings in a highly personal manner.

Each work on perception by psychologists went back to first principles, the premise that people's knowledge of the world derives from the senses, and stimuli acting upon the senses. Also important are past learning and motivation. Such studies emphasise that man has only a finite capacity for perceiving and for storing information, and that in apparently identical circumstances individuals behave differently. Thus, one psychological study found that, 'all individuals have a given space preference... defined as a desired level of social contact, and when placed in the same spatial situation, providing all possess identical levels of information, they will behave differently.'[8]

The acceptance that human beings may behave in a seemingly irrational fashion is expressed in Simon's model of *satisficing* behaviour; an individual may be content with one of a series of outcomes that he takes as 'satisfactory', without seeking to optimise, that is, find the 'best' outcome. Clearly this view of behaviour allows full scope for individuals to respond to circumstances in varying ways. These relationships have been expressed diagramatically (by Downs[9]).

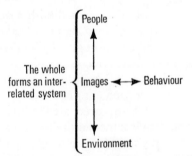

Lynch concentrated on real 'legibility' of environment, as perceived by people and reflected in their daily behaviour as they moved about their home areas. Thus he was interested in the ease with which people could actually recognise the parts of a city and organise them into a coherent pattern. He collected information on people's 'perceived city' in interviews, using devices such as making them describe their routes to work or draw maps of their neighbourhood. His analysis confirmed that 'there seems to be a public image of any given city which is the overlap of many individual images'[10] From people's city images he concluded that there are five significant types of element in the perception of the physical structure of a city—paths, nodes, edges, districts and landmarks. Lynch's findings, and design principles based on them, have had widespread influence on planners and architects and his analytical methods have also been much used.

Techniques focusing on space perception have been applied at widely varying geographical scales. There have been neighbourhood studies, such as Eyles' on Highgate village in London—in which he noted that people tended to stretch the extent of the village in the direction of their own home, and that the size of the village they depict becomes smaller with increased length of residence.[11] A national study was one of 'mental maps' of Britain, by Gould and White.[12] In essence, they presented lists of different parts of Britain for ranking in order of preference as residential areas to several groups of school-children. From the lists of preferences drawn up by individuals, they produced a statistical result for each group of children living in the same area, which could then be compared with the preference maps of the groups of school-children who lived in other parts of the country. They found a general pattern which recurred through all groups' preferences, wherever they lived, but on to which, predictably, a local variation was superimposed. Their suggestions as to further research centre on clarifying the influences forming both the 'general' and the 'local' preferences, but they caution, 'images are clearly shaped by the varying flows of information to which people are subjected, but it seems an almost impossible task to specify such flows properly'.[13]

Perception of other people

One perception element which is of some significance for planners is the individual's reaction to the presence of other people.

Much has been written (and much disputed) about the psychological and, indeed, physiological, effects of different densities of people, particularly residential densities. A few years ago most of the emphasis was on the possible strains caused by too many people, but growing concern now also focuses on disturbances which can result from insufficient contact with other people.

It is clear that the pleasure derived from some activities can be considerably diminished if an individual feels overcrowded. So far, techniques to measure this aspect of perception have not been too successful, but research continues. Work carried out by the Dartington Amenity Research Trust on Dartmoor, in which they attempted to deduce people's tolerances of others from the results of questionnaire surveys, has been described by Butterfield: 'People were asked whether there were too many, too few or about the right number of other people present for their own enjoyment. Most people replied "about the right number"— possibly with some sense of pleasing the interviewer, but there was only a weak correlation between those replying "too many" and the busier times of the day. One man said there were too many people present for his enjoyment when at that time there was only one other person present on the riverside picnic site at which he was being interviewed. (Possibly he felt he was being overcrowded by our interviewer.)'[14]

In the USA, the ORRC classification of recreation resource areas, which ranges from 'wilderness' to the equivalent of our country parks, takes into account the effects of the presence of people, as well as the natural beauty of the landscape, as a determinant of the perceived character of an area.[15]

Senses other than visual

So far, I have discussed perception of what can be seen, of space and of other people. There remain the factors of noise, smell and vibration. These have received increasing attention as planners invested more and more of their time in grappling with the environmental effects of traffic and as suffering communities pressured local and central government to face up to their responsibilities.

The many studies on the noise effects of motorways have

402

generally been concerned either to find appropriate building treatment to reduce the disamenity produced or to incorporate such effects into cost-benefit analyses of the development possibilities. Apart from studies connected with motorways, there have been numerous environmental studies of the effects of traffic in parts of cities—especially those deemed of particular architectural or historic interest—and in countryside recreation areas.

Several techniques for measuring aspects of the environmental effects of traffic have been developed by research workers at Imperial College, in association with Buchanan, and used in studies such as those in Greenwich and the North-East of London, in Edinburgh and in the New Forest.[16] I have mentioned before Hills' suggestion of the Environmental Passenger Car Unit, which would weight different vehicle types according to their effect on the environment. The findings in the New Forest Study, for example, were that the noise, smell, vibration and visual intrusion of cars all affect people's enjoyment.

Evaluation of different aspects of perception

Now that the notion of uniform and easily identified sensual reactions has largely been displaced by a realisation of the complexity of people's values in these matters, much depends on the development of subtle and indirect ways of establishing people's environmental preferences, and how they are affected by different aspects of their surroundings.

Some planners have great hopes of forms of gaming and simulation, which encourage people to express their likes in ways that appear fairly informal and analagous to the every-day world. The 'planner's fruit machine' (a method of priority evaluation) which appeared at a recent public exhibition of Camden's planning ideas, was an interim product of research of this type conducted by Social and Community Planning Research to identify and measure the trade-off values of people's preferences.[17]

Meantime, public attention has been well and truly directed to the difficulties of 'putting a price on amenity' by such exercises as the Roskill Commission's investigations of possible sites for London's third airport.[18]

But, as Gregory has said, 'the preservation of amenity is not the only worthy cause on which money should be spent', and 'there is not much to be said for a system where the price of basic utilities is raised in order to preserve the amenities of the comparatively well-to-do'. From his analysis of 'five of the most celebrated planning controversies of the last decade', he concluded—'In the years ahead there will be no shortage of general exhortation. But of one thing we may be quite certain: making the choices will become an even more perplexing and thankless task.'[19]

References

1 Cullen, G., 'Notation', in *Architect's Journal*, 12 July 1967.
2 Fines, K. D., 'Landscape evaluation: a research project in East Sussex', in *Regional Studies*, page 41, **2** (1968).
3 Brancher, D. M., 'Critique', in *Regional Studies*, page 91, **3** (1969).
4 *Op. cit.* (2) above, page 41.
5 Lynch, K., Appleyard D. & Meyer, J. R. *The View from the Road*, MIT Press, Cambridge, Massachusetts (1964).
6 see *Methods of Landscape Analysis*, Landscape Research Group Symposium (1967).
7 Mason, D., 'Camden discovers a way of quantifying environment' in *Municipal Engineering*, page 2428, 20 November 1970.
8 Huff, D. L., 'A topographic model of consumer space preferences', in *Proceedings of Regional Science Association*, page 160, Paper 6 (1960).
9 Downs, R. M., *The role of perception in modern geography*, Seminar Papers Series A, 11, Department of Geography, University of Bristol (1968).
10 Lynch, K., *The Image of the City*, Harvard University Press (1960).
11 Eyles, J. D., *The Inhabitants' Image of Highgate Village (London)—an example of a Perception Measurement Technique*, LSE Graduate School of Geography Discussion Paper 15 (1968).
12 Gould, P. R. & White, R. R. 'The mental maps of British school-leavers', in *Regional Studies*, page 161, **2** (1968).
13 *Op. cit.* (12) above, page 181.
14 Butterfield, J. H., 'The capacity and management of recreation resources in the countryside', in *Recreation Land Use Planning and Forecasting*, PATRAC, page 37 (1969).

404

15 Bureau of Outdoor Recreation, Department of the Interior, USA, *Outdoor Recreation Space Standards* (1967).

16 Buchanan, C. & Partners, *North East London*, a Report to the Greater London Council (1970); and *Greenwich and Blackheath Study*, a Report to the Greater London Council (1971), for example.

17 Hoinville, G., *Evaluating Community Preferences: a Summary Report of SCPR Development Work*, published by Social and Community Planning Research (1970).

18 As discussed in Frost, M. J., *Values for Money: the Techniques of Cost-Benefit Analysis*, Gower Press (1971); see also Mishan, E. J., *Cost-benefit Analysis—an Informal Introduction*, Unwin, London (1971).

19 Gregory, R., *The Price of Amenity: Five Studies in Conservation and Government*, Macmillan, page 307 (1971).

See also:

Burton, I., 'The quality of the environment: a review', in *Geographical Review*, page 472, **58** (1968).

Countryside Commission, *Recreation News*, 23, October 1970—outline of Landscape Evaluation Research Project at Manchester University.

Craik, K. H., 'The comprehension of the everyday physical environment', in *Journal of the American Institute of Planners*, page 29, **34** (1968).

Crowe, S., *Symposium on National, Regional and Local Landscape Plans*, Institute of Landscape Architects, May 1971.

Denham, C., *Attitudes towards the Environment: Analyses of Aspects of the Environment in a Social Setting*, LSE Graduate School of Geography Discussion Paper 18, (1968).

Ewald, W. R. (Ed), *Environment for Man; the Next 50 Years*, Bloomington, USA (1967), especially C. Alexander, 'The city as a mechanism for maintaining human contact' and S. Orr, 'The city of the mind'.

Goodey, B., *Perception of the environment*, CURS Occasional Paper 17, University of Birmingham (1971).

Hall, P., 'Valuing amenity with special reference to landscape', at 1971 Symposium.

De Jonge, J., 'Images of urban areas: their structural and psychological foundation', in *Journal of the American Institute of Planners*, page 266, **28** (1962).

Leopold, L. B., 'Landscape Esthetics', in *Natural History*, page
37, **78**, 8 (1969).
Linton, D. C., 'The assessment of scenery as a natural resource', in
Scottish Geographical Magazine, page 221 (1968).
Murray, A. C., *Power Station Siting: Visual Analysis,* in Proceedings
of a Symposium on Methods of Landscape Analysis, held in London,
May 1967; includes also Tandy, C. R., *The Isovist Method
of Landscape Survey.*
Peterson, G. L., 'A model of preference: quantitative analysis of
the perception of visual appearance of residential neighbourhoods',
in *Journal of Regional Science*, page 19, **7** (1967).
Thomas, R. J., 'The cash value of the environment', in *Journal
of the Institute of Municipal Treasurers and Accountants,* October 1968.
Yi-Fu Tuan, 'Attitudes towards environment: themes and
approaches', in *Environmental Perception and Behaviour,* edited by
D. Lowenthal, Research Paper 109, Department of Geography,
University of Chicago (1967);
see also—Lowenthal, D., and Prince, H. C., 'English landscape
tastes', in *Geographical Review*, page 186, **55** (1965).
Waller, R. A., *The Valuation of Amenity,* W. S. Atkins &
Partners (1965); and Thomas, R. J., 'The cash value of the
environment', in *Arena*, page 164, **82** (1967).
Waller, R. A., and Thomas, R. J., 'Environmental quality—its measure-
ment and control', in *Regional Studies,* page 177, **4,** 2 (1970).
Wood, L. J., 'Perception studies in geography', in *Transactions:
Institute of British Geographers,* page 129, 50, July 1970.